THE TANOAK TREE

THE TANOAK TREE

AN ENVIRONMENTAL HISTORY OF

A PACIFIC COAST HARDWOOD

FREDERICA BOWCUTT

Foreword by
FRANK KANAWHA LAKE

UNIVERSITY OF
WASHINGTON PRESS
Seattle and London

A portion of the royalties of this book go to Native Americans
fostering tanoak wellness.

© 2015 by the University of Washington Press
Printed and bound in the United States of America
Design: Dustin Kilgore
Composed in Chaparral, a typeface designed by Carol Twombly
19 18 17 16 15   5 4 3 2 1

UNIVERSITY OF WASHINGTON PRESS
www.washington.edu/uwpress

Library of Congress Cataloging-in-Publication Data
Bowcutt, Frederica.
The tanoak tree : an environmental history of a Pacific Coast hardwood /
Frederica Bowcutt ; foreword by Frank Kanawha Lake.
    pages   cm
Includes bibliographical references and index.
ISBN 978-0-295-99464-2 (hardcover : acid-free paper)
1. Tanoak—Pacific Coast (U.S)—History. 2. Hardwoods—Pacific Coast
(U.S)—History. 3. Tanoak—Ecology—Pacific Coast (U.S)
4. Pacific Coast (U.S.)—Environmental conditions. 5. Pacific Coast
(U.S.)—Economic conditions. I. Title.
SD397.B4B69 2015
634.9'72—dc23

                                                    2014045924

Dust cover, frontispiece, and paperback cover: Tanoak (*Notholithocarpus
densiflorus*) with acorns. Previously called "dense-flowered oak" (*Quercus
densiflora*). From Thomas Nuttall, *The North American Sylva*, vol. 4 (1865),
plate V. Lithograph by Thomas S. Sinclair, ca. 1841–1849. Hand-colored.
Courtesy of New York Public Library. The image was copied and slightly
modified from the earliest-known image of tanoak published in 1841 as
tab. 380 in Hooker, *Icones Plantarum*. Photograph of solo acorn courtesy
of the U.S. Forest Service, the National Agricultural Library, and the
USDA-NRCS PLANTS database.

Dedicated to my beloved husband,
Rob Saecker

CONTENTS

FOREWORD

ACCORDING TO MANY CALIFORNIA INDIANS, ALL THINGS IN THIS world were and still are spirits. It was in the Beginning Time that these spirits manifested their physical forms, preparing for a time when humans would come. These spirits would instruct the humans on how to use, steward, and respect all of creation, even if people did not fully understand everything the spirits did and would do in this world. Among the Karuk and Yurok Tribes, one story tells of Tanoak, one of several oak spirit sisters transforming themselves for the coming of humans to this land. In preparation, each oak sister wove her basket cap as fine as she could, to be attractive to the humans. The time came, but Tanoak was not done with her cap. She took her cap, turned it inside out, and told the other oak sisters, "It's OK if my cap is rough-looking." Although her cap was unfinished and not scraped clean as it should be, she went on to say, "Humans will still like me the best." The other oaks had nicer-looking caps, but Tanoak did not mind; her acorns made the best soup.

Out of all the available oaks and oaklike nut trees, tanoak acorns are some of the most relished and prized among the tribes of northern California. Beyond the nutritional value the tree provides, the tanoak fulfills significant ecological, economic, and traditional roles for California Indians. The knowledge tribes gained over millennia about tanoak forests and trees started from this Beginning Time and continues today. Many tribes believe that the Creator and the spirits themselves taught the first humans how to manage, utilize, and perpetuate tanoaks across the landscape. Although, from then to now, how could anyone even comprehend and fully understand all that this amazing tree embodies? It would take generations of building this knowledge from the individual life experiences and interactions of people, places, and tanoaks.

When gathering tanoak acorns for food across the landscape, one begins to understand that it is the uniqueness of individual trees, the history and context of place, and a multitude of other factors that form the relationships between people and forests. Beyond the acorns that provide food for people, stock animals, and wildlife, tanoaks have a variety of other uses. The wood is popular for furniture, flooring, cabinets, and firewood, among other things. The bark, used for tannins, was historically important to the regional economy. Moreover, tanoak-dominated forests host many other useful species that benefit wildlife and people. This tree is important to many, from the tribes who depend on it as a food source to the seasoned timber workers who generate products for the general public, who marvel at the wood's beauty. Yet many people today do not even realize or understand all that this tree provides to the environment and society. Fortunately, though, tribes, public agencies, universities, private and nonprofit organizations, and members of the public are focusing heightened attention on the tree through management, research, and restoration efforts. It is this call for awareness, understanding, and respect for tanoaks that author Frederica Bowcutt shares in this book.

Frederica explores and reveals the great complexity and challenges that people, places, and tanoaks have endured up to this day and what the future may hold. Her passion and respect for this tree are reflected in the story line, which offers an epic tale of the influence the tanoak tree has had on the ecology and economies of the places where it grows as well as on the lives of those who use it. The book presents a range of fruitful and tragic outcomes for tanoaks. Currently, sudden oak death syndrome—for which there is no known cure—is one of the greatest threats tanoaks face. How land managers choose to respond to this disease will affect the tree's persistence on the landscape and its continued use into the future. The absence of a cure for sudden oak death has increased tensions over treatment options, with no consensus on the best way of protecting the trees from this fatal disease. There is, however, hope that natural resistance among individual trees or a particular management treatment, such as fuels reduction and prescribed fire, will prove effective. Or perhaps a novel vaccine will be discovered that can be applied to non-infected trees and will reduce or alleviate the pathogen problem when integrated with specific forestry treatments.

Of course, the other threat with unknown future consequences is global climate change, which has increased the occurrence of drought conditions in California to record levels. Associated shifts in fire and other ecological processes are only beginning to be identified and understood. Unfortunately, the available science lacks sufficient information on how to respond to the effects of sudden oak death and climate change at different sociocultural and ecological scales. As a result, traditional and local knowledge of tanoaks will be all the more important in defining the metrics of what to study, identifying how and what to monitor, and determining which indicators of wellness are useful at the acorn, tree, forest, and landscape levels. Given all these complexities, the reader begins to understand the threats, stressors, and challenges facing tanoak trees in the modern world. This book provides context and some hope in a future of uncertainty for this magnificent tree.

An appreciation for tanoaks comes from many sources and experiences. Many of us will know the tree based on what we have learned from others, some of us will form a bond and a relationship with it that will last or be remembered for a lifetime, and a small number of us will engage in use and stewardship of tanoaks that will continue for generations to come and sustain people, places, and forests. Each person, in his or her own capacity, influences the fate of this beautiful tree.

As a traditional acorn gatherer, tanoak forest steward, and scientist who has respect and reverence for the tanoak tree, I applaud the author's effort to share her knowledge and experiences in this important and carefully researched book.

Frank Kanawha Lake
(Karuk-Seneca-Cherokee-Mexican)
Research Ecologist, USDA Forest Service,
Orleans, California
January 2015

ACKNOWLEDGMENTS

MY INTEREST IN TANOAK BEGAN WHILE I WAS WORKING ON MY
dissertation in ecology at the University of California, Davis. Over the past
nearly twenty years, while teaching in interdisciplinary teams at the Evergreen State College in Olympia, Washington, that interest expanded into an
investigation of the historical context of current threats to native biodiversity through a case study of one plant species. My University of California
professors, particularly David Robertson, Gary Snyder, Bruce Hackett, and
Carolyn Merchant, supported my early efforts to link botany and California's environmental history, for which I am grateful.

The Evergreen State College helped fund my research and created a fer-
tile interdisciplinary environment for the development of my ideas. Many
of my humanities colleagues at this public liberal arts college advised in
the earlier stages, including Sandy Yannone, Sean Williams, Sonia Wieden-
haupt, Zahid Shariff, Joli Sandoz, Therese Saliba, Bill Ransom, Susan Pre-
cisio, Barbara Perkins, Linda Moon-Stumpff, Helena Meyer-Knapp, Jeanne
Hahn, and Nancy Allen. Former students Eve Rickert and Luke Painter assisted with the early literature research. Librarians graciously provided expert research assistance at multiple public institutions: Bancroft Library,
California History Section of the California State Library, University of
California, Davis; the Evergreen State College; Humboldt State Univer-
sity; Oregon State University Libraries Special Collections and Archives;
University of Washington, Seattle; and the U.S. National Archives and Records Administration. Special thanks to Joan Berman at Humboldt State
University library; Andrea Heisel, Sara Huntington, Sarah Pedersen, Liza
Rognas, and Jules Unsel at the Evergreen State College library; and archivist
Amy Kasameyer, with the University and Jepson Herbaria Archives housed
at the University of California, Berkeley. Miko Francis and Nancy Brewer,
the staff at Evergreen's interlibrary loan office, worked tirelessly for years
tracking down obscure and often old primary sources. I also thank the various historical societies and museums that assisted me with my research,

including Curry County Historical Society, the Forest History Society, Fort Bragg–Mendocino Coast Historical Society, Grace Hudson Museum and Sun House, Marin History Museum, Mendocino County Historical Society, Oregon Historical Society, and the Santa Cruz Museum of Art & History.

I am grateful to Oxford University Press, the California Botanical Society, the U.S. Forest Service, and the California Department of Fish and Wildlife for permission to rework and republish portions of this book that were previously published. For support in the writing of "Tanoak Target: The Rise and Fall of Herbicide Use on a Common Native Tree," published in the journal *Environmental History* in April 2011, I credit my generous Evergreen colleagues Martha Henderson (geographer), Sam Schrager (American Studies and folklorist), and emeritus faculty member Matt Smith (political economist). Michael Pfeifer, who formerly taught American history at Evergreen also commented on the "Tanoak Target" manuscript. In addition, I received insightful feedback from ethnobotanist M. Kat Anderson at the U.S. Department of Agriculture (USDA), National Resources Conservation Service; members of the American Society of Environmental History Mark Ciouc, Bruce Thompson, Neil Maher, and Cindy Ott; and two anonymous reviewers. Dominique Bachelet, Eric Engles, and Rob Saecker suggested changes on earlier drafts of the "Tanoak Target" article. Common Counsel Foundation supported a delightful and productive writer's retreat at the Mesa Refuge in Marin County, California.

In partnership with the U.S. Forest Service, the California Botanical Society published "Tanoak Landscapes: Tending a Native American Nut Tree" in the tanoak issue of *Madroño*, edited by Susan Frankel, who solicited the essay. Frankel is the sudden oak death (SOD) research leader at the U.S. Forest Service's Pacific Southwest Research Station. For support during the writing process, I am grateful to the following individuals, in addition to the issue editor, who read drafts and gave valuable feedback: Tamara Caulkins, Lisa Hintz, Judith Larner Lowry, Rob Saecker, and three anonymous reviewers. Hawk Rosales, executive director of the InterTribal Sinkyone Wilderness Council, and Sherrie Smith-Ferri, executive director of the Grace Hudson Museum, commented on sections pertaining to Native peoples. Dave Rizzo, University of California plant pathologist, commented on an earlier version of the section discussing sudden oak death.

The California Department of Fish and Wildlife invited me to contribute an article for the centennial issue of its journal, the first issue devoted entirely to plants. The article "Tanoak Conservation: A Role for the California

Department of Fish and Wildlife" was reviewed by Cherilyn Burton, Ed Guerrant, and Frank Lake, for which I am grateful. Linda Perkins and Steve Schoenig also consulted on the draft. For the evolution section, Diane Erwin skillfully gave me a crash course in analyzing *Lithocarpus* macrofossils at the University of California Museum of Paleontology on the Berkeley campus and also reviewed that portion of the text that addresses evolutionary history. In her University of Washington lab in Seattle, Estella Leopold gave me access to her reference pollen collection and fielded my questions about the microfossil record. Thomas Denk and Guido Grimm both at the Swedish Museum of Natural History in Stockholm provided helpful feedback on the discussion of tanoak evolution. University of California paleobotanist James A. Doyle commented on an earlier version of that section.

I am particularly thankful for the insightful feedback and gracious support I have received over multiple years from Susan Frankel and Kat Anderson. Both commented on the book manuscript, along with Richard Cobb and an anonymous reader. Sarah Gage critiqued the "Bark" and "Weed" chapters. Feedback from Jim Anderson, Tamara Caulkins, and John Shelly helped me refine the "Hardwood" chapter. For the "Weed" chapter, Tim Harrington and Steve Schoenig provided constructive criticism, David Bakke reviewed the table of herbicides, and Patty Clary consulted on data. Ted Swiecki and other plant pathologists as well as foresters fielded sudden oak death questions during the writing of the "Plague" chapter. Zoltán Grossman commented on the "Landscapes" and "Partnerships" chapters. Mollee Mullins gave helpful feedback, particularly on the glossary, and make significant contributions to the index. Michael Brackney mindfully mentored me in the craft of creating an index. Marianne Keddington-Lang, Ranjit Arab, Tim Zimmerman, Mary C. Ribesky, Laura Iwasaki, and Natasha Varner kindly guided me through the publication process at the University of Washington Press.

I benefited from multiple opportunities to lecture on my tanoak research, including for the Association for Women in Science, the Evergreen State College, Jepson Herbarium at the University of California, Berkeley, the Society for Applied Anthropology, the University of Washington Botanic Gardens, the Washington Native Plant Society, the U.S. Forest Service, and Centralia College. California family and friends kindly hosted me during research trips, including Kat Anderson, Mark Harrington and Dixie Dursteler, Judy Irvin, Gabriele Ludwig, Kate Mawdsley, Melissa Nelson and Colin Farish, David and Jeannette Robertson, Steve Schoenig and Carol

Hillhouse, Carrie Shaw and Marc Hoshovsky, Mike and Susan Swezy, and Eileen Zar. Washingtonian friends Anne Fischel, Ruth Hayes, Peter Randlette, Laurie Meeker, and Maria Trevizo encouraged me in countless ways. My husband, Rob Saecker, made this work possible with his love, respect, patience, and good cooking

THE TANOAK TREE

INTRODUCTION

Plants seldom figure in the grand narratives of war, peace,
or even everyday life in proportion to their importance to humans.
Yet they are significant natural and cultural artifacts,
often at the center of high intrigue.

—LONDA SCHIEBINGER

EARLY ONE MORNING IN THE AUTUMN OF 1902, A SINKYONE IN-
dian man danced and sang on the rocky rugged Lost Coast of northern
California to renew the world and reaffirm the earth. In the forest nearby lay
tanoak trees, stripped of their bark. Stacks upon stacks of peeled tanbark
waited near Needle Rock on the marine terrace below. Like big cinnamon
sticks neatly arranged, the bark would soon be loaded onto schooners and
taken to tanneries in San Francisco, over a hundred miles to the south. The
prized bark from tanoaks was a key ingredient for making heavy leather, a
commodity consumed in large quantities in a pre-plastic world. While Jack
Woodman prayed for a cure to the destruction he witnessed, the Creator
appeared and said, referring to the naked tanoak trunks left to rot, "It looks
just like my people lying around . . . with all their skin cut off." The Creator "saw men breaking rocks and plowing up grass" but "felt worst about
the tanbark," because "Tanoak has big power."[1] Its nutritious and delicious
acorns were a staple for Native peoples from southwestern Oregon to the
central coast of California for millennia. On a landscape scale, indigenous
people once fostered the health of tanoak as an important food plant.

This case study of tanoak examines the interplay of economic, ecological, and cultural factors that made the tree a crucial resource for Native

Americans, a useful one for nineteenth-century industries, and an expendable one for twentieth-century lumber companies. Because of its distinctive properties, the tanoak played multiple roles in the industrial development of the West. Acorns produced by tanoaks are nutritious for people as well as pigs, cattle, and other livestock. Tanoak bark contains high concentrations of tannins, which can be used for tanning leather. Tanoak wood is useful for flooring, furniture, cabinetry, tool handles, and other wooden objects but less profitable to harvest than conifers. Tanoaks grow rapidly after the clear-cutting of Douglas-fir forests, thereby crowding out more commercially valuable conifers. In roughly a century, this indigenous totem food plant was transformed into an early cash crop in California and Oregon and then became a target of chemical weeding. Changes in economic organization and technology resulted in tanoaks not only losing their value as a tannin source but also becoming viewed as obstacles to the growing of more lucrative species. As a result, a policy of tanoak eradication came to prevail in industrial West Coast forests.

Native hardwoods on the west coast of North America have been killed on a landscape scale in industrial forests since the middle of the twentieth century in order to favor softwoods (conifers). Common hardwood herbicide targets include maple, alder, and oak. Tanoak killing emerged in West Coast industrial forests because tanoak could not be integrated into centralized, global-scale production of pork, leather, and wood, despite its utility and early profitability for all three industries. Tanoak could not compete with faster-growing and ultimately more easily processed species such as cereal grains, black wattle (*Acacia decurrens*), coast redwood (*Sequoia sempervirens*), Douglas-fir (*Pseudotsuga menziesii*), and eucalyptus (*Eucalyptus* spp.).

For social and environmental reasons, Native peoples, timber workers, and local environmental activists questioned herbicide use on tanoaks for decades. Despite its important ecological roles in forest ecosystems, beginning in 1950, most industrial foresters advocated killing this native hardwood species in order to favor conifers such as Douglas-fir. Ironically, beginning in the late nineteenth century, foresters initially defended tanoak from bark overharvesters and detractors with little success. Foresters became influential on a landscape scale in tanoak management when their advice served the goal of simplifying West Coast forests for the purpose of maximizing softwood production, in part by adopting green revolution strategies from agriculture and mechanization approaches designed to reduce dependency on labor.

Today tanoak still deserves conservation attention due to its cultural and ecological importance. Tanoak preservation in parks theoretically safeguards this foundation species against the unintended consequences of commerce. However, an exotic disease, sudden oak death, first detected in North America in the mid-1990s, poses a serious threat. Many state and federal parks are already infested. This magnificent tree, along with its relative American chestnut (*Castanea dentata*), reminds us that even common plants can rapidly become threatened. A century ago in North America's eastern deciduous forests, a non-native disease inadvertently introduced on an imported Chinese chestnut (*Castanea mollissama*) began to spread. Within decades, the once widespread American chestnuts succumbed to chestnut blight and no longer produced nutritious nuts for people, livestock, and wildlife in most of its native range.[2] Today, a similar fate may await tanoak. This particular tree's story teaches us about the limits and failures of government regulation of industry.

Ever since the horticultural trade accidentally introduced the pathogen that causes sudden oak death to North America, millions of tanoaks have died, and an unknown number are infected. In roughly twenty years, the lethal disease has spread extensively to the south and north of San Francisco, with disjunct outbreaks as far away as southwestern Oregon despite efforts to contain it. Currently no cure exists for infected trees, and thus far tanoak exhibits little genetic resistance to the exotic water mold, *Phytophthora ramorum*, that causes the disease. Fortunately, large areas remain uninfected. The southernmost tanoak populations near Santa Barbara and inland populations away from the coast are probably too dry to foster sudden oak death. However, these populations may not fare well with global climate change if conditions get too much drier. Computer models rank uninfected areas on the northern coast of California as at high risk for infection. The current epidemic of sudden oak death warrants concern because, although tanoak can't compete as an industrial, monocultural crop, its persistence may be critical to the continued production of more commercially valuable species that do, such as Douglas-fir.

Tanoak's history traces a common trajectory of American expansionism and industrial capitalism leading to environmental decline and more centralized control over land use, with one important twist. Radical downsizing of the West Coast softwood timber industry beginning in the late twentieth century created an opportunity to catalyze significant changes in forest products industries. Currently local initiatives to favor fair and sustainable trade in West Coast hardwoods, including tanoak, show promise as a means of improving forest ecosystem health. Also contemporary efforts by indigenous peoples to reestablish traditional burning practices offer hope, given evidence that suppressing fires in order to protect conifers compromised tanoak health and made the tree vulnerable to decline. Partnerships between local timber-based communities, tribes, public foresters, and educated consumers offer the potential to change forest use in ways that are more democratically determined, socially just, and ecologically sound.

This interdisciplinary book draws evidence from diverse fields including American history, anthropology, economic botany, environmental history, ethnobotany, forestry, horticulture, industrial chemistry, natural history, plant science, wildlife biology, and wood science. Primary sources include business records, diaries, government reports, historic photographs, letters, nature journals, scientific journal articles, and trade journal articles. Given the long period of time covered and the integration of evidence from many disciplines, I relied on secondary sources at times. I also interviewed and corresponded with a variety of experts such as ecologists, environmentalists, ethnobotanists, evolutionary plant biologists, foresters, horticulturalists, Native Americans (including individuals with expertise in traditional ecological knowledge), plant pathologists, and postglacial vegetation scientists.

THE BEAUTIFUL TREE

Truth is relative to culture,
that what one people takes for good, beautiful,
and true may be thought as the reverse by another.

—JAMES R. JACOB

IN THE KASHAYA POMO LANGUAGE, TANOAK IS CALLED *CHISHKALE*, which translates to "beautiful tree."[1] In his 1889 description of tanoak, the first botany professor at the University of California, Berkeley, Edward L. Greene, called tanoak "the most remarkable of all North American oaks" and listed it "among the most beautiful of Californian forest trees."[2] One booster of tanoak as a source of fine-grained wood claimed in 1891 that "[i]t is not generally known that this is one of the most beautiful of all the hardwoods of America or, for that matter, of any other country."[3] In his multivolume treatise *The Silva on North America*, Charles Sprague Sargent ranked it among "the most interesting inhabitants" of U.S. forests in 1895.[4] He claimed that no other western North American oak tree surpassed "the best representatives of [tanoak] in massive beauty, in symmetry of outline, or in richness of color." Sargent described how "in early spring the elongated tender shoots and unfolding leaves coated with bright hairs, appearing like masses of flowers against the dark background of foliage, light up the dark coniferous forests" where it often grows.[5]

One late nineteenth-century writer for a San Francisco newspaper compared old-growth tanoak groves in Mendocino County to Druidic temples because of their lofty branches and pleasing forms, a romantic reference to the lost sacred oak groves used in the ancient Celtic religion of the British

Isles and Europe.⁶ George Sudworth, a nationally recognized tree authority who worked for the U.S. Forest Service for more than four decades, remarked in 1908: "Economically a tree of the greatest importance in Pacific forest, both for its valuable tanbark and for the promise it gives of furnishing good commercial timber in a region particularly lacking in hardwoods."⁷ Yet despite high praise, most Americans remain unfamiliar with this common associate in the coast redwood forests of the United States.

Tanoak occurs in a monospecific genus, meaning only one species exists in its genus on the planet. The tree variety, *Notholithocarpus densiflorus* var. *densiflorus*, grows from southwestern Oregon through the California Coast Range to near Santa Barbara, with inland populations occurring through the Siskiyou Mountains and from the southern tip of the Cascade Range along the western slopes of the Sierra Nevada to Yosemite National Park.⁸ Much of its coastal distribution overlaps with that of coast redwood, but due to its greater tolerance of drought, tanoak extends farther inland. The shrub variety, *N. densiflorus* var. *echinoides*, occurs in "scattered locations in the Siskiyou region and the Sierra Nevada to Mariposa County."⁹ This "dwarf form . . . is more common at higher elevations in the north-eastern range of the species, particularly on serpentine."¹⁰ A mutant shrublike form (*N. densiflorus* forma "attenuato-dentatus") grows in Yuba County in the northern Sierra Nevada.¹¹ The mutant is used in horticulture due in part to its rarity and its unusual and beautiful narrow leaves, which are deeply toothed and taper to a very narrow apical tip. Given that this mutant's maximum height is roughly eight feet, it adapts to small urban gardens much better than the full-size tanoak trees. In California, tanoak is more common than any other hardwood tree, which includes all flowering trees.¹² Despite being abundant in much of its range, tanoak's global distribution is very limited.

The most ancient trees are estimated to be as old as three hundred to four hundred years.¹³ According to the U.S. Forest Service, 109 inches is the largest diameter on record, which was measured on a 100-foot-tall tanoak in Humboldt County with a 76-foot-wide crown.¹⁴ Although significantly shorter at 65 feet in height, the limbs of another ancient tree reported farther south reached 60 feet in width. This enormous tree with a circumference of 227 inches grew near Rock Spring in Mount Tamalpais State Park, just north of San Francisco (fig. 1.1).¹⁵ Throughout its range, 180 years appears to be a typical maximum age in unlogged forests.¹⁶ It is often difficult to reliably determine the age of a tanoak due to heart rot and the high frequency of suckering if killed to the ground. Its hard wood also makes coring a tanoak

FIGURE 1.1 Old-growth tanoak tree on Mount Tamalpais in Marin County, California, north of San Francisco, ca. 1942. Courtesy of the Forest History Society, Durham, North Carolina.

FIGURE 1.2 Tanoak in open prairie with robust canopy, a legacy of frequent, low-intensity fires set by Native people. Ukiah, California, ca. 1903. Photograph by A. O. Carpenter. Courtesy of the University and Jepson Herbaria Archives, University of California, Berkeley.

trunk to count growth rings a challenge. Tanoak's overall shape varies greatly depending on growing conditions, like other plants. However, two common forms of this evergreen tree exist, one in full sun (fig 1.2) and another in shade (see fig. 8.2). In open stands dominated by hardwoods or scattered in prairies, tanoaks form a broad, dense crown and a short trunk with robust horizontal branches that can reach to the ground. In shady, dense coniferous forests, tanoaks often grow as tall as 150 feet, with a branchless trunk that is clear for 30 to 80 feet.[17] Taller trees with long trunks growing with coniferous competition lend themselves to wood production, while trees grown in sunny exposures generate a greater abundance of food in the form of acorns. Generally, the height of a medium-size tree typically ranges from 50 to 90 feet , with a maximum height recorded at 208 feet.[18] Diameter at breast height in mature trees typically ranges from 6 to 48 inches .[19]

Willis Linn Jepson, a University of California botany professor from 1899 to 1937, wrote that tanoak is "exceptionally well-fitted by its reproductive powers, vigor and shade endurance to take part in the struggle for continuous possession of the land"—hence its other common name, sovereign oak.[20] In response to fire, tanoak can quickly rise from the ashes when previously dormant epicormic buds are activated to sprout from a burl below or near ground level or from the root system. The ability to form a burl as a sapling makes tanoak well adapted to recover if it dies down to the ground after a frost, drought, or fire. Tanoak can be in a repressed state for a long time in the understory and spring to life when released from competition after conifer logging.

Tanoak is a resilient evergreen capable of withstanding drought and frost. Its simple leaves alternate on the stem. Notorious for being highly variable, the leaves are "leathery to brittle" with serrated to toothless edges and often revolute margins (fig. 1.3).[21] The lateral veins off the midrib typically are parallel and unbranched all the way to the leaf margin, which lends the tree the appearance of being related to chestnuts. The usually smooth and shiny leaves are densely wooly on the underside initially, but much of the hair wears off with age.[22] Dense hairiness on new leaves and young twigs reduces water loss. The thick, grayish-brown bark becomes fissured with age.

As is typical of the beech family (Fagaceae), tanoak produces separate female and male flowers on the same plant, a condition known as monoecism. Each small, simple unisexual flower lacks petals (fig. 1.4). Although each flower is tiny, collectively the males put on a show in a kind of inflo-

FIGURE 1.3 Tanoak. Unknown photographer, U.S. Forest Service, 1966.
Courtesy of the National Agricultural Library and USDA-NRCS PLANTS
Database, http://plants.usda.gov/java/largeImage?imageID=lide3_011_avp.tif.

rescence called a "spike," with each flower lacking an individual stalk. In
the words of Donald Culross Peattie, author of *A Natural History of Western
Trees*, the abundant yellowish-white male spikes "light up the tree like can-
dles at Christmas" (fig. 1.5).[23] The small, solitary female flowers aggregate at
the base of the erect male catkin, each subtended by a small bract. Tanoaks
can flower in any season except winter, but blossoms typically appear in
June, July, or August with coastal and low-elevation trees blooming earliest.[24] Drought during pollination fosters greater seed set.[25] Once pollinated,
acorns mature after two years.[26] Tanoak trees begin bearing acorns in abundance between thirty and forty years of age.[27] Coppice growth in the form of
burl sprouts can begin producing acorns as young as five years old.[28]

Although botanists, foresters, and plant pathologists have completed

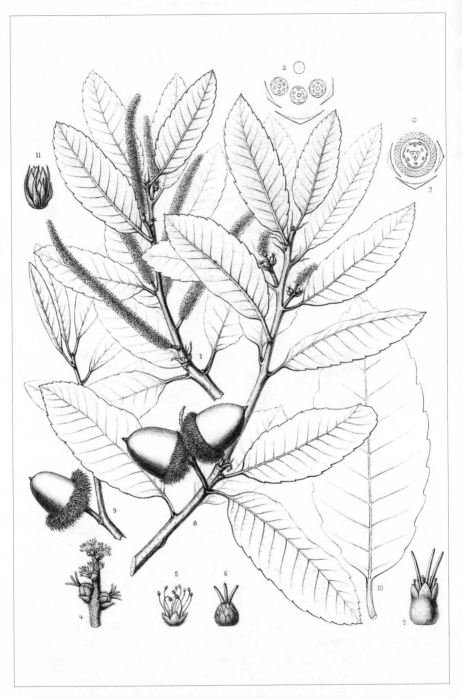

FIGURE 1.4 Tanoak twig with female flowers, male flowers, male catkins, and acorns. Illustration by Charles Edward Faxon, ca. late nineteenth century. From Sargent, *The Silva of North America*, tab. 438.

M.S del. J.N.Fitch.lith.

Vincent Brooks,Day&Son Ltᵈimp.

L.Reeve & Cᵒ London.

FIGURE 1.5 Tanoak portrait in *Curtis's Botanical Magazine*. Detail of female flowers in upper left, acorns and empty acorn cap in lower left, and male flower close-up in center at bottom of image. From Prain (1917), tab. 8695. Courtesy of Biodiversity Heritage Library.

much research on tanoak, a full understanding of the organisms and ecological processes affected by it remains incomplete. Until recently, tanoak
was widely believed to be wind pollinated, like oaks in the genus *Quercus*.
Although self-fertilization does occur, and some wind pollination is likely,
most female tanoak flowers are insect pollinated.[29] Volunteer citizen scientists assisted in making this new discovery; however, the insect species
observed remain to be systematically identified. Further research is recommended to study the significance of tanoak pollen as a food source in
pollinator communities.[30] Tanoak's pollination ecology has multiple implications for conservation. Insect pollination can significantly increase genetic diversity within a plant's populations, which can ultimately affect the
plant's ability to adapt to changing environmental conditions.

These nut-bearing trees feed numerous animal species. Many wildlife
species cache tanoak acorns for later consumption, including acorn wood-
peckers (*Melanerpes formicivorus*), Steller's jays (*Cyanocitta stelleri*), and at
least four species of squirrels.[31] One tanoak nut hoarder, the dusky-footed
woodrat (*Neotoma fuscipes* ssp. *fuscipes*), is an important prey of the northern spotted owl (*Strix occidentalis* ssp. *caurina*). Other predators of tanoak
herbivores include coyotes (*Canis latrans*), cougars (*Puma concolor*), and
fishers (*Martes pennanti*).[32] Because tanoaks produce their abundant nut
crop in the fall, they provide a critically important food source for bear and
deer that fatten on the acorns, building a reserve and insulating layer for
winter. Even the now extinct, endemic California grizzly bear (*Ursus arctos*
ssp. *californicus*) enjoyed tanoak acorns given its former distribution.[33] In
addition to deer and bear, other important game species benefit from the
tanoak mast, such as band-tailed pigeon (*Patagioenas fasciata* ssp. *fasciata*),
wild turkey (*Meleagris gallopavo* ssp. *intermedia*), and feral pig (*Sus scrofa*).
Various species of native mice (*Peromyscus* spp.) also consume the acorns.[34]
(For a partial list of wildlife species that eat tanoak acorns, see table 1.) In
addition, mule deer (*Odocoileus hemionus*) browse its leaves.[35]

Various salamanders and rodents use tanoak for cover and/or nest-
ing.[36] Because tanoaks often grow in the shade of taller coast redwood
and Douglas-fir, they help to create forests with multilayered tree canopies favorable to northern spotted owls and other animals (fig. 1.6).[37]
A variety of birds forage for insects on tanoak, including red-breasted
sapsuckers (*Sphyrapicus ruber*), dusky flycatchers (*Empidonax oberholseri*),
mountain chickadees (*Poecile gambeli*), brown creepers (*Certhia americana*), Nashville warblers (*Vermivora ruficapilla*), and yellow-rumped war-

TABLE 1. Some Wildlife Species That Consume Tanoak Acorns

Animal Type	Common Name	Scientific Name
Birds	Acorn woodpecker	*Melanerpes formicivorus*
	Band-tailed pigeon	*Patagioena fasciata* ssp. *fasciata*
	Pacific varied thrush	*Ixoreus naevius* ssp. *naevius*
	Steller's jay	*Cyanocitta stelleri*
Mammals	American black bear	*Ursus americanus*
	California ground squirrel	*Spermophilus beecheyi*
	Columbian black-tailed deer	*Odocoileus hemionus* ssp. *columbianus*
	Douglas squirrel	*Tamiasciurus douglasii* ssp. *mollipilosus*
	Dusky-footed woodrat	*Neotoma fuscipes* ssp. *fuscipes*
	Mule deer	*Odocoileus hemionus*
	Northern flying squirrel	*Glaucomys sabrinus*
	Northern raccoon	*Procyon lotor*
	Townsend's chipmunk	*Tamias townsendii*
	Western gray squirrel	*Sciurus griseus*

Sources: Based on Roy, "A Record," 4; and Fryer, "*Lithocarpus densiflorus* in Fire Effects Information System."
Note: Nomenclature follows the Integrated Taxonomic Information System.

blers (*Dendroica coronata*).[38] The brown creeper may also eat acorns.[39]

   Tanoaks are host to a variety of fungi, including many that play critical ecological roles in forests. A variety of ectomycorrhizal fungi form mutually beneficial relationships with tanoaks in which they grow around the roots and between cell walls, allowing for increased water and mineral uptake by the plant in exchange for carbohydrates produced by the plant through photosynthesis. Two University of California researchers found 119 taxa of ectomycorrhizae growing on tanoak roots in northern California, which they believed to be an underestimate due to their sampling method.[40] Their estimated species richness of root-associated fungal taxa was 265. Researchers predict that *P. ramorum* will cause a decline in ectomycorrhizal fungi, which is troubling, given their significance in "ecosystem function through their control over decomposition, nutrient acquisition, and mobilization

FIGURE 1.6 Northern spotted owl perched in a tanoak tree in northern California, 1985. Photograph by Paul Chesley. Courtesy of the photographer and National Geographic Creative.

and regulation of succession in plant communities"; thus their decline "will likely disrupt the function and structure of these forests."[41] In coast redwood forests and some other ecosystems, tanoak is the dominant or only ectomycorrhizal host.[42] Northern flying squirrels, another important prey for northern spotted owls, consume fungi that grow on tanoak roots.[43]

Tanoak logs, snags, and forests produce a variety of edible fungi coveted by many Californians. One of the most treasured mushrooms hunted in tanoak stands is the American matsutake (*Tricholoma magnivelare*), also known as tanoak mushroom (fig. 1.7). It is harvested for local consumption and for export. Multiple northwestern California tribes particularly value the American matsutake, including the Hupa, Karuk, Wailaki, and Yurok.[44] They typically combine autumn mushroom hunting with tanoak acorn and

FIGURE 1.7 American matsutake, or tanoak mushrooms (*Tricholoma magnivelare*), harvested by LaVerne Glaze, Karuk-Yurok. Photograph by Frank K. Lake. Courtesy of Frank K. Lake and LaVerne Glaze.

huckleberry harvesting.[45] Native peoples from northwestern California still consume several other species of fungi that grow from tanoak, including oyster mushroom (*Pleurotus cornucopiae*), black trumpet (*Craterellus cornucopioides*) and lion's mane (*Hericium erinaceus*).[46] Choice "oyster mushrooms will repeatedly fruit from rotting . . . tanoak . . . snags and logs until the decay is too advanced."[47] Shiitake mushrooms (*Lentinula edodes*) can be cultivated on whole tanoak log chips.[48]

For more than a century, botanists believed tanoak to be an evolutionary link between oak (*Quercus*) and chestnut (*Castanea*) based on morphological features. The tanoak acorn resembles that of *Quercus*, but its upright male catkins echo those of *Castanea*. In 1840, two British botanists wrote the original description for tanoak and assigned it to *Quercus* but described tanoak as a "remarkable plant [that] has very much the appearance of a *Castanea*."[49] Willis Linn Jepson in 1909 adopted the revised tanoak name that placed it in the southeast Asian genus *Pasania*, claiming it to be "equally related to" oaks and chestnuts.[50] Currently, the genus *Pasania* is included within *Lithocarpus*. Charles Sprague Sargent's 1922 manual of North American trees called tanoak an oak-chestnut "intermediate" and favored its inclusion in the genus *Lithocarpus*.[51] However, genetic research published in 2008 indicates that tanoak is more closely related to oaks, chestnuts, and Asian chinquapin (*Castanopsis*) than it is to the southeast Asian genus *Lithocarpus* and the North American chinquapin in the genus *Chrysolepis*, which is now considered a sister taxon to *Lithocarpus*.[52] Consequently, a new monospecific genus was established for the North American tanoak, *Notholithocarpus*.

The fossil record of tanoak remains unresolved. When tanoak was moved to *Notholithocarpus*, the North American paleospecies assigned to the genus *Lithocarpus* were not automatically placed in the new genus.[53] To date, paleobotanists have not determined whether the fossils ascribed to the genus *Lithocarpus* in North America require reassignment. In addition, multiple paleospecies are disputed. In the words of paleobotanist Alan Graham, "In the older literature identifications were often made on the basis of limited, fragmentary, poorly preserved specimens; and the level of accuracy has proven to be less than spectacular."[54] Because of the extreme range of leaf variation in *Lithocarpus*, their macrofossils are difficult to identify with certainty when preserved fruits don't occur with the fossilized leaves. For this reason, *L. klamathensis* and *L. weidei* are disputed species.[55] Based on leaf shape, venation, and acorn cupule characteristics preserved in macrofossils, *Lithocarpus nevadensis* did grow in Nevada 10-15 million years ago at 6,000 feet or more under a much warmer and wetter climate than exists today at that elevation.[56] Based on macrofossil specimens that include an acorn cap, also housed at the University of California Museum of Paleontology, *L. coatsi* dated to the Eocene also appears to be a defendable species and grew in present-day Nevada.[57] This puts the oldest known *Lithocarpus* fossil in North America at more than 33.9 million years old.

Although helpful in distinguishing other members of the Fagaceae family from one another, microfossils of pollen are unlikely to further refine the current understanding of tanoak evolution. Researchers studying Quaternary vegetation in southwestern Oregon found that fossilized pollen of tanoak resembles chinquapin pollen.[58] This was corroborated by light microscopic study of extant tanoak and chinquapin pollen from Estella Leopold's reference collection at the University of Washington, Seattle. Two Swedish paleobotanists, Thomas Denk and Guido Grimm, found pollen ornamentation highly useful in delineating evolutionary lineages within the genus *Quercus* when examined with a scanning electron microscope.[59] However,

Denk doubts that pollen can be used to distinguish *Notholithocarpus* from *Lithocarpus*.[60] Although pollen micromorphology such as shape and pollen wall sculpting has been used successfully in various taxonomic studies of some groups within the Fagaceae family, within the chestnut subfamily Castaneiodeae it is "relatively uniform."[61]

The beech family (Fagaceae), to which tanoak belongs, originated in the Northern Hemisphere. Although widely considered a natural group derived from a shared ancestor, evolutionary relationships between taxa within the family remain "far from resolved."[62] Bidirectional migration reputedly occurred between Eurasia and North America via the North Atlantic and Bering Land Bridges.[63] However, two evergreen taxa, *Castanopsis* and *Lithocarpus*, appear to have migrated only over the Bering Land Bridge; based on the fossil record, this occurred "by at least the mid-Eocene."[64] During periods of glaciation, sea level dropped enough to link the Eurasian and North American continents. Later isolation caused by the rising sea level allowed for the evolution of novel species, including tanoak and American chinquapin (*Chrysolepis*). Uplift of mountain ranges and the Nevadaplano due to tectonic activity in western North America may have begun in the Cretaceous more than 65 million years ago.[65] Subsequent down-drop of land to the east of the present-day Sierra Nevada mountain range contributed to the formation of a rain-shadow effect that caused tanoak's range to shrink to areas that still received moisture from storms moving across the Pacific Ocean. Between 15 and 14.5 million years ago, "development of a cold current along the eastern North Pacific Ocean" resulted in drier summer conditions east of the Sierra Nevada and the Cascade Range.[66] During this period of time in the Miocene, a Mediterranean climate resembling today's dry-summer–wet-winter regime developed relatively rapidly "from a summer moist climate" on the west coast of North America.[67]

Judging from the fossil record, the ancestors of tanoak probably enjoyed a broader distribution. Like its common associate coast redwood, tanoak is a relict of a wetter climate, which has shaped its current distribution. Recent genetic research reinforces the notion that tanoak is a paleoendemic, a relict of "an ancient and formerly widespread broad-leaf evergreen flora, which persists today in the Indochinese tropics" where summer rainfall is the norm and killing frosts are not.[68] Despite its long evolutionary history involving the ability to morph in ways that allowed it to survive significant changes in climate and landforms over millions of years, economic activity threatens its future.[69] This book tells the story of how a valued food plant on the western coast of North America became, in the eyes of some, a valueless species that could not adapt to a new social order. This account examines how tanoak ultimately became a native weed to be exterminated and the many attempts to tend to and defend this beautiful tree.

2

ACORNS

Human ideologies, religions, value systems, and moral codes
have been, and continue to be, at the heart of . . . the story all over the
world whenever people differ in opinion about their natural resource
lands and how they should be used and managed.

—SAM H. HAM

TANOAK IS ONE OF THE MORE RELIABLE ACORN PRODUCERS, rarely failing completely and bearing bumper crops more frequently. Annual nut production in most nut-bearing trees worldwide varies significantly, with heavy crops every two to five years. As with other members of the beech family, masting, or variable annual nut production, evolved in tanoak to limit the population size of seed-eating animals. In addition to reducing "loss . . . to specialist insect seed predators," masting "increase[s] the effectiveness of nut dispersal by scatter hoarding rodents and corvids" such as jays and crows.[1] Tanoaks "are heavily laden almost every alternate year and complete seed crop failures are rare," helping to give it the reputation of being the heaviest acorn producer of all Pacific Coast oak species.[2] Tanoak trees typically begin to bear an abundance of acorns when they are between 30 and 40 years old, "although 5-year-old [burl] sprouts also have produced fairly heavy crops."[3] A mature tanoak tree bears more than 200 pounds of nuts on average in a good year, with estimates as high as 1,000 pounds annually for old-growth trees.[4] Tanoak acorns typically exceed the size of a hazelnut.

Tanoak acorns formed the basis of a California Indian acorn economy for thousands of years (fig. 2.1) and remain a highly valued food among indigenous tribal peoples. In northern California, at least after American settlement, salmon was the only other food consumed in larger quantities. Indigenous peoples gathered and favored acorns from multiple oak species. Northwestern tribes in particular often preferred tanoak acorns when obtainable.[5] E. W. Gifford, an academic expert on acorn eating, or balanophagy, in California, ranked tanoak number one in popularity and black oak (*Quercus kelloggii*) second.[6] Although the notion is controversial, anthropologist Martin Baumhoff defended rating as important "because in many areas people would travel a long way to a single tree of a preferred species while ignoring nearby groves of an undesirable species."[7] Three remnant Tolowa tanoak groves totaling nearly five hundred mature trees along the Smith River were estimated to produce per season "14.4 tons . . . of usable food materials when dried."[8] In addition to their role as a staple food, tanoak acorns could be used as medicine. Among the Kashaya Pomo, tanoak acorns functioned as cough drops as the tannins suppressed coughing,[9] and the Ohlones used a tanbark decoction to treat facial sores and loose teeth.[10] Oak saplings, including tanoak, provided strength in heavy-duty baskets, including the hopper basket used during acorn pounding, with an oak rim where women rested their legs in order to hold the basket in place around the mortar.[11] In baby baskets, the sapling protected the infant's head. Tanoak was highly regarded by the Sinkyone, who considered "dreams of tanoak . . . a sign of good luck."[12]

Multiple characteristics of the acorns contribute to tanoak's popularity as a staple food among many California Indian tribes. A thicker shell makes the delicious nut more resistant to fungal and insect attacks.[13] Tanoak acorns store for years, making them a desirable trade item. For example, the Karuk (or Karok) swapped tanoak acorns for "white deer skins, obsidian, dentalia shells, and Sugar Pine nuts" with Shasta people.[14] Tanoak reliably produces an abundance of generous-sized acorns. Compared to grains like wheat, tanoak acorns are low in protein but higher in caloric value due to their superior levels of nutritious fats.[15] Nutrition scientist Linda Ellen Gilliland's study, completed in 1985, reported that protein and fat content varied significantly in acorns and confirmed that protein content is low and fat and carbohydrates are moderately high in traditional tanoak acorn foods (see table 2). Unfortunately, she did not analyze mineral content for tanoak foods.[16] A study published in 2007 indicated that tanoak acorns are rich in gallic acid and ellagic acid.[17] Both of these polyphenolic compounds are known to function as antioxidants in the human body, potentially re-

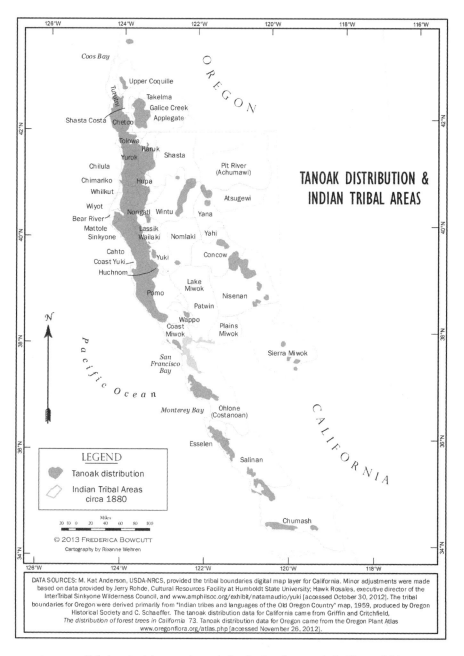

DATA SOURCES: M. Kat Anderson, USDA-NRCS, provided the tribal boundaries digital map layer for California. Minor adjustments were made based on data provided by Jerry Rohde, Cultural Resources Facility at Humboldt State University; Hawk Rosales, executive director of the InterTribal Sinkyone Wilderness Council, and www.amphilsoc.org/exhibit/natamaudio/yuki [accessed October 30, 2012]. The tribal boundaries for Oregon were derived primarily from "Indian tribes and languages of the Old Oregon Country" map, 1959, produced by Oregon Historical Society and C. Schaeffer. The tanoak distribution data for California came from Griffin and Critchfield, *The distribution of forest trees in California* 73. Tanoak distribution data for Oregon came from the Oregon Plant Atlas www.oregonflora.org/atlas.php [accessed November 26, 2012].

FIGURE 2.1 Tribal territorial map and tanoak distribution. Cartography by Rixanne Wehren.

ducing oxidative stress and the risk of cancer. The researchers also assayed fatty acid composition and determined that palmitic acid, oleic acid, and linoleic acid are present in the greatest concentrations.[18] Palmitic acid is a saturated fatty acid that is also found in palm oil and coconut oil. Recent studies challenge earlier claims that it can lead to cardiovascular diseases and cancer.[19] The other two fatty acids are widely recognized as providing significant health benefits. Oleic acid is a monounsaturated omega-9 fatty acid also found in olive oil, and linoleic acid is a polyunsaturated omega-6 essential fatty acid. Humans need dietary sources of essential fatty acids.[20] More research is needed on the nutritional value of these nuts. Acorns are soft enough to chew without processing, but the tannins must be removed to make them useful as human food.[21] Compared to most acorns, tanoak nutmeats are significantly bigger, making them easier to process.

Tanoak acorn harvesting occurred and continues to occur during autumn. Based on the ethnographic record, Karuk families gathered for roughly a month in October.[22] When the tree variety of tanoak failed to produce enough, the Karuk harvested acorns from the shrub variety.[23] The Yuki collected tanoak acorns "far up in the mountains in November when they were ripe" at higher elevations.[24] In order to leave enough for animals, "many native people in northwestern California . . . stop acorn harvest after November."[25] Collecting often occurred some distance from winter residences. The Tolowa moved to the inland edge of the redwood belt for a month to gather nuts before moving back to coastal villages.[26] Pomo ethnographer Fred Kniffen remarked that "no trip was too long to make for these highly desired nuts."[27] Families picked up fallen acorns under tanoak trees. Some tribes used sticks to knock down acorns, but others sanctioned this practice as harmful to the trees as it can cause nuts in their first year of development to fall off, thus reducing the next year's harvest. Pomo men climbed mature trees or, if the trees were smooth barked, used "a sapling or a fallen redwood as a ladder" and then stamped "on the branches to shake" acorns down.[28] Women used openwork burden baskets, which were loosely woven, to transport the harvest.[29]

Annual first acorn ceremonies preceded consumption of the nuts each autumn.[30] Among the Sinkyone, this ceremony lasted five nights.[31] In 1940, Mary Socktish, an officiate of the Hupa's first acorn feast, recounted the associated rituals. Typically, in early October and rarely in late September, she and several other women harvested the earliest ripe tanoak acorns. The night before the feast, she prayed for "plenty of acorns," addressing her

TABLE 2. Nutritional Composition by Percentages of Select Acorns Compared to Barley and Wheat

Species	Fats	Fiber	Carbohydrates	Protein
Black oak (*Quercus kelloggii*)	11.1–18	11.4	55.5	3.4–4.6
Blue oak (*Q. douglasii*)	4.8–8.1	9.8	65.5	3.0–5.5
Canyon oak (*Q. chrysolepis*)	8.7	12.7	63.5	4.1
Coast live oak (*Q. agrifolia*)	14.5–16.8	11.6	54.6	3.1–6.3
Oregon white oak (*Q. garryana*)	4.5	12	68.9	3.9
Valley oak (*Q. lobata*)	4.2–5.5	9.5	69	2.8–4.9
Tanoak (*Notholithocarpus densiflorus*)	12.1	20.1	54.4	2.9
Barley	1.9	5.7	71.0	8.7
Wheat	1.8	2.3	69.4	12.3

Sources: Adapted from Basgall, "Resource Intensification among Hunter-Gatherers," 25; and Baumhoff, "Ecological Determinants," 162.

request to "the acorn 'boss'—Yinukatsisdai, the god of vegetation." Several other women assisted her in praying for a good harvest most of the night in the "sacred living house." After bathing at three in the morning in the cold river, the women began to skin, winnow, pound, and sift the shelled acorns. Around sunrise, the women took the acorn meal to the river for leaching and cooking at the feasting place. "While the stones are heating, we prepare fall salmon, broiling it on sticks around the fire. . . . After the acorn meal is all cooked, about two o'clock in the afternoon, a messenger is sent to notify the people to come to the feast. The people come along a special trail." Socktish warned: "Whoever wastes acorns at any time will not have plenty."[32]

Indigenous peoples developed food technologies for storing, processing, and cooking tanoak acorns to yield a sweet, nutty meal rich in complex carbohydrates and essential fatty acids. Storage inside homes helped to protect against rodents.[33] Among the Lassik, all tanoak acorns were stored inside while other acorn types were stored outside, indicating at least in part the high value placed on tanoak acorns.[34] Pomo women reduced spoilage by drying whole tanoak acorns in the sun before storage, using ultraviolet radiation to kill mold and other fungi. California Indian people used a hammerstone to crack open acorns placed on a flat rock.[35] The Karuk kept hulled tanoak acorns in their homes after drying them on basket plates. The drying acorn meats were occasionally shaken and then rubbed and winnowed to remove the thin skin adhering to the meats that is exposed when the shell is removed.[36]

Outdoor storage allowed for significant stockpiles. Many tribes created granaries where they stored excess acorns for future daily use, feasts, and trading.[37] Sometimes these were far away from a village. Made from woven tule (*Schoenoplectus acutus*), coppice growth of willow or other woody plants (wattle), and/or conifer boughs, these silos often perched on branch legs that raised them off the ground. Construction practices varied among tribes and over time. Essie Parrish, a Kashaya Pomo leader and healer, demonstrated construction of a tanoak acorn cache on a stump in 1960.[38] During the winter months, when fresh foods were scarce, stored acorns became an even more important part of the diet.

Many preparation methods existed. Initially, indigenous peoples processed the nuts either hulled or unhulled but never crushed. Several tribes—including the Yurok, Hupa, Pomo, and Yuki—immersed or buried acorns whole in order to extract the bitter-tasting tannins.[39] The Karuk prepared unpulverized tanoak nuts by placing them in a hole and pouring water over them "for several weeks until they became soft and turned black."[40] For a southwestern Pomo preparation method, the nuts were placed in a pool with the hull cracked but left on, and after four or five months, the mushy, tannin-free acorns were shelled and cooked whole.[41] As with cheese, yogurt, and wine, fungi sometimes factored into acorn preparation. After several weeks in a Pomo home, hulled but still whole nuts molded. After the greenish patina was rubbed off by hand, women ground the nuts and used them like vinegar and salt to give dishes a sour flavor.[42] Sometimes people roasted or boiled the whole nuts; however, removing enough of the tannins from whole nuts by leaching them in water or mud required a great deal more processing time.

Thousands of years ago, women developed a much faster way of processing acorns. Pulverizing and then leaching became the preferred mode of preparation and dominated in areas where acorns served as a staple food.[43] This radically faster leaching process liberated a "vast new food supply of high nutritive value."[44] In California's North Coast Ranges, anthropologists have uncovered milling implements as much as five thousand to seven thousand years old.[45] From archaeological sites in the southern end of the north

Coast Ranges, "the slab and handstone represented the primary milling technology until about 3,000 B.P., after which the mortar and pestle became increasingly more important."[46] A flat milling slab combined with an elongated stone or mano typically served to grind the hard, smaller seeds of mostly grassland plants (pinole), while the stone mortar and pestle primarily pulverized acorn meats and other oily nuts.[47] Pinole was made from a variety of grassland seeds such as tarweed (*Madia*) and California oat grass (*Danthonia californica*). Oak logs with depressions sometimes served as mortars, too.[48] In Potter Valley and other areas in northwest California, women used oak mortars.[49] Bottomless basket hoppers on their mortars kept meal in place during the acorn-pounding process.

The practice of pounding acorns and then leaching the meal with water in a sand basin or basket became widespread between 4,000 and 2,000 BCE (fig. 2.2).[50] Before leaching, Karuk women sifted the acorn meal "in a tight, flat basket, the coarse stuff being removed by tapping the basket with a stick."[51] Sifting practices varied among different indigenous peoples, but essentially it involved separating out the still coarse material so that it could be repulverized more finely. The Karuk used increasingly warmer water during the leaching process. When whites introduced metal pots in the mid-nineteenth century, Round Valley Reservation cooks adapted to leaching almost entirely with warm water, which reduced leaching time,[52] but traditional cultural practitioners persisted with the slower, cold-water method.[53] Heated water extracts the tannins faster, but cold water leaves more of the nutritive value behind, including the high-quality fats. Periodic taste testing during the leaching process indicated when the bitter tannins had been adequately removed. Some people like a little bitterness, while others favor the "sweet" or bland taste of a more leached acorn food. Most people eat prepared acorns with salmon, venison, or honey. The preferred consistency of tanoak acorn food varies from a watery soup to a thick porridge.

In a worldwide comparison, the acorn food technologies of California are among the most developed.[54] People across the globe used (and continue to use) acorns from various oak species as food, but tannin removal practices varied or were lacking entirely. Indigenous people in central Arizona ate only unleached sweet acorns, neglecting acorns with more tannin that yielded a bitter taste. This was true in Mediterranean regions as well, such as Spain. In Mexico, people neglected acorns entirely as food. Most tribes on the east coast of North America boiled acorns before pulverizing them

FIGURE 2.2 Mrs. Freddie (Hupa) leaching acorn meal in 1902 with an open-weave acorn-collecting basket (left). Photograph by Pliny E. Goddard (neg. no. 15-3329). Courtesy of the Phoebe A. Hearst Museum of Anthropology and the Regents of the University of California.

to make them palatable, as did people in Japan. On the island of Sardinia in the Mediterranean Sea, people boiled and then ground acorns but mixed clay rich in iron oxide into the meal to counteract the tannins, in the same way Pomo women do when making acorn bread from black oak acorns.[55] People in the southeastern United States and Persia pounded and then leached acorns, as did the California Indians.[56]

Once the pounded acorns were leached of the bitter tannins, California Native women cooked tanoak acorn porridge or soup by placing hot rocks in baskets with two sticks often with loops at the ends. To prevent the baskets from burning, the women kept the hot rocks moving with wooden paddles. Cooks used extreme caution in their selection of rocks, so that the red-hot rocks would not explode when dunked in water to rinse off ashes before they were placed in the cooking basket.[57] Many women inherited their cooking rocks from female relatives. This method of cooking was fast, and the delicious result was served in dedicated basket bowls or cups. Karuk cooks gave the cake that formed on hot cooking rocks to children as a special treat.[58] Sometimes the Karuk used hot coals to bake patties from tanoak acorn paste.[59] The Kashaya Pomo preferred (and still prefer) to make cereal and soup from tanoak acorns and favor black oak or valley oak acorns for unleavened acorn bread prepared in an earth oven.[60] Along with other abundant native foods such as pinole and salmon, tanoak acorns made possible a settled existence on a relatively small area. Multiple species of oaks generated roughly a pound of food daily over the course of a year.[61] A single well-tended, healthy tanoak grove could meet the needs of a tribal village without supplemental irrigation or inordinate amounts of physical labor.[62]

ACORNS REPURPOSED AS LIVESTOCK FODDER

Americans repurposed the preexisting cultural landscape by importing the European practices of using acorns as livestock fodder and unfenced lands as a grazing commons. Many Euro-Americans met their domestic needs as well as raised excess for the market by fattening semi-feral hogs on tanoak acorns in the fall before slaughter. The resulting fat-rich ham and bacon that "spat all over you" was an indicator of the favored "acorn-fed hog."[63] Using salt to preserve the meat enabled transport without refrigeration. Humboldt County exported 90,000 pounds of bacon and 36,100 pounds of pork in 1881. Humboldt Pork Packing Company alone had sold more than 400,000 pounds of pork by 1881.[64] In neighboring Mendocino County, hog raising also became "an extensive business" by 1882 and was most profitable in well-developed tanoak groves located in valleys.[65] Hog claims could be lucrative and required little capital investment beyond acquiring suitable land. Local meat production helped to meet the burgeoning needs of Pacific Coast cities and mining camps.

Some California settlers converted cash earned from livestock grazed in tanoak groves and associated prairies into capital to help establish a softwood industry. For example, Mr. McKee, who established a homestead in Humboldt County in 1871, sold "ham and bacon to nearby stores and lumber camps." McKee also drove a cattle herd more than a hundred miles and sold it to Fort Ross, a former Russian outpost north of San Francisco. With the money, McKee purchased a sawmill in San Francisco and brought it back to the Mattole River Valley.[66]

By the 1930s, in response to market demand, some indigenous people in northern California favored peeling tanoak bark on the Hoopa Valley Indian Reservation and burning to increase grasslands for raising cattle.[67] Leonard Radtke, the forest supervisor with the U.S. Indian Service tried to make an economic argument in defense of tanoak by quantifying the value of the acorns as hog fodder.[68] His analysis indicated that it was not cost-effective to convert tanoak stands to grasslands. Ironically, while he wistfully described the disappearing noble savage dependent on tanoak acorns, he chastised the modern Indians adapting to the new cultural landscape that favored land use driven by commercial interests over traditional practices. Radtke's unpublished 1937 report remained obscure and unpersuasive against the economic incentives even for Native Americans to produce beef over pork and thus favor grasslands over tanoaks.

Limited use of oak acorns as cattle and hog forage continued into the present, but according to Rancho Santa Ana Botanic Garden researcher Carl B. Wolf, by 1945 tons were "largely wasted."[69] Although tanoak acorns tested low in protein relative to barley, their high fat and carbohydrate content combined with their ease of harvesting led Wolf to conclude that tanoak acorns enriched with protein could be a valuable livestock feed. But as the grazing commons became enclosed as private property, pig production shifted from open range foraging to increasingly centralized and industrialized indoor piggeries dependent on grains grown in monocultures. Use of feedlots came to be favored over open range beef production, a transition also made possible by cheap grain-based feed. American consumers helped to change land use practices by demanding familiar foods and cheaper prices gained in part through greater efficiency in commodities production.

While assimilation efforts beginning in the late 1800s resulted in most Native peoples shifting to wheat as a staple, tanoak acorns remained a culturally important food. Lulu Johnson, a Yuki woman, still prepared tanoak, or shō'-kish, acorn soup, mush, and pancakes for her family in the 1950s when they had "a longing for the taste of the nuts."[70] While fire suppression, livestock grazing, and development diminished acorn crops throughout California, in the twentieth century, the automobile increasingly facilitated travel to optimal locations for gathering acorns, which might vary from year to year. Some people facilitated the process by shifting their collecting to mowed landscapes such as cemeteries. Others were forced to gather at higher elevations than their ancestors had; this often required a shift in schedule to ensure ripeness. Adaptability continued to be key with keeping tanoak food traditions alive and vibrant.

In the new cultural landscape, logging of old-growth forests in northern California became celebrated work from the late 1800s to the 1960s, while female agency as significant producers of local food faded from view. Yet this labor-intensive work represented an important economic contribution in many indigenous homes as well as a traditional way to maintain cultural identity and health. In 1964, anthropologist Samuel Alfred Barrett produced a film on tanoak acorn use, *The Beautiful Tree, Chishkale*, as a part of the American Indian Film Project, made in collaboration with Essie Parrish and her family.[71] "As a cultural leader," Parrish promoted "the maintenance of Native traditions" (figs. 2.3, 2.4).[72] Barrett focused on what he perceived as authentic practices and intentionally did not document the adaptation of new tools like shovels, rakes, and metal meat grinders and pots to facilitate acorn harvesting and processing. "[I]n general Native food systems had substantially changed since contact, and most anthropologists did not want to describe such creole or mixed customs."[73] Due to his romanticism, Barrett opted to present indigenous people as static. In reality, indigenous women had creatively repurposed the garden and culinary tools of Euro-American culture to serve their needs when obtaining and preparing tanoak-based foods.

FIGURE 2.3 Essie Parrish gathering acorns, Kashaya, Sonoma County, 1960. Photograph by Josepha Haveman (neg. no. 15-19440). Courtesy of the Phoebe A. Hearst Museum of Anthropology and the Regents of the University of California.

FIGURE 2.4 Essie Parrish preparing acorn meal, Kashaya, Sonoma County, 1960. Photograph by Josepha Haveman (neg. no. 15-19554). Courtesy of the Phoebe A. Hearst Museum of Anthropology and the Regents of the University of California.

BARK

The many cargoes of this bark which are annually
landed in San Francisco from the northern coast counties may
make botanists apprehensive of a final extinction of the tree.

—EDWARD L. GREENE

THE CULTURAL LANDSCAPE CREATED BY INDIGENOUS PEOPLE FOR
the purpose of producing tanoak acorns was already in transition before
American settlement. With the exception of northern California and
southwestern Oregon, Spanish colonists and their descendants, known as
Californios, usurped oak woodlands and prairies on which to produce beef
for local consumption, with the by-products of tallow and hides intended
primarily for export. Boosters of American commerce chided the Californios for building their economy on these raw resource exports. One such
booster, John Hittell, published an account in 1882 of the Pacific Coast's potential for commerce and industrialization. Indeed by the start of the Civil
War, the golden state had already become "the most commercialized state
in the nation."[1] Hittell originally came to California in 1849 as a gold seeker
but soon became a San Francisco–based journalist and prolific author.[2] He
acknowledged in his 1882 assessment of California that Spaniards imported
the cattle and sheep, which "furnished a regular supply of material for the
tanneries of the missions,"[3] and the practice of using oak bark to process
leather. As early as 1792, the Spanish mission community of Santa Clara
tanned two thousand hides using oak bark.[4] Cattle ranching dominated
land use among the Californios. Both the Spanish and the Californios exported the majority of hides untanned. One agent serving an East Coast

importer bragged in 1836 that he had secured the largest cargo to date from California, which included thirty-nine thousand hides.[5] Hittell asserted that because the region lacked a large tanning industry, West Coast residents paid high prices for imported leather products while exporting their raw materials to be processed elsewhere.[6] Americans like Hittell justified seizing control of natural resources by claiming that they would be more enterprising and less wasteful than the Californios.

Tanning dependent on oak bark represented a dramatic change from preceding indigenous modes of processing animal skins. Before European colonization, Native Americans typically used the chamois tanning method, which yielded pliable leather that was especially useful for making clothing. Using animal brains, livers, and fat, they traditionally converted buckskins or deer hide into soft leather.[7] The Russians operated a California tannery at Fort Ross from 1814 to 1841, shipping most of the resulting leather to their Sitka colony in Alaska and trading a small amount with the Spanish.[8] An Aleut Indian from Kodiak used both methods at the Sonoma Coast fort, preferring the chamois method for tanning deer and wild goat hides. According to K. Khlebnikoff, the resulting product made "excellent pantalones."[9] Hittell dismissed indigenous tanning practices, saying that "the process was tedious, and the stock of such leather in proportion to the population was very small."[10] Native peoples made limited use of tanoak bark. The Tolowa used a dye made from tanoak bark to color their nets and make them less visible to fish.[11] Tannins have a history of being used to preserve fibers such as cloth sails for ships as well as fishnets, so the Tolowa's nets may have lasted longer.[12] The Ohlones (also known as the Costanoans) prepared a dye from tanoak bark as well and used a tanbark decoction as a treatment for facial sores and loose teeth.[13] Some tribes used oak bark in tanning, but the historical record is unclear about whether this occurred before or after colonization and whether the species used included tanoak.[14] In line with social Darwinist ideologies of the time, Euro-Americans justified displacement of Native peoples in northern California in part by claiming that they used natural resources inefficiently, as evident from their tanning practices.

The high concentration of tannins in tanoak bark enabled tanneries to produce durable heavy leathers. Willis Linn Jepson estimated tannin content as high as 10-29 percent in tanoak bark.[15] In a world still dependent on horses for travel, commodities like saddles and other equestrian gear, travel trunks, and even stagecoaches, all made with heavy leathers, were in high demand. The tanned hides of animals also literally kept the cogs of industry turning in the form of leather mechanical belts. Beginning in the mid- to late nineteenth century, after rubber could be vulcanized, industrial belts were made first from natural latex and then, in the early twentieth century, from petroleum-based synthetic rubber.[16] The moderate Mediterranean climate of California enabled quicker leather production than on the Atlantic coast or in northern Europe. It took only three or four months to produce harness leather in California, and leather for shoe soles took four to five.[17] Manufacturers in less temperate climates would speed up the process by adding chemicals, which also compromised the leather's quality by making it more pervious to water and less tough.[18] In contrast, California manufacturers could use just water and tanbark.

Tannins are mildly acidic, organic, phenolic, plant-produced compounds that vary in molecular size. Small tannin molecules dissolve easily in water and are known as hydrolyzable tannins.[19] These combine with other kinds of tannin molecules to form a complex mixture in tree bark. Because "tannins bind strongly to proteins denaturing them," they are useful in leather tanning.[20] Tannic acid from tanoak, used historically for tanning, was derived from tannins found in the tree's bark. In addition to their industrial uses, the bitter taste, negative impact on animal enzyme systems, and toxicity of tannins are significant deterrents to insect feeding.[21] And tannins function to protect plants against fungal attack.[22]

The term "tanbark" refers to bark from any species of plant that is used for tanning. The common name "tanbark oak" refers specifically to tanoak, which was the most prized, and most often utilized, source of tanbark in California. Tanoak bark supplied "practically . . . all the tanners' bark used" on the West Coast.[23] Bark harvesters who supplied tanners peeled the tanoak bark over a three-month period, typically beginning in May in the Santa Cruz area. The sap needed to be running, which in northern California more often occurred from mid-May to mid-July.[24] Bark peelers removed four feet of bark from the base of the standing tree before felling it (fig. 3.1). Then they peeled farther up the trunk and even large branches, as long as the bark was at least a half inch thick (fig. 3.2).[25] Small trees were often jayhawked, meaning that the girdled tree was left standing after the bark at the base had been peeled.[26] Peeled bark was set aside to dry nearby to reduce its weight. Peelers kept busy hauling the bark out of the forest through August and September. If the bark was not hauled out and shipped to a tannery, it was covered (or shedded) and allowed to season before it was

FIGURE 3.1 Crew of tanoak bark peelers in the Bear River or Mattole River watershed south of Eureka, California, ca. 1907. Photograph probably by Ray Jerome Baker (photo ID 1999.01.0066). The Swanlund/Baker Collection, Humboldt State University Library Special Collections, Arcata, California.

FIGURE 3.2 Peeling tanoak bark, date and photographer unknown. Courtesy of the University and Jepson Herbaria Archives, University of California, Berkeley.

1953

FIGURE 3.3 Tanoak bark curing shed in Briceland, California, ca. 1907. Photograph by Ray Jerome Baker (photo ID 1999.01.0063). The Swanlund/Baker Collection, Humboldt State University Library Special Collections, Arcata, California.

shipped or processed into extract (fig. 3.3). Curing it under cover prevented the precious tannins from being leached out by winter rains.

The preparation of leather was a multistep process. Tanners took salted, scraped, and dried hides and washed them thoroughly, getting rid of the salt and any remaining blood, meat, or dung. Then a strong lime solution was used to loosen hair shafts. Another thorough washing removed the lime and the remaining hair. The time-consuming process of tanning leather began with placing the hides in a progression of stronger tanning solutions, from weak, previously used tanning liquid to the tannin-rich solution derived from freshly leached bark. The liquid, or "liquor," was made from ground bark combined with water and heated in order to extract the tannins and other active compounds.[27] The tanners placed hides in the dark tea or a decoction to soak in vats for months. The last steps involved scrubbing the coating that developed off the hides, which were then dried, oiled, and greased.[28]

Sonoma County's Alexander Valley was reputedly the site of the first American-staffed tannery. It was built in 1840 solely for the use of the owner, Cyrus Alexander, who obtained tanbark nearby and traded with Native people for shells as a source of lime.[29] In 1843, John Sutter established a small tanyard at Fort Sutter in Sacramento. Although he purchased Fort Ross from the departing Russians in 1841, he opted not to transfer their tanning equipment to Sacramento but instead sold Fort Ross entirely in 1845.[30] A short-lived Los Angeles tannery established in 1854 imported tanoak bark from farther north.[31] Several tanneries formed in Stockton by 1858, which were initially dependent on live oak bark, but as they depleted that resource they shifted to tanoak bark.[32] By the 1860s, there were many tanneries near San Francisco Bay and a short distance from it. Santa Cruz supported seven tanneries by 1868, which collectively consumed roughly 300 tons of bark per month.[33] Due to its large populations of tanoak, Humboldt County's third-largest industry from the late 1880s to the early 1900s was leather manufacturing.[34] Tanneries continued to be established throughout the range of tanoak into the early twentieth century.

Tanoak bark enabled the advancement of capital as California industrialized. Leather manufacturers centralized much of their production in urban settings in order to maximize access to cheap labor sources, such as Chinese and European immigrants (fig. 3.4). Access to an abundance of water was also important for washing hides, and the many rainless, warm

FIGURE 3.4 Tannery letterhead promoting the "Monarch of oaks," 1907. From the San Francisco Bay area tannery in Benicia operated by Kullman, Salz & Company. From *Jepson Correspondence Letters received and written by Willis Linn Jepson Concerning Tan Oak*, vol. 29, 1902-1916. Courtesy of the University and Jepson Herbaria Archives, University of California, Berkeley.

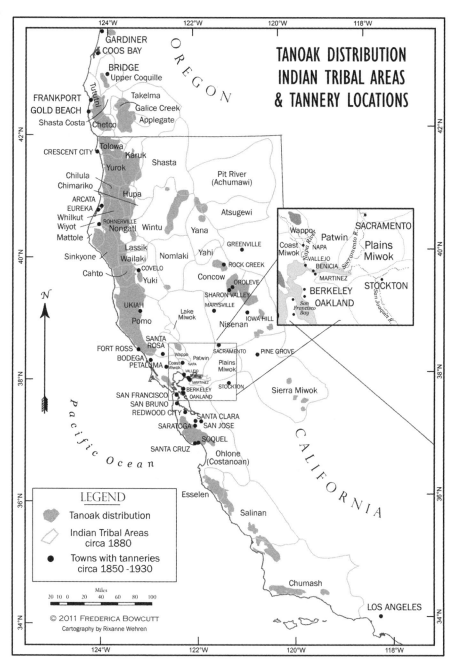

FIGURE 3.5 Tanoak's distribution in relation to tribal boundaries and tannery locations. Cartography by Rixanne Wehren.

days were a bonus for drying them. The discovery that tannin could be leached out of ground tanoak bark and even foreign tanbark with a setup similar to a coffee percolator also fostered urban tanneries.[35] The thick liquid extract could be shipped much more cheaply than heavy and cumbersome bark. All told, Americans established tanneries in roughly forty towns and cities within the range of tanoak or within a relatively short distance (fig. 3.5). By 1858, the tanning industry in California had "already almost driven Eastern leather out of the market."[36] As of 1866, annual leather sales in San Francisco exceeded $1 million.[37] Due to its high quality, well-known New York and Pennsylvania boot and shoe manufacturers bought San Francisco heavy leather. Leather tanned with tanoak bark was also exported to China and Hawaii as early as 1866.[38]

San Francisco was a major consumer of tanbark oak. The city stank, literally, from approximately fifty tanneries. The rotting flesh still stuck to the hides reeked, while animal skins were left to cure in vats of oak bark decoction for months. According to one early northern Californian, San Francisco controlled the Pacific Coast market.[39] Based on 1881 estimates, California used about 28,000 tons annually, with 16,000 tons (57 percent) going to San Francisco tanneries.[40] An 1889 estimate put annual consumption at nearly 50,000 tons.[41] Hittell estimated the value of the bark from tanoak used in California that year at $560,000.[42] As demand increased, the bark rose in value. In 1882, tanners paid $14 to $18 per cord.[43] Oregon tanoak bark fetched the highest price in the country in 1906, with an average price of $26.66 per cord. In the same year, a cord of the bark was worth $20.48 on average in California, possibly because the tree is more widespread and abundant than in Oregon. In contrast, the cheapest tanbark in 1906 was from New Jersey, at $6.81 per cord, and the national average was $9.32 for other less desirable and more abundant native species such as hemlock (*Tsuga*), chestnut, and *Quercus*.[44] By 1919, a cord of tanoak bark delivered to a tannery fetched $32.[45]

Bark from tanoak proved so desirable that after tanneries depleted nearby tanoak populations in the San Francisco Bay area and the Santa Cruz Mountains, they imported bark from northern hinterlands (figs. 3.6–3.11). The most extensive stands of tanoak occurred from the mouth of the Russian River in Sonoma County north of San Francisco through Mendocino, Humboldt, and Del Norte Counties.[46] Initially, however, this mother lode of tanoak was poorly connected to urban centers of leather manufacturing and consumption. In the late nineteenth and early twentieth centuries, treach-

FIGURE 3.6 Hauling tanoak bark on donkeys, then transferring bark to wagons in the Bear River or Mattole River Watershed south of Eureka, California, ca. 1907. Photograph by Ray Jerome Baker (photo ID 1999.01.0412). The Swanlund/Baker Collection, Humboldt State University Library Special Collections, Arcata, California.

FIGURE 3.7 Wagon loaded with tanoak bark being pulled up a steep hill by a steam donkey, Bear River or Mattole River Watershed south of Eureka, California, ca. 1907. Photograph by Ray Jerome Baker (photo ID 1999.01.0048). The Swanlund/Baker Collection, Humboldt State University Library Special Collections, Arcata, California.

FIGURE 3.8 Wagons loaded with dried tanoak bark from the Bear River or Mattole River Watershed south of Eureka, California, ca. 1907. Oak-prairie mosaic vegetation in background. Photograph probably by Ray Jerome Baker (photo ID 1999.01.0062). The Swanlund/Baker Collection, Humboldt State University Library Special Collections, Arcata, California.

FIGURE 3.9 Loading large quantities of tanoak bark onto a steam schooner destined probably for San Francisco tanneries. Photograph by A. O. Carpenter, Westport, California, ca. 1900. Courtesy of the Mendocino County Historical Society and Grace Hudson Museum & Sun House, Ukiah, California.

FIGURE 3.10 Loading tanbark onto the small schooner *Rio Rey*, Usal, California, 1895. The narrow-gauge railroad provided access for extraction of tanbark and coast redwood from the lower reaches of the Usal Creek watershed in Mendocino County. Courtesy of California Department of Parks and Recreation.

FIGURE 3.11 Dried tanbark load with crew of workers on Gualala Mill Company locomotive no. 4, near Bourne's Landing, just north of Gualala, California. The tanbark rolls were shipped out by schooner from Bourne's Landing. Note the sacks of broken tanbark on the third of the eight four-wheel railroad flat cars. Photo by A. O. Carpenter, ca. 1890. Collection of Grace Hudson Museum & Sun House, Ukiah, California.

erous "dog-hole" ports allowed tanbark and redwood to be shipped from the coastline of these northwestern counties to San Francisco and other urban destinations (fig. 3.10). Narrow-gauge railroads also facilitated the movement of forest resources to market, but they remained an expensive form of transport (fig. 3.11). Alluvial plains and other flat or gently sloping areas proved most cost-effective for such significant capital investments. Sailboats and steam schooners in tandem with donkeys and horse-drawn wagons continued to carry tanbark from more rugged and remote areas until extensive roads provided better access.

To reduce the expense of transporting the heavy and unwieldy bark long distances to urban centers, some tanneries shifted to producing tanoak bark extract near the trees and then transporting barrels of extract. In 1902, Wagner Tannery, based in the Central Valley, established Pacific Oak Extract Works in the remote northern California town of Briceland. From its Humboldt County facility, it shipped barrels of tanning liquor for soaking hides to its Stockton tannery. Workers reduced 2,200 pounds of dry bark (the equivalent in volume of one cord) to fifty gallons of extract weighing about 550 pounds.[47] The annual consumption of tanoak bark by Pacific Oak Extract Works alone was about 2,000 to 3,000 cords.[48]

Tanoak bark enabled an increasingly lucrative American tanning industry on the Pacific Coast. From 1851 to 1907, 861,000 cords of tanbark with an approximate total value of $15,498,000 were harvested in California.[49] By 1918, tanoak had contributed more than 30 million gallons of tannin extract to the U.S. leather industry.[50] However, non-sustainable use of tanbark posed a serious threat to the tanning industry. Within decades of the Pacific tanning industry's beginning, tanoak was suffering signs of depletion. The market all but collapsed in the 1920s due to overexploitation. Although there were other sources of tanbark in California, such as species in the genus *Quercus*, tanoak bark was used almost exclusively.

TANOAK BARK CONSERVATION

In 1882, the U.S. Forest Service warned that tanoak bark consumption could not be sustained beyond thirty years at the current rate.[51] Conservationists in general attempted to convince the industry to make production practices more sustainable. Nationwide concern about deforestation had led to increasing interest in European scientific forest management practices beginning in the 1870s. Many reformers argued that without government intervention, laissez-faire capitalism would lead to forest resource depletion. Franklin B. Hough, who later became the first chief of the Division of Forestry, advocated for reform in the 1870s because the timber industry, which had already depleted eastern forests and those of the Great Lakes region, was now assaulting West Coast forests.[52] California established a State Board of Forestry in 1885.[53] In its first report, it defended regulation of the industry, claiming that deforestation resulting from "unregulated supply and demand" would make future generation of wood products difficult or impossible.[54]

State foresters ranked tanoak among the most abused tree species in their first biennial report for 1885-1886: "There is probably no tree which has been so systematically wasted as this oak." As soon as new roads were constructed within tanbark oak stands, they noted, the bark was extracted, "leaving the valuable wood to perish on the ground."[55] In its plea for conservation, the board concluded that "there is nothing more important to the welfare of this commonwealth than the preservation of its splendid forests."[56] In its third biennial report, the California State Board of Forestry persisted in its concern for tanoak, claiming in 1890 that although it was originally associated with coast redwood "in great quantity, [it] has been cut out, and . . . [has] practically disappeared."[57] The excellent reputations of California's manufacturers of heavy leather depended on tanoak bark. As the availability of tanoak bark decreased, its economic value increased, driving "barkcutters . . . to invade places once considered impracticable . . . to get at this precious product."[58] Peelers lacked incentives to conserve the unregulated resource.

Because tanoak was "fast approaching the vanishing point," the California Board of Forestry promoted scientific management in order to avert a "bark famine."[59] State foresters developed recommendations based on information from plantations of various bark crop plants grown around the world. Partial bark stripping of cinchona trees in India for malaria medicine led to the suggestion that tanbark could be harvested sustainably if tanoak trees weren't girdled.[60] The board also promoted the introduction of black wattle (*Acacia decurrens*) and other acacias for tannin production, given the similarities between the climate in California and their native Australia (fig. 3.12). Black wattle appeared superior to tanoak for sustainable use because it grew faster and withstood bark stripping better, yet was of comparable value as a tanning agent.[61] California state foresters argued that black wattle could yield profits, citing the handsome returns for tanning reagents generated from a seven-year-old plantation on one hundred acres in South Australia.[62] The new wattle-growing industry in the Australian colonies emerged in part because the colonists had depleted wild stands for domestic use and to export bark to Britain.[63] In an 1882 forestry report submitted to the U.S. Congress, Hough noted that, based on their success as ornamentals, "Australian wattles will do well" in California as alternate sources of bark.[64] A test plantation in the southern California beach town of Santa Monica exhibited very promising growth as of 1890, as did other plantings in the state.[65]

Many people defended tanoak. The 1891 annual report of California's State Board of Horticulture includes F. H. Clark's lament for the annual destruction of 180,000 tanoak trees and twenty-five square miles of forest:

> Every season the "peeler" has to penetrate farther into the forests to procure the bark he covets. . . . He *must*, to realize a profit on his contract, mow down, as relentless as Death, the great and small, the growth of a century, the saplings of but a few years' life. He leaves behind him the stark naked skeletons of great trees intermingled with the dying young. It is a war of extermination, in which the young and old, alike defenseless, fall before the weapon of a crude civilization, the keen, relentless ax of the woodman.[66]

A trade magazine claimed in 1900 that the highly valuable bark of tanoak put the species in danger of extinction.[67] Preservationist John Muir opposed industrial use of the bark, which "rapidly destroyed" tanoak.[68] Muir's friend Willis Linn Jepson, a prominent University of California botany professor, documented that in 1907 peelers harvested 25,000 cords by peeling 100,000 trees.[69] In response to the environmental impacts of industrialization in California, Muir and Jepson helped to found the Sierra Club, which would advocate for nature preservation including old-growth coast redwood groves with tanoak. Two historians noted that "with any care at all, such as is given in Europe to forests," the tanoak bark resource was "inexhaustible."[70] The British had harvested tanbark from *Quercus* for centuries, favoring "trees coppiced at 25 to 30 years when the bark was easy to strip and gave a better overall yield than older trees."[71]

FIGURE 3.12 An early promoter of *Acacia* cultivation for plantation production of tanbark, Englishman John Vanderplank gave black wattle seeds from Australia to Afrikaners in the mid- to late-nineteenth centuries. Vanderplank, here portrayed as a member of the social elite, offers a female white colonist black wattle seeds while her husband stands by ready to defend a new social order that promises them social mobility. The disengaged yoke to the right symbolizes their male progeny's future freedom from manual labor and subservience. The tool used to unlock the yoke rests at the bare feet of their son leaning on a future black wattle tree. He will profit from the plantation-grown tanbark cultivated with the labor of Africans, symbolized by the black boy pictured above his head. Howes, *Vegetable Tanning Materials*, facing title page.

Despite years of warnings about overharvesting, the tanning industry depleted the tanbark oak resource. It became scarce, expensive, and unreliable in its availability. Tanneries shifted increasingly to imported tanbark and tanning extract from other vegetable tannin sources such as quebracho (*Schinopsis balansae*), wattle (*Acacia*), mangrove (*Rhizophora*), and Sicilian sumac (*Rhus coriaria*). California tanners also began to use chromium-based tanning agents for lightweight leathers and to experiment with its use for manufacturing heavy leathers.[72] Leather could be tanned in a matter of hours using chromium salts, whereas tanning with vegetable tannins took a month or more. Thus, mined chromium salts overtook renewable vegetable tannins due to their greater efficiency despite the reduced quality of the product. Pacific Oak Extract Works closed in 1922 after twenty years of operation, because the owners "ran out of tan bark."[73] By 1928, most Pacific Coast tanneries had closed.

By the mid-twentieth century, increasing reliance on imported tanbark and tannin-rich extracts provoked exploration for other American sources of vegetable tanning reagents. During World War II, access to many foreign imports ended or was severely limited, including South American quebracho extract, African wattle extract, and Italian sumac bark.[74] A. K. Salz Tannery in Santa Cruz, which still relied on tanoak bark, sold 100 percent of its production during the war to the U.S. military.[75] Nationwide in 1947, American chestnut supplied nearly 90 percent of the domestic vegetable tanning reagent, which wasn't expected to last much longer because of the chestnut blight.[76] Landowners were liquidating the bark and wood resources associated with the trees before or shortly after chestnut blight killed them. Foreign-sourced tannin use in the United States dropped to roughly 45 percent by 1952.[77] But investigations into native sumacs from the eastern United States led to the conclusion at midcentury that without better processing methods and possibly a breeding program to improve tannin quality, tannin production from sumacs would "probably never become an important industry."[78] Other plants given serious consideration include spruce (*Picea*) and canaigre (*Rumex hymenosepalus*).[79] Indeed, much earlier, canaigre had gained the attention of a University of California researcher whose findings were published in a treatise on the herbaceous plant in 1894, dubbing it the "tanners dock."[80] However, post–World War II labor costs in the United States made it increasingly difficult to compete with foreign vegetable-tanning reagents and imported leather.

Despite the renewed interest in domestic sources of vegetable tannins, several biological and ecological factors discouraged continued commercial use of tanoak. Trees that established after bark extraction occurred in an area took time to reach a size suitable for profitable bark harvesting. In addition, tanoak trees resprouted after being peeled and cut down. According to Jepson, one stump could produce "as many as 1,400" sprouts, which, after thirty years, were reduced to "four to eight of the most vigorous poles" after natural thinning occurred.[81] Regrowing bark commercially would require thinning the sprouts manually, entailing high labor costs, followed by decades of growth. If trees survived being girdled, those left standing never again produced bark of commercial value.[82]

GLOBAL COMPETITION

Sometime before 1947, the United States went from being a large exporter of native tanning materials to importing as much as 60-70 percent of the vegetable tannin it used, mostly from South America and Africa.[83] While attempts to grow Australian black wattle for tanbark in California failed, acacias thrived in plantations in South Africa. First planted in Natal as a test, possibly as early as 1846, wattle plantations increased significantly in number after 1886, once they had proved their commercial value.[84] Between 1904 to their peak in the 1960s, wattle plantations in South Africa increased from roughly 79,000 to 741,000 acres.[85] Global competition undermined the tanoak conservation arguments of foresters. In less than one hundred years of extraction, harvestable tanoak bark had become hard to find. Conservationists failed to change tanoak-bark harvesting practices in part because tanners turned to cheaper foreign vegetable tannins and faster-acting mineral-based tanning agents.

Even the oldest tannery in the West turned to chromium salts and then closed altogether. In operation from 1861 to 2001, A. K. Salz Tannery depended heavily on tanoak bark for more than a century.[86] Its famed "California Saddle Leather" trademarked product owed its "golden sheen" to tanoak bark (figs. 3.13–3.18).[87] Another trade magazine claimed that the unique golden russet color was "not readily obtained with any other tanning material."[88] Over time, the Santa Cruz–based tannery hauled the bark from increasingly remote forests in the surrounding Santa Cruz Mountains. Although it modernized in 1957, it sought to combine modern ma-

FIGURE 3.13 Unknown bark harvester removed green bark from a tanoak tree, probably in Santa Cruz County, California, 1955. Used with permission from the Lezin Family and the anonymous copyright holder.

FIGURE 3.14 Tanoak bark drying at the A. K. Salz Tannery in Santa Cruz, California, 1955. Collection of the Santa Cruz Museum of Art & History. Gift of the Lezin Family. Used with permission from the anonymous copyright holder.

chinery with traditional vegetable-tannin-based leather-making methods. In trying to maintain the renowned quality of its products, the tannery continued to use tanoak bark in its tanning process, which required forty days.[89] Part of its modernization effort included making tannin extract closer to the forests where the bark was harvested in an attempt to reduce hauling costs. But after World War II, "the scarcity of tan bark and the pressures of competition caused the tannery to change its method from vegetable tanning to the use of chrome as the principal tanning agent."[90] Despite the shift to faster tanning agents, the company could not compete with foreign leather producers and closed in 2001.[91] Tanoak-dependent tanning in the United States shifted to less labor-intensive production using mined minerals and then relocated in order to utilize cheaper labor sources and raw resources from foreign ecosystems and plantations.

FIGURE 3.15 Tanoak bark transported with a forklift at the A. K. Salz Company tannery complex, Santa Cruz, 1955. Collection of the Santa Cruz Museum of Art & History. Gift of the Lezin Family. Used with permission from the anonymous copyright holder.

FIGURE 3.16 Two unknown A. K. Salz Company employees removed hides from tan pits of tanoak tanning liquor, Santa Cruz, 1955. Used with permission from the Lezin Family and the anonymous copyright holder.

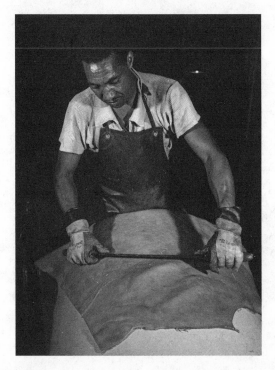

FIGURE 3.17 Hand scudding removed the remaining fine hair roots after chemical and mechanical removal of flesh and hair. Henry Everly, employee of A. K. Salz Company, Santa Cruz, 1955. Collection of the Santa Cruz Museum of Art & History. Gift of the Lezin Family. Used with permission from the anonymous copyright holder.

The non-sustainable harvesting of tanoak bark lent credence to foresters' claim that neither industry nor locals could be trusted to manage forest resources responsibly. Yet foresters who opposed the early forest products industry shifted to a less confrontational position. They began placing greater focus on transitioning the timber industry from mining old-growth forests to raising plantations of single-age trees. With the decline of the California tanning industry, tanoak needed culling, so the cash crops, coast redwood and later Douglas-fir, could grow better without competition from weeds. Scientific forestry offered solutions to the perceived problem of tanoak's sovereign hold on the landscape after old-growth forest logging.

FIGURE 3.18 California Saddle Leather, produced at A. K. Salz Company, was glazed on both sides to add shine after tanning and subsequent scudding, Santa Cruz, 1955. Used with permission from the Lezin Family and the anonymous copyright holder.

WEED

Who among us should we trust with the power to decide how nature
should be managed? . . . There is no genuine disinterestedness, no objective
or neutral authority whose exercise of power wins universal assent.

—JAN E. DIZARD

TANOAK, ONE OF CALIFORNIA'S MOST COMMON NATIVE FLOWER-
ing trees, is the target of herbicides in industrial forests. Chemical weeding
favors coast redwood and Douglas-fir. Throughout tanoak's range, historical, physical, ecological, and economic influences led foresters and timber
producers to prioritize softwood over native hardwoods like tanoak. The
term "softwood" refers to wood from cone-bearing trees such as coast redwood and Douglas-fir; "hardwood" refers to wood derived from flowering
trees such as tanoak, madrone (*Arbutus menziesii*), alder (*Alnus*), and maple
(*Acer*). Killing hardwood species deemed weeds resulted in "competitive
release" for softwood species and "type conversion" from one kind of forest to another.

In 1878, the American transcendentalist Ralph Waldo Emerson asked
the rhetorical question "What is a weed?" and then answered it: "A plant
whose virtues have not yet been discovered."[1] By that definition, tanoak
is not a weed because its virtues are numerous and well documented. Its
branches bear plump nuts that feed people and other animals. Deer use
them to fatten up in the fall, to build a reserve and insulating layer for
winter. Squirrel, feral pig, turkey, band-tailed pigeon, raccoon, coyote, and
fox relish the fleshy plant embryo inside the hard-shelled fruit. Tanoak
roots hold the soil after logging and other forms of disturbance. The canopy

creates a surface on which fog can condense. The tree's leaves add organic material to the soil when they drop. The secondary xylem tissue yields fine-grained wood for cabinets and hardwood floors. Tanoak bark produces some of the best vegetable-tanned leather for heavy-duty uses such as for shoes, saddles, and luggage. Yet despite its utility and ecological importance, by the mid-twentieth century, the focus of foresters shifted to eradicating tanoak because it had little economic value and competed with economically valuable species such as Douglas-fir and coast redwood.

Government foresters began using herbicides on public forests to control hardwoods and brush and promoted the practice to private landowners as scientific management. Softwood producers saw tanoak as usurping space that could support more profitable conifers: "Loggers and foresters, in particular, considered hardwoods as troublesome weeds that impeded harvesting and logging operations, increased slash disposal problems, dominated cut-over areas, and interfered with growth of high value conifers.... Many landowners and loggers viewed California hardwoods as a nuisance to be dealt with by disposal rather than by management."[2] The authors of a *Weed Science* article in 1976 lamented the vast acreage in northern California and southwestern Oregon "infested" by tanoak that could be producing coast redwood and Douglas-fir instead.[3] For maximizing Douglas-fir wood production, total tanoak removal was deemed "necessary, ... while productive, mixed stands can be achieved by removing 50% or more of tanoak cover."[4] Because "initial changes in vegetation ... have long-lasting effects on stand development," foresters emphasized "careful planning and early intervention" as essential to successful management of Douglas-fir and tanoak.[5] With chemical weeding, foresters hoped to decrease tanoak competition for light, water, and soil nutrients. The challenge was how to remove tanoaks efficiently and in a cost-effective manner.

WESTERN U.S. SOFTWOOD INDUSTRY

Establishment of a softwood industry on the West Coast faced numerous challenges.[6] Land laws had favored farmers over timbermen in the mid-1800s, making it difficult to legally acquire tracts large enough to support a well-capitalized mill. That had changed with the Timber and Stone Act of 1878 and subsequent shifts in government land policies. Despite industry's increasing ability to supply the market with West Coast softwood products, demand lagged until wood use habits changed, in part through advertising that educated consumers about unfamiliar species. Beginning in the 1880s, the Division of Forestry systematically tested the attributes of various woods to identify the best uses of different species.[7] Scientific knowledge about relative strength, hardness, and so on, expanded the list of native raw resources. Coast redwood proved decay-resistant enough to be used in place of hardwoods for railroad ties. With this discovery, demand in the West for eastern oak railroad ties declined. After 1889, Douglas-fir became the primary lumber for home construction and was exported across the country, replacing the hardwoods traditionally used for this purpose.[8]

In part because of new uses for redwood and Douglas-fir wood, the predicted national hardwood famine failed to materialize, and eastern forests recovered after logging faster than expected. As the cost of wood increased, builders developed less wasteful practices and new construction methods, such as reinforced concrete.[9] At the same time, railroad companies, "the single largest user of timber," radically reduced consumption by adopting milled, creosoted ties over hand-hewn untreated ones; they also redesigned trestles to be less wasteful.[10] Between 1900 and 1914, use of wood impregnated with chemical preservatives increased radically as wood prices rose due to reduced availability.[11] Although American forests had begun to recover from past logging by the 1920s, foresters continued to warn against timber famine, but "this was . . . a softwood famine that they feared" most.[12]

Softwood logging intensified, with new technologies and transportation networks increasing the impact on tanoak. With the introduction of the steam donkey in the 1880s, selective logging had given way to clear-cutting.[13] In order to drag logs to a central staging area, the steam donkeys needed a clear field (fig. 4.1). Before clear-cutting the old-growth coast redwoods, peelers would first harvest all the associated tanoaks, including the imperfect and young trees that used to be left in place. There was no incentive to conserve because the early lumber companies typically burned after felling, "to facilitate the getting out of the redwood logs by wire cable and donkey engine," which killed or damaged the tanoak, making "peeling difficult or impossible."[14] Whatever was not extracted was leveled and left on the forest floor as waste. Beginning in the late 1800s, investors installed private narrow-gauge railroad systems into previously inaccessible terrain and purchased specialized equipment for milling giant old-growth redwoods.[15]

Engineering a new cultural landscape for mercantile America required more extensive transportation infrastructure that would move goods from farms and forests to cities. Such a transformation of the land also called

FIGURE 4.1 Logging with an early Dolbeer steam donkey in Humboldt County, California, near the Mad River, ca. late nineteenth century. Surrounding hills logged for the John Vance Mill & Lumber Co. Photograph by A. W. or Edgar Ericson (photo ID 1999.02.0410). From the Ericson Collection, Humboldt State University Library Special Collections, Arcata, California.

for rural producers to supply urban demand. Enticing settlers to remote northern California required some marketing. One 1911 promotional map promised a paradise of cheap land suitable for hunting and growing familiar foods with access to "unlimited markets" (fig. 4.2). In the 1930s and 1940s, the Caterpillar tractor combined with trucks and revolutionized logging.[16] Along with new state highways and federal freeways, they helped to make it profitable to log Douglas-fir stands in steep terrain.

Greater access combined with increased wood demands during and after the Second World War resulted in a dramatic rise in the rate of cut. Even before the United States entered the war, production increased significantly to supply American allies. After the war, a surge in suburban developments for returning soldiers and their new families created an enormous market for dimensional lumber from softwoods. More softwood extraction, particularly in Douglas-fir-dominated forests, resulted in more tanoak

The Promise of Paradise - 1911

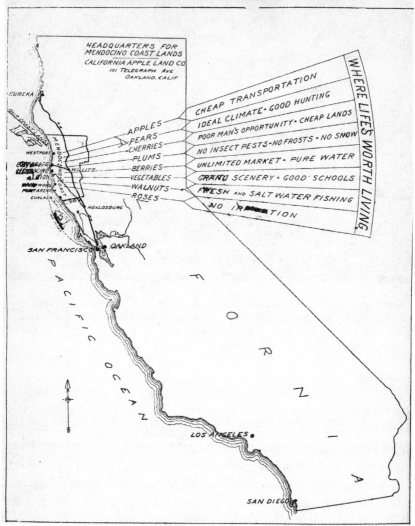

FIGURE 4.2 Boosters promoted northern California as a haven for aspiring agrarian yeomen seeking the good life with access to hunting and fishing, a favorable climate for food plants, and a transportation infrastructure linked to markets. The California Western Railroad (aka the Skunk Train) connected Fort Bragg to the town of Willits and the Northwestern Pacific rail line in 1911. Courtesy of *Mendocino Beacon*.

thickets, because Douglas-fir doesn't stump-sprout like coast redwood. As a result, tanoak outcompeted Douglas-fir in the early years of regeneration and delayed the production of harvestable softwood. Clear-cutting favored tanoak during the decade or more after logging. Willis Linn Jepson had labeled tanoak "an aggressive tree" and found it "exceptionally well-fitted by its reproductive powers, vigor and shade endurance to take part in the struggle for continuous possession of the land"—hence the common name "sovereign oak."[17] Coppice growth on tanoak emerged from buds located under the bark at the base of the trees. "Fairly extensive, nearly pure stands of coppice growth appear on cutover areas," William M. Harlow and Ellwood S. Harrar note in their dendrology textbook, making the land unproductive from a short-term economic perspective.[18]

Emanuel Fritz, a forestry professor at the University of California, Berkeley, warned in 1949 that clear-cutting and subsequently broadcast slash burning damaged the soil and reduced chances for reforestation. Instead, he proposed an ecosystem approach that allowed tanoak and brush species to rehabilitate the soil by maintaining its moisture and friability, which ultimately would enable conifers to reassert themselves. Fritz saw solid tanoak and brush intrusions as an indicator of excessive logging and advocated lighter cutting.[19] State and federal foresters as well as private timberland owners opted not to follow his advice. Today, however, burning slash piles or leaving woody debris to decompose on-site has replaced broadcast burning after logging.

TANOAK SPROUTING CREATES COMPETITION FOR CONIFERS

Competition pressure for conifers can increase significantly two to three years after logging or burning due to vigorous sprouting from injured tanoak.[20] This vegetative growth originates from buds "under the bark at the base of the tree," which are located primarily on underground burls.[21] Sprout densities of frequently more than eight thousand stems per acre diminish conifer regeneration, survival, and growth.[22] Logging mixed conifer-tanoak forests older than seventy years typically causes "a dense cover of vigorous sprout clumps within 3 to 6 years."[23] When tanoak coverage exceeded 50 percent, "the annual basal area growth of a Douglas-fir seedling [declined] by 37% or more."[24] Growth in height also began to decline.[25] On decade-old plantations, Douglas-fir that remained shorter than tanoak might not even survive, thus thwarting "crown closure" and resulting in "a few widely spaced 'crop trees.'" Early intervention is critical according to foresters, because "[s]uch heterogeneity in stand structure is not correctable by thinning or hardwood removal."[26] According to some studies, removal of tanoak alone did not significantly increase rates of Douglas-fir growth unless the rest of the plant species in the forest understory were suppressed. "Hardwood removal stimulated understory development, which subsequently limited height and diameter of Douglas-fir."[27] But one eleven-year study suggests that, "with adequate site preparation, Douglas-fir seedlings can be established and grown among tanoak sprout clumps with no significant reductions in seedling survival."[28]

Burl formation in tanoaks begins early, "when seedlings are 3-5 years old. By age 12, they are usually well developed and have prominent buds."[29] However, the capacity to sprout develops slowly in tanoak.[30] Although young tanoak can't sprout as vigorously as older individuals, they can produce sprouts after being damaged including "newly germinated seedlings whose tops were killed by frost 7 days after they emerged above ground."[31] Mature, undisturbed tanoaks also sprout as a survival strategy. "In old stands, 70% had basal sprouts" that, while shade tolerant, can also survive removal of the main trunk.[32] Sexual reproduction through acorns is much less effective than asexual reproduction through sprouting from the burl. In one study in southwestern Oregon, nine to thirteen years after clearcutting, one to eight tanoak seedlings established per hectare despite a ready supply of acorns, while burls produced "18,000 to 31,000 sprouts per hectare."[33] Because seedlings establish slowly and sprout less vigorously, tanoak removal at this developmental stage in a forest means that "reestablishment of a dense understory with the capacity for vigorous sprouting is likely to take more than 100 years . . . and if the seed supply is limited, then one treatment in alternate 60- to 80-year conifer rotations may effectively eliminate tanoak as a competitor."[34]

STUMP TREATMENTS

In the late 1940s, the U.S. Forest Service experimented with applying herbicides to the cut stumps of tanoak in order to reduce competition for conifers.[35] The results of one of these early studies were published in 1950 by G. H. Schubert, who concluded that because the herbicide treatments killed tanoak or diminished sprouting, stumps should be treated immediately after tanoaks were felled for firewood. Delays in treatment resulted in significant reductions in herbicide absorption and translocation, because air bubbles and/or exudates quickly clog the vascular tissue after logging. Schubert noted that stand improvement resulted from "this simple treatment of the stumps."[36] Among the first pesticides tested were the phenoxy herbicides 2,4-D and 2,4,5-T, separately and combined. Painting or daubing herbicide directly onto the stumps proved more effective and cheaper than spraying the stumps.[37] Over decades, researchers experimented with different treatment times and mixtures. "Oil soluble herbicides, like triclopyr ester, require an organic carrier . . . [; however,] diesel is not the best because it burns living tissue. Vegetable oil is better. Water soluble herbicides, like glyphosate or triclopyr amine, can be applied with a water carrier."[38] October proved to be the best time for "giving nearly complete control,"[39] but February also worked well.[40] Tests were also made on undiluted applications of 2,4-D and 2,4,5-T. Subsequent experiments tested other pesticides such as Garlon, which effectively killed tanoak as a stump spray.[41] As "undesirable . . . weed trees," tanoaks were also "removed to increase forage production" using the stump treatment method.[42]

FOLIAGE SPRAYING

One weed researcher reported in 1958 that "aerial foliage spray of 2,4-D or 2,4,5-T . . . lightly damaged" tanoak.[43] In 1964, researchers tested foliar spraying with 2,4,5-T alone and mixed 1:1 with 2,4-D found them "equally effective" on tanoak in the Six Rivers National Forest.[44] They noted that mixing with diesel, not just water, worked better and that multiple applications were required for "full control." The U.S. Forest Service researchers concluded that it would be "more practical on most areas" to use aerial herbicide treatments to suppress tanoak than to try and manage the vegetation through on-the-ground foliage spraying.[45] Weeding tanoak through the use of aerial herbicide applications in forests became a widespread practice in the 1960s and 1970s due to economies of scale. The thick waxy cuticle coating the leaves of conifers made them more resistant than broad-leaved plants to autumn applications. Conifer needles also shed liquid poison better than the broad leaves of hardwoods.

Tests of foliar applications in the Six Rivers National Forest indicated that nine years after final treatments, chemical control of tanoak worked better than manual control. "When the study began [in 1978], 2,4-D was the foliage-active herbicide most often applied to forest plantations in

California, and Garlon was a new cut-surface and foliage-active herbicide recommended for use in young forest plantations threatened by" leathery-leaved species like tanoak.[46] Garlon 4 combined with 2,4-D applied twice as a foliar spray resulted in significantly less tanoak coverage compared to 2,4-D used alone as a foliar spray.[47] These treatments occurred a few years after conifer logging, hardwood thinning, and broadcast burning, when tanoak sprouts and seedlings were young and therefore easier to control. Douglas-fir seedlings were planted in 1981. The plots treated with the Garlon 4 and 2,4-D combination became conifer dominated, with 95 percent coverage of Douglas-fir after nine years. In comparison, Douglas-fir foliar coverage measured 99 percent in plots where tanoaks were cut with chain saws and then sprayed with Garlon 3A twice. The researchers listed this treatment as a combined manual and chemical release.

In southwestern Oregon, use of herbicides to favor conifers over tanoaks increased during the 1980s when an economic downturn catalyzed efforts to improve the profitability of industrial forests with more aggressive silviculture. In an effort to solve "important forest management problems" such as tanoak competition, the Forestry Intensified Research (FIR) program formed in 1978 as a cooperative effort between Oregon State University's College of Forestry and the Forest Service's Pacific Northwest Research Station with support from the Bureau of Land Management (BLM), relevant counties, and the southwest Oregon forest products industry.[48] The FIR program spent millions on research to try and "solve the chronic reforestation problems in southwestern Oregon."[49] Researchers affiliated with the FIR program, the Forest Service, and others experimented with treating tanoak using a wide variety of herbicides (see table 3).

CUT-FRILL TREATMENTS

The cut-frill (also cut-surface and "hack and squirt") treatment gained favor over other approaches to tanoak control when opposition to aerial herbicide spraying became widespread in the 1980s. Tree trunks were hacked with an ax, typically entirely around, and then herbicide was applied to the fresh wounds. This allowed for a reduction in herbicide use because the active ingredient entered the vascular system of the plant directly instead of through the leaves. Applicators could direct the herbicide only onto target trees, reducing the impact on those that were not targets. Marketable conifers and other non-target species sometimes suffered negative effects

TABLE 3. Partial List of Herbicides Used on Tanoak

Type of Herbicide	Trade Names	Active Ingredient	Use	Notes
2,4-D	Many different formulations, including Weedar 64, Weedone LV4, Weedone LV6, 2,4-D Amine 4, and Formula 40	2,4-dichlorophenoxy acetic acid	Aerial, foliar, cut-frill, and stump	Not classified by the EPA as a human carcinogen due to conflicting data (EPA Class D); sometimes contaminated with dioxin.
2,4,5-T	Many different formulations with different trade names, including Weedone 2,4,5-T and Esteron 245	2,4,5-trichlorophenoxy acetic acid	Aerial, foliar, cut-frill, stump	No longer sold in the United States due to the known toxicity of the contaminant dioxin; lost EPA registration.
Glyphosate	Many different formulations with different trade names, including Accord Concentrate, Rodeo, Accord XRT, and Roundup	N-(phosphonomethyl) glycine	Aerial, foliar, cut-frill, stump	Listed as a noncarcinogen by the EPA (Class E).
Imazapyr	Arsenal Applicator's Concentrate, Chopper Gen2, Polaris AC Complete, and Polaris SP	Salt of imazapyr	Aerial, cut-frill	Listed as a noncarcinogen by the EPA (Class E).
Metsulfuron	Escort XP	Metsulfuron-methyl	Aerial	Not registered for use in California. According to the EPA, not likely to be carcinogenic to humans based on the results of carcinogenicity studies in rats and mice.
Picloram	Tordon 22K and Grazon	4-amino-3,5,6-trichloropicolinic acid	Cut-frill	Not legal for sale in California.
Triclopyr	Many different formulations with different trade names including Garlon 3A (amine form), Garlon 4 Ultra (ester form), and Pathfinder II	Triclopyr formulations are either produced as amine salts or oil-soluble esters	Foliar, cut-frill, stump	Not classified by the EPA as a human carcinogen due to conflicting data (EPA Class D).

from aerial herbicide treatments.[50] The cut-frill method was also attractive to softwood producers because aerial applications of herbicides resulted in "relatively poor control of resprouting species" like tanoak.[51]

Initial tests in the 1950s using the cut-frill method of tanoak control led researchers to advocate for stronger concentrations of herbicides. The research forester D. F. Roy did find that 2,4,5-T mixed with diesel oil was "the most effective killer" and that "tanoaks with smaller diameters were killed more easily by poisoning."[52] Roy also noted that the slow death of tanoaks after treatment could be beneficial by providing "shade to young conifers."[53] A test in 1964 of 2,4-D, 2,4,5-T and picloram applied on ax-injured tanoak trunks in Ukiah, California, provided "acceptable control for 10 years following application."[54] After a decade, basal area growth of Douglas-fir in the treatment area "increased by 260, 451, and 405 percent . . . with 2,4-D, 2,4,5-T, and picloram, respectively."[55] Triclopyr amine mixed with water proved effective for reducing an established tanoak canopy in favor of underplanted Douglas-fir. After five growing seasons, the competitive release did result in significantly greater growth rates for Douglas-fir as compared to control plots. Although roughly 60 percent of the hardwood canopy died back in response to the cut-frill treatment with triclopyr, extensive resprouting by the seventh year led the researcher to conclude that additional herbicide treatments might be necessary to protect the planted Douglas-fir.[56] "The recovery of the hardwoods in the understory, relative to the growth of the conifer seedlings, indicates that hardwood sprouts may kill weaker conifer seedlings, and that additional sprout control may be necessary to ensure that a sufficient number of Douglas-fir achieve merchantable size within an acceptable time."[57]

Picloram worked well for cut-frill treatments, but its product registrations ended in California in 1988.[58] Although new product could not be sold within the state, existing stock, already sold, could be used up. Picloram's product registrations remain active in Oregon, the only other state where tanoak is native. However, the Oregon Department of Agriculture lacks a mechanism for knowing whether foresters continue to use it on tanoak within the state. In 2012, roughly twenty pesticide products registered for use in Oregon forests contained picloram.[59] By 2014, the number had dropped to two.[60]

Imazapyr is currently a favorite for cut-frill treatments. The first product containing this herbicide was registered for use in California in 1998.[61] Mendocino Redwood Company began experimenting with imazapyr in 1999, and

Humboldt Redwood Company adopted its use in 2008, its first year of business.[62] Imazapyr allowed both companies to reduce their herbicide use to as little as 10 percent of the volume of Garlon they had been using. According to the shared website for Mendocino Redwood Company and Humboldt Redwood Company, "less herbicide is used with this method than with foliage or aerial spraying."[63] Research in the southern United States based on urine assays indicates that cut-frill applications measurably reduce pesticide exposure for forest workers over backpack spray foliage treatments.[64] According to the Environmental Protection Agency (EPA), imazapyr is "*practically non-toxic* to mammals, birds, honeybees, fish, and aquatic invertebrates. . . . Most accidental exposures raise only minimal concern. The major uncertainties regarding potential toxic effects in animals are associated with the lack of toxicity data on reptiles and amphibians."[65] However, a more recent study on the impact of this herbicide on endangered Oregon spotted frogs (*Rana pretiosa*) indicates that "imazapyr use in wetland restoration poses a low risk of direct toxic effects on juvenile[s]."[66] Given common amphibian sensitivities to other pesticides, further study is needed.

Although its tanoak treatments are "currently conducted at a financial loss," Mendocino Redwood Company is "encouraged by the results" it is getting from treating standing tanoak trees with small amounts of imazapyr.[67]

> As the standing tanoak trees gradually lose their leaves, they continue to provide shade and shelter for the conifers newly planted underneath. As the decomposition of the tanoak accelerates, the fine limbs and then the trunks slowly decompose which returns 100% of the biomass to the soil thus increasing soil fertility and moisture holding capacity. This is particularly beneficial to forest soils where decades of continual burning have left the soils depleted and vulnerable to erosion.[68]

On its website, the company states that "once the tanoak has been brought back into balance with other species, . . . [its] forest of the future will not require either herbicides or the same use of heavy harvest prescriptions."[69] In its work to encourage conifer dominance, Mendocino Redwood Company supplied Mendocino Forest Products with wood generated from thinning tanoak in 1999 and 2000. Mendocino Forest Products retooled a defunct softwood mill to process tanoak into flooring, wood chips, and firewood. According to Mendocino Redwood Company's website, the "operation was designed to offset the costs of the tanoak removal program but operated at a loss and has been closed."[70] Due to the regional decline in the timber industry, a diminishing number of companies continue to use herbicide to weed tanoak. Most of the remaining companies, like Mendocino Redwood Company, continue the practice in order to increase commercial softwood production. However, it is difficult to quantify the amount of acreage being treated with herbicides to kill tanoak, as companies are not required to be fully transparent about their practices. Based on county pesticide use reports, the use of imazapyr on forests in Mendocino County increased between 2009 and 2010 from 159 pounds to 5,886 pounds.[71]

WARNINGS AGAINST HERBICIDE USE

Warnings against overzealous tanoak control came from the ranks of professional foresters as early as 1956. In the article "Killing Tanoak in Northwestern California," Douglass F. Roy claims that, because of its valuable wood, the tanoak "may contribute substantially to forest products" in the future and thus "should not be killed promiscuously but only when it interferes with the objectives of management."[72] Roy also noted that tanoak played important ecological roles in the forest ecosystem. Six years later, he lamented, "Management of forest lands often begins with extensive practices based upon scanty information."[73] Two U.S. Forest Service researchers writing nearly twenty-five years later concluded, "Because tanoak and conifers intermingle over much of tanoak's natural range, and control of sprouting tanoak is difficult and expensive, management of both on the same acre of land seems logical."[74]

RACHEL CARSON'S CRITIQUE

In her 1962 book *Silent Spring*, Rachel Carson titled her chapter on aerial pesticide spraying "Indiscriminately from the Skies" and claimed, "Not only the target insect or plant, but anything—human or nonhuman—within range of the chemical fallout may know the sinister touch of the poison." Carson sharply criticized the adoption of chemical weeding by foresters, stating,

> An unknown but very large acreage of timber-producing lands is now aerial sprayed in order to "weed out" the hardwoods from the more spray-resistant conifers. . . . The chemical weed killers are a bright new

toy . . . [T]hey give a giddy sense of power over nature to those who wield them, and as for the long-range and less obvious effects—these are easily brushed aside as the baseless imaginings of pessimists. The "agricultural engineers" speak blithely of "chemical plowing" in a world that is urged to beat its plowshares into spray guns.[75]

Carson called it "the shotgun approach to nature" and explained that "spraying also eliminates a great many plants that were not its intended target."[76] She warned against a myopically utilitarian view of nature: "Our attitude toward plants is a singularly narrow one. If we see any immediate utility in a plant we foster it. If for any reason its presence [becomes] undesirable or merely a matter of indifference, we may condemn it to destruction forthwith."[77]

GRASSROOTS ENVIRONMENTAL ACTIVISM

Use of herbicides to weed forests contributed to the creation of environmental activists in rural communities most affected by aerial spraying. Rural residents clashed with industrial softwood producers, claiming that aerial herbicide spraying increased cancer rates, reproductive problems, and water contamination in their communities.[78] Grassroots environmental advocacy organizations formed, such as Citizens against Toxic Herbicides (now defunct); Northwest Coalition for Alternatives to Pesticides, in Eugene, Oregon; Californians for Alternatives to Toxics, based in Arcata, California; and the Environmental Protection Information Center, in Garberville, California. A campaign to stop the spraying ensued (fig. 4.3).

Despite growing concerns about its safety, in the 1970s, the U.S. Department of Agriculture applied the phenoxy herbicide 2,4,5-T on millions of acres annually, including on forests nationwide in order to release conifers from hardwoods and other broad-leaved plant competition.[79] Controversy over 2,4,5-T resulted in a court decision against the U.S. Forest Service in 1977, which prompted a short-lived suspension of the use of the herbicide on tanoak in national forests in Oregon. The presiding federal judge expressed concern that the U.S. Forest Service had not adequately or objectively evaluated different herbicide treatments, nontoxic alternatives, or human health impacts in the assessment of its vegetation management practices.[80] In 1979, a staff writer for the *New Yorker* published a book that argued for stronger regulation of 2,4,5-T and other dioxin-containing sub-

FOREST SERVICE TO SPRAY
5½ MILLION ACRES WITH

FIGURE 4.3 "Money trees is what we want!! Ha Ha Ha Ha Ha . . ."
R. Crumb, ca. 1986. Courtesy of R. Crumb.

stances based on numerous studies of experiments with primates and other lab animals as well as anecdotal evidence resulting from accidental human exposures.[81]

Critics also claimed that 2,4-D, like 2,4,5-T, contained the contaminant dioxin, which was linked to miscarriages, birth defects, and other health problems.[82] In an act of civil disobedience, members of a group that included pregnant women threatened to handcuff themselves to trees in 1979 in an effort to prevent the Bureau of Land Management from spraying 2,4-D near

Grants Pass, Oregon. They met their objective by occupying the area "until the spraying season ended."[83] Environmentalists based in southern Oregon won a major victory in 1983 when their efforts resulted in a ten-year moratorium on all herbicide use on U.S. Forest Service and BLM land.[84] That year, the U.S. Forest Service stopped aerial herbicide applications entirely and never resumed the practice. BLM ended herbicide use "under a 1984/1987 court mandated injunction . . . except for the control of noxious weeds."[85] In 1985, "the Environmental Protection Agency (EPA) cancelled the use of 2,4,5-T and of silvex, a chemical analog," at the peak of "the most controversial and turbulent period in the history of forest pest management." Forest managers lamented the loss of "the best tool of all."[86]

Most government agencies and timber companies shifted to applying herbicide directly to cut stumps or wounded tanoak trunks; however, citizen action against herbicide use extended to non-aerial applications. In 1994, the Mendocino County Board of Supervisors unanimously adopted a resolution to "protect Mendocino County forest lands and residences from the extreme high fire danger caused by the girdling and/or use of herbicides resulting in dead but not downed hardwoods." The supervisors requested "an immediate halt to any practice which leaves large acreages of killed hardwoods standing but not downed."[87] Although not legally binding, the resolution communicated a widespread sentiment among county residents. The attempt to end spraying was triggered in part by a significant increase in hardwood poisoning. According to a 1994 article in the *Sacramento Bee*, 700 acres in Mendocino County were sprayed in 1992 as opposed to 6,180 acres in 1994 as of August.[88] Just to the north in Del Norte and Humboldt Counties, three companies alone sprayed roughly 4,474 acres in 1994: Louisiana-Pacific Corporation, Rellim Redwood Company, and Simpson Timber Company.[89]

Although political action and legal challenges essentially brought an end to aerial herbicide spraying on tanoak by the mid-1980s, Simpson Timber Company continued to aerially spray herbicides such as 2,4-D and Garlon 4 on forests surrounding homes on the Yurok Reservation in northern California, a practice it had begun in the 1970s (fig. 4.4). In addition to owning ancestral Yurok lands off the reservation, Simpson owned more than 50,000 acres of the reservation.[90] According to a 1992 *San Francisco Chronicle* article, cancer and miscarriage rates were above normal on the reservation, and many Native people blamed the herbicides. Lawrence (Tiger) O'Rourke, a Yurok building contractor, said, "I say it amounts to genocide."[91] By tribal

FIGURE 4.4 Tribal members protested herbicide spraying to kill tanoak and other native plants on the Yurok Reservation and elsewhere in northern California forests. Demonstration at the Simpson Timber Company facility, Arcata, California, March 30, 1992. Left to right: Margo Robbins (Yurok), Carole Lewis (Yurok), George Lewis (Yurok), Carol Williams (Yurok), Josey Conrad (Karuk), and Nancy Richardson (Karuk). Photograph by Joseph Audisio. Courtesy of Patty Clary and Californians for Alternatives to Toxics.

ordinance, herbicide use had been banned on the nearby Hoopa Valley Indian Reservation since 1978.[92] According to Hupa tribal member Merv George, "The tribe never liked herbicides because of how they impacted wildlife, watersheds, and subsistence gathering."[93] In 1996, the Yurok Tribe passed a resolution banning pesticide use on its lands because of the threats they pose to human health, clean air, and water quality.[94]

Conflict continued over the use of glyphosate-containing herbicides such as Garlon. In 2006, a lawyer representing the conservation group California Oak Foundation claimed that BLM's own assessment of a proposal to increase herbicide use on its lands in seventeen western states failed to provide adequate information for informed public scrutiny, nor did it sufficiently consider the negative impacts of increased herbicide use on oak woodlands and the many indigenous species dependent on them.[95] When the virulent, exotic plant disease sudden oak death started to spread, in part through infected tanoaks, in 2009, BLM attained an amendment to the 1980s injunction preventing herbicide use except on noxious weeds. The amendment allowed for use of glyphosate on the native tanoak to limit the impacts of sudden oak death.[96] The legal right to use glyphosate on BLM lands was reaffirmed in 2011, and imazapyr was added in the same year to the list of acceptable herbicides for use on tanoak on sites infected with sudden oak death.[97]

HERBICIDE HUMAN HEALTH RISKS

Critics claimed that increased cancer rates, reproductive problems, and water contamination in their communities resulted from aerial herbicide spraying on neighboring forests. Anecdotal evidence linked birth defects, mutations, miscarriages, and a host of other health problems to 2,4-D and 2,4,5-T. However, it was very difficult to prove cause and effect, particularly when symptoms often appeared years after exposure.[98] A spokesperson for Californians for Alternatives to Toxics described Garlon as "highly mobile and persistent in soils" and untested by EPA for "safety when . . . mixed with diesel and other chemicals," a common pre-application practice.[99] EPA does not require listing of inert ingredients.[100] Herbicide critics pressed for full disclosure and testing of inert ingredients and contaminants, as well as active ingredients, for acute and chronic toxicity. They also argued that everyone has the right to know when and to what herbicides he or she may be exposed and to opt out through notification before spraying occurs.

Foresters promoted herbicide use to control brush, sometimes without a complete understanding of the long-term human health and ecological impacts. In the case of 2,4,5-T, U.S. Forest Service professionals were not adequately educated about chemicals, responsive to and empathetic toward concerned members of the public, and transparent enough about their plans for spraying tanoak and other species.[101] In part because of this breach of the public's trust, many people in northern California remain adamantly opposed to pesticides. In 2012, David Bakke, pesticide use specialist for the Pacific Southwest Region, acknowledged that had the U.S. Forest Service known then what the world knows now about the hazards of 2,4,5-T, it would not have used the herbicide.[102] He also noted that, as with any activity, it is impossible to eliminate all risk when using herbicides. The

U.S. Forest Service's completed risk assessments on the herbicides it uses for vegetation management are available online.[103] Oregon State University's Environmental Toxicology and Chemistry Program and Environmental Health Sciences Center partnered on creating fact sheets on pesticides used in forestry and addressed issues of risk.[104]

THE CONTROL-OF-NATURE PARADIGM

Many critics of herbicide use object to the paradigm of control. Rachel Carson concluded in *Silent Spring*: "The 'control of nature' is a phrase conceived in arrogance, born of the Neanderthal age of biology and philosophy, when it was supposed that nature exists for the convenience of man."[105] In a 1996 article in *Conservation Biology*, two ecologists, C. S. Holling and Gary Meffe, called "command and control" ideology "the pathology of natural resource management" and claimed that it "usually results in unforeseen consequences for both natural ecosystems and human welfare in the form of collapsing resources, social and economic strife, and losses of biological diversity. . . . An ultimate pathology emerges when resource management agencies, through initial success with command and control, lose sight of their original purposes, eliminate research and monitoring, and focus on efficiency of control."[106]

Within natural resource management professions heavily influenced by industry, the rise of conservation biology represents an ecological reform movement that could bring foresters back to the radical roots of their profession. Arguably, a paradigm shift to an ecosystem approach, which allows for "a broader array of methodologies and techniques . . . including those that take longer to produce results,"[107] is already occurring in natural resource management. Long-term research on eradicating all tanoaks from forests with herbicides indicates that an absence of tanoaks can foster black stain root disease, which is potentially lethal to Douglas-fir.[108] The elimination of other hardwood species elsewhere on the West Coast similarly resulted in "greater incidence of root rots on Douglas-fir."[109]

HERBICIDE ALTERNATIVES

Political and legal challenges to herbicide use spurred researchers to actively explore alternative ways of releasing conifers from tanoak competition, including mechanical removal, grazing, mulching, burning, botanical oils, vinegar, and biological control.[110] Manual removal of "tanoak sprouts with axes or chainsaws" proved to be "rarely effective, and often expensive."[111] One study in the King Range National Conservation Area, a BLM holding in northern California, found no statistically significant difference in tanoak clump density between treated and untreated plots after five growing seasons. The researchers, including tanoak expert Philip McDonald, attributed their results to the massive root systems of tanoak clumps that make it "impractical to remove them with hand tools."[112] A study published in 1988 observed that monthly removal of competing vegetation including tanoak did result in significantly greater growth in height and diameter of Douglas-fir. However, the researcher, Annabelle Jaramillo, concluded that monthly clearing "is impractical."[113] U.S. Forest Service researchers noted that uprooting tanoak stumps, grinding them to prevent sprouting, and burning were "untested on a large scale" and generally were too expensive to offer viable alternatives.[114] In areas they manage for conifers on the Hoopa Valley Reservation, "tribal foresters are exploring alternative vegetation management techniques to achieve their diverse goals."[115] To reduce tanoak numbers in these areas, they tried double decapitation of sprouts using machetes without success. A later study by the U.S. Forest Service found that more aggressive manual vegetation control combined with mulching was effective, but the treatment was deemed too expensive.[116]

Manual removal of tanoak raised concerns among traditionalist Native peoples who favor tanoak as a food source. A Pomo Indian from Sherwood Rancheria said in an anonymous 1995 interview, "Everybody is focused on fir and redwoods but it's the tanoak that really needs attention. . . . People are taking tanoaks to run mills [to use as biofuel in on-site cogeneration power plants]. Chipping it up and burning it."[117] He explained that this tree is critical to indigenous cultural renewal. Hawk Rosales, executive director for the InterTribal Sinkyone Wilderness Council, echoed concern about mills chipping these acorn trees. "Each year there are fewer of the productive tanoak trees that are so necessary for the maintenance of California Indian peoples' traditional cultures."[118]

Multiple attempts to control tanoak by means of herbicide alternatives led to the same conclusion: they generally are more expensive, and most are also less effective. Grazing was determined to benefit sheep and cattle but make no significant dent in competition from tanoak. The Hupa Tribe tested burning with flamethrowers or weed burners. But "repeated destruction" did not inhibit tanoak sprout formation; quite the opposite, "formation of callus tissue led to even more sprouts."[119] Mendocino Red-wood Company defended its pesticide use on tanoak at a public meeting in Westport, California, on April 5, 2011, stating it had experimented with girdling, shade mats, vinegar, and other methods but was unable "to control [tanoak] without use of herbicide."[120]

Hamstrung by resistance to herbicide use on public forests, public for-esters hoped to adapt biological control for a new purpose: controlling a native species as opposed to a nonnative and invasive plant. They advocated research on insect pests and diseases of tanoak, "to explore their role in po-tential biological control of this and other hardwood species."[121] U.S. Forest Service researchers observed that abnormal and dead sprout clumps occur in otherwise healthy tanoak stands and suggested that fungi or obscure viruses in the rootstocks could be the cause. From this, they deduced, "The chance of a virus being the cause of decline was intriguing because of the possibility for developing a viral herbicide."[122] Unlike chemical herbicides, pathogens reproduce, potentially making control elusive. Introducing dis-ease-causing organisms risks unintended changes in ecosystem function. With the unintentional introduction of *Phytophtora ramorum*, competition from tanoak continues, as affected individuals die to the ground and re-sprout.

CONCLUSIONS

A hundred years encapsulate tanoak's shift from cash crop to trash tree. When scientific forestry was first established in North America, foresters advocated that the impacts of intensive tanoak bark harvesting be miti-gated through conservation and black wattle plantations. To better accom-modate commercial interests in softwood production, they shifted their focus in the mid-twentieth century and concentrated primarily on eradi-cating tanoak. The U.S. Forest Service funded decades of research on the use of herbicides to increase softwood productivity after the collapse of California's tanbark industry. This public investment in scientific manage-ment of conifer plantations and naturally regenerated stands of conifers after logging helped to make the American dream of home ownership more affordable for the middle class. Cheaper dimensional lumber for framing residential structures contributed to the increasing size of the average American home, which went from an average of 983 square feet in 1950 to nearly 2,600 square feet in 2013 for new construction.[123] Tanoak became a weed when its commercial value diminished relative to other tree species, not because its virtues remained undiscovered, as Emerson intimated with his definition of a weed.

HARDWOOD

Working citizens who believe in saving both the trees and
the people do not have to submit to the request to leave quietly.
Instead, the first task is to resist false choices; the second is to work
with optimism towards a future that embraces both healthy
forests and inclusive democratic community.

—**BEVERLY BROWN**

TANOAK WOOD HAS A LONG HISTORY OF USE, INCLUDING FOR
heating, flooring, cabinets, furniture, construction and finishing lumber,
veneer, tool handles, barrels, wood chips, paper pulp, and industrial biofuel.
Despite its abundance in northern California and southwestern Oregon, to
date it has not achieved its commercial potential, but it may become more
widely used in the future. Hardwood production from tanoak also has the
potential to help reduce continued conflict over logging that uses herbicide
for weeding, particularly in northern California. If a forest-based industry
is to continue with support from local communities on the Mendocino and
Humboldt County coast, tanoak wood production will likely have to be adopted and not just for low-end products like biofuel and paper pulp. However, tanoak's ability to dominate after logging combined with economic
factors will make this difficult to achieve. Many attempts have been made
to use tanoak wood commercially, but most producers couldn't overcome
a variety of challenges, including high production costs and competition
from red oak and other eastern U.S. hardwood species. Government subsidies and environmental philanthropy might help establish a viable trade in
tanoak wood and promote conservation of this foundation species. But cur-

rent economic incentives to ship unprocessed logs of various tree species to Asia and repurpose working forests into subdivided, private ranchettes for retirement and second homes are already making sustainable, community forestry efforts a challenge.

EUROPEAN INFLUENCES

Some of the reasons tanoak wood is not used commercially on any significant scale can be traced back to European influences. In the seventeenth century, the Englishman Francis Bacon promoted the idea of centralized planning that relied on science to improve upon nature's productivity for the benefit of people. In his utopian novel *New Atlantis*, this germinal thinker of the scientific revolution featured a research facility, Salomon's House, where scientists studied natural resources with the intent of managing them.[1] Expanding on Bacon's plan, European botanists assisted in rearranging the distribution of profitable plants on a global scale beginning in the eighteenth century, their aim being to maximize production and minimize labor costs. By providing technical support, they helped establish plantations in various American, African, and Asian colonies. Colonial plantation production focused on addictive substances (such as tobacco, opium, sugar, coffee, tea, chocolate, and cocaine), medicinals (e.g., cinchona bark, the source of quinine), staple foods (e.g., wheat and rice), spices (e.g., black pepper and ginger), and industrial resources, including rubber and wood. Through correspondence and publications, botanists shared information about growth requirements gleaned from experimental gardens in Europe and European colonies all over the world. Science empowered European nation-states to profit from the educated use of nature.

Decision making became centralized in Europe and was heavily influenced by scientists in service of commerce, which led to conflict because it undermined the ability of local communities to decide the best ways of working with nature and the land around them. It interfered with their right to self-determination. During the nineteenth century, "the combination of a developing rural capitalism and a centralized bureaucratic state, which protected and sponsored it," eroded the sovereignty of rural French communities, diminishing their food security and access to firewood and other forest resources.[2] Residents of the Ariège region of the Pyrenees, engaged in civil disobedience in response to Paris-based foresters taking control of forests in the French hinterlands. Their uprising came to be known as the War of the Demoiselles, or War of the Maidens, because men hid their identities by dressing as women while resisting the loss of local rights to manage lands held in common.[3] In nineteenth-century colonial Java, the rise of state forestry led to resistance from local communities who saw their forest use rights threatened, a conflict that persists today.[4] In the twentieth century, similar efforts to defend local control emerged in forests with tanoak when changes in forest management, which were in part state-funded, led to mistrust of industrial approaches to extraction and production. In the United States, killing tanoak as a weed species provoked the widespread perception that foresters were neither objective about tanoak's value nor adequately responsive to local concerns about toxic exposures to herbicides. This perception persists today in many rural communities in northern California.

Tanoak's place in European history is linked to exploration of the New World and the search for natural resources of value to the nation-states of Europe. Botanical prospecting for oaks occurred in North America in the late eighteenth and early nineteenth centuries because the military strength and commercial enterprises of European superpowers, like France and Britain, depended on oaks for making seaworthy ships. Britain's first treatise on forest management, *Sylva: Or, a Discourse of Forest Trees*, published in 1664 by John Evelyn, was inspired in part by anxieties about deforestation that might negatively affect the Royal Navy in the future.[5] In addition, metallurgists favored charcoal made from oak wood for iron smelting.[6] As the French and English depleted their oaks, they explored North America for alternate sources. In 1785, King Louis XVI of France sent André Michaux to the newly formed United States as a plant prospector. Although he wrote a monograph on the North American oaks,[7] tanoak was not included, as Michaux never encountered it.

Early in the nineteenth century, the London Horticultural Society sent the resource scout David Douglas to North America to seek out oaks, new fruit tree varieties, and potentially profitable garden plants. Although the Eastern Seaboard was no longer a British colony, the Pacific Coast was still contested terrain at the time of Douglas's collecting trips. California was a fragile, poorly protected, and newly independent Spanish colony under the jurisdiction of Mexico.[8] Traveling north of Santa Cruz Mission in 1831, Douglas encountered coast redwood for the first time.[9] Because tanoak is a common associate of these now iconic conifers, he likely also observed the leathery-leaved, evergreen acorn tree. However, the exact location of his collections of tanoak is unknown because he lost his field notes and his collection labels are vague. Sir William Jackson Hooker, one of the most influential botanists of the nineteenth century, formally named tanoak with a Glasgow University colleague in 1840.[10] The following year, Hooker republished the official Latin description and added the earliest known image of tanoak.[11] Also in 1841, he became the first official director of the Royal Botanic Gardens at Kew, near London, the premier botanical research institution of the British Empire.[12] One of Douglas's specimens at Kew is dated 1833, and other one lacks a date.[13] Hooker and Arnott used one or both of these specimens; the historical record is unclear as to which is the type specimen, but that ambiguity was common at the time, as designation of a type specimen is a more recent requirement.[14] Hooker's 1841 illustration appears to have been based primarily on the undated specimen.

The naming of tanoak by European botanists marked the beginning of new kinds of relationships between people and tanoak. In her book *Possessing Nature*, Paula Findlen explained that "natural history . . . was a form of inquiry designed to record the knowledge of the world for the use and betterment of mankind. . . . Collecting was one way of maintaining some degree of control over the natural world."[15] Formally classifying and naming tanoak according to the accepted scientific method of the time marked it as a natural resource to be used. The intent to exploit was made clear by André Michaux's son, François André, who authored *The North American Sylva: A description of the forest trees of the United States, Canada, and Nova Scotia considered particularly with respect to their use in the arts and their introduction into commerce*.[16] Europeans welcomed the new trees from North America into the cadre of other natural products that could be sold in the marketplace. For example, Douglas-fir, also introduced by Douglas, was transplanted to various British colonies, including Australia, New Zealand, and South Africa, as a softwood plantation tree. This North American conifer performed well in cultivation, becoming "the most important timber tree in the international forestry trade" during the twentieth century.[17]

Tanoak underwent multiple name changes between 1840 and 2008 as botanists attempted to classify the acorn-bearing tree with leaves resembling those of a chestnut. After more than ninety years of name stability, between 1917 and 2008, botanists changed tanoak's name again in response to new genetic information. It took nearly 170 years to settle on the current accepted scientific name for tanoak after the initial christening. In 1840, tanoak was added to Europe's inventories of potentially valuable trees of the world. Hooker collaborated with G. A. Walker Arnott to formally name tanoak *Quercus densiflora* "under the authority of the Right Honorable the Secretary of State for Colonial Affairs."[18] In 1866, Danish botanist Anders Sandøe Ørsted changed the name to *Pasania densiflora*.[19] Although he agreed that it belongs in the beech family (Fagaceae), Ørsted argued that tanoak differed too much from European oaks to warrant placing it in the genus *Quercus*. The male catkins don't droop like "true" oaks, and the acorn cups have slender spreading scales. Although botanists currently exclude tanoak from *Quercus* based on evolutionary analyses, the many common English names indicate a widespread and long lasting perception of kinship: burr oak,[20] California oak,[21] chestnut oak,[22] Coast chestnut oak,[23] dense-flowered oak, Spanish oak,[24] tanoak, tanbark oak, sovereign oak, and water oak.[25]

Increasingly, nineteenth-century European botanists thought the genus for oaks, *Quercus*, was overused and argued for subdivision. Dutch botany professor Frederick Anton Willem Miquel (1811-1871) added a new subgenus, *Lithocarpus*.[26] Before Ørsted changed tanoak's generic name to *Pasania* in 1866, a German botanist, Carl Ludwig von Blume (1796-1862), elevated *Lithocarpus* to full genus status based on Javanese specimens.[27] A year later, Alfred Rehder renamed the California hardwood *Lithocarpus densiflorus*, claiming it to be the only species in North America with numerous related species in Southeast Asia. Based on classical languages from Europe, the new scientific name for tanoak described some of its morphological characters, features evident in its external form and used in classification. *Lithos* means "rock" and *karpos* means "fruit" in Greek, referring to the hard nuts.[28] The Latin *densiflora* refers to the dense arrangement of tiny flowers in the male catkins. Rehder agreed with Ørsted that tanoak differed enough to warrant separating it from *Castanea* (the chestnuts) and not lumping it with *Quercus* (the "true" oaks).[29] However, Rehder did not find *Pasania* a satisfactory name given that the genus name *Lithocarpus* is older and therefore has seniority.[30] According to the International Code of Botanical Nomenclature, each plant bears only one legitimate binomial, and the first published name that best reflects evolutionary lineages takes precedence, beginning with the names published by Carl Linnaeus in *Species Plantarum* in 1753. A 1916 article in the Tokyo Botanical Society's journal changed tanoak's name to *Synaedrys densiflora* (Hook. & Arn.) Koidz, but this name was not adopted.[31] In 2008, botanists changed the name again, based on genetic research placing tanoak in the genus *Notholithocarpus*, to reflect its closer relationship to *Quercus*, *Castanea*, and *Castanopsis* (Asian chinquapin). The researchers

FIGURE 5.1 Fattening pigs on *Quercus* acorns in November before slaughtering them in December, Europe, ca. 1500. Pig herders' used the sticks in their hands to knock acorns down from the oak trees. Detail from a page in the calendar section of a prayer book, reproduced in Wieck, Voelkle, and Hearne, *The Hours of Henry VIII*, folio 6.

FIGURE 5.2 Oak (*Quercus*) honored as the glorious protector of the British Empire, personified by Britannia with a seedling in hand and sailing vessels made of oak wood in the background. From Wheeler, *The Modern Druid* (1747), reproduced in Harris, Harris, and James, *Oak: A British History*, 115.

concluded that North America's chinquapin (*Chrysolepis*) is more closely related to the Southeast Asian *Lithocarpus* than tanoak is to either.[32]

Naming New World plants like tanoak facilitated expansion of global commerce and European nation-states in part through the use of hinterlands for raw resources. In the process, European cultural practices were exported around the world. In regions of Europe with oaks, farmers fattened pigs on the autumn mast of acorns (fig. 5.1), and Euro-American settlers extended the practice to tanoak acorns in the late 1800s and early 1900s. Similarly, European practices around wood use influenced Euro-American settlers' perceptions of tanoak wood and its value. Until the nineteenth century, Europeans favored oaks. They used its wood for building castles, churches, homes, barns, and other structures.[33] Standard post-and-beam construction involved the use of heavy-timber framing, which depended primarily on oaks. This medieval European-style of construction was widely adopted in the American colonies using oaks in the genus *Quercus* and "remain[ed] common until 1840."[34] Oak wood was used in both Europe and the United States to make furniture and to build ships critical for commerce and the military (fig. 5.2). But by the late 1840s, iron rapidly began to replace wood in shipbuilding.[35] A fateful battle in 1862, during the American Civil War, marked the end of wooden naval ships, which proved vulnerable to the new ironclads.[36]

In response to deforestation and the resulting wood famines that followed, the idea of managing forests through science and maximizing production of desired goods in a sustained way gained momentum. During the nineteenth century, scientific forestry emerged as another way of seeing wood as an industrial resource. In that shift, oaks became less valued in Europe. German and French foresters began to promote softwoods at the expense of hardwood species in the early nineteenth century. Heinrich Cotta (1763-1844) founded the world's first forestry school and developed industrial forestry in Germany. Informed by emerging forestry professionals, Germans reforested degraded forestlands during the nineteenth and twentieth centuries with spruce (*Pinus*) and pine (*Picea*), which grow faster than hardwoods and therefore were better for meeting the needs of an industrializing economy. Later improvements in the knowledge of wood properties combined with advances in structural engineering also helped to increase demand for softwoods in industrialized nations.

American forestry was built particularly on German, Prussian, and French forestry practices, albeit slowly at first. In his germinal book *Man and Nature*, published in 1864, George Perkins Marsh advocated for scientific management of forests, claiming "that the sooner a natural wood is brought into the state of an artificially regulated one, the better it is for all the multiple interests which depend on the wise administration of this branch of public economy."[37] F. P. Baker, U.S. commissioner to the 1878 Paris Universal Exposition, doubted that the European-style forestry showcased at the world's fair could be applied in the United States due to the absence of "a strong central state, and without cultural support for conservation." He questioned whether Americans "would support the level of governmental interference that gave European foresters unrestrained authority."[38]

The expansiveness of the North American landscape, with its well-developed forests, also caused naysayers to question the ability of U.S. foresters to import European forestry practices. European foresters predicted that Americans would fail to adopt scientific forestry, believing that they'd never be able to convert all the old-growth redwood forests to efficient plantations.[39] Vegetation type conversion in forests dominated by such enormous trees seemed unachievable; however, technological innovations allowed the American timber industry to log these native forests. Foresters then proposed establishing young conifers in order to avert wood shortages that could limit industrial production and hamper economic growth (figs. 5.3, 5.4). Between 1922 and 1931, Union Lumber Company sprouted and transplanted about 3.5 million trees on some eight thousand acres, 90 percent of them redwood.[40] The rise of the softwood industry in the West combined with the emphasis placed on managing conifers at the expense of hardwoods created the preconditions for later use of herbicides on tanoak.

TANOAK WOOD WASTE

Americans used enormous amounts of wood for constructing and operating railroad systems during the late nineteenth century. According to a mid-1880s estimate, 17 million acres of forest were destroyed to supply enough railroad ties for the existing tracks in the United States and another 567,714 forested acres were needed annually to replace rotted railroad ties.[41] Eastern oaks furnished more than 60 percent of the wood for these ties.[42] Tanoak wood could be of limited use for railroad ties after it was treated with preservatives.[43] However, the added expense was a disincentive for using the wood in this way, and untreated tanoak wood, particularly the sapwood, decomposed quickly when left unprotected in the elements making

FIGURE 5.3 Coast redwood bareroot stock being grown at the Union Lumber Company Nursery for use in reforestation, with sunflower windrow in the background, Fort Bragg, California, August 25, 1923. The nursery closed in 1931 because natural reforestation proved more successful than planting unirrigated seedlings. Courtesy of Fort Bragg–Mendocino Coast Historical Society Archives, Georgia-Pacific Donations, Union Lumber Co. Collection.

FIGURE 5.4 Unidentified conifer tree planter probably with bareroot redwood seedlings replanted after logging of old-growth forests, Campbell Creek watershed north of Fort Bragg, California, ca. 1920s. Union Lumber Company in Fort Bragg promoted its use of forest farming over forest mining or "cut and run" practices. Courtesy of Fort Bragg-Mendocino Coast Historical Society Archives, Georgia-Pacific Donations, Union Lumber Co. Collection.

it unsuitable for railroad ties. [44] In contrast, old-growth redwood heartwood resisted decay and could be processed in the forest with an ax into "split stuff," including railroad ties, thereby reducing production and transportation costs relative to using milled and treated tanoak wood for railroad ties.

Native North American oaks supplied wood for cabinetry, furniture, flooring, construction timbers, finishing lumber, firewood, barrels, charcoal, and many other items. Despite widespread use of related species, the tanning industry prized tanoak bark for curing leather and wasted most of the wood in the process of tanbark extraction. Between 1849 and 1918, half a billion board feet of tanoak wood were squandered by bark peelers. [45] This waste galled University of California botany professor Willis Linn Jepson, who complained that "100,000 trunks 10 to 100 feet long and 1/2 to 4 feet in diameter are left annually to rot on the ground," with an estimated 5 percent being "cut into firewood." [46] He argued that prompt seasoning would eliminate most of the checking that tended to result when tanoak wood was handled in an unskillful manner; it could then be put to the same kinds of uses as *Quercus* wood, "and a stupendous annual waste" could be eliminated. [47] But most tanoak wood was used for firewood or charcoal production, if it was harvested at all, [48] with a small percentage utilized for mine timbers and furniture. [49] In 1868, the Santa Cruz region reportedly sent several thousand cords of firewood annually to San Francisco while its coopers made staves for flour and lime barrels from the best part of the tanoak trunk after bark stripping. [50]

Tanoak couldn't compete commercially with coast redwood and, later, Douglas-fir, because of its lower volume. Tanoak trees suitable for milling occurred in scattered stands over the landscape, making harvesting more expensive. U.S. Forest Service researcher Douglass Roy concluded that for economic reasons, "land managers cannot invest money to manage these inclusions." [51] Without adequate access in steep terrain, extracting heavy tanoak wood often proved prohibitive in terms of cost. Even with access, the "mechanics of skidding and loading heavy, not-always-straight hardwood logs often caused additional expenses." [52]

Many justified the waste of tanoak wood out of ignorance of tanoak's properties. Henry Bolander reported at an October 1865 meeting of the California Academy of Sciences, "Its wood is absolutely useless; . . . wet like a sponge when cut; [and] . . . extremely perishable. At Mendocino City log-men call it Water Oak." [53] According to a much later source, a tanoak "tree literally oozes water when it is felled." [54] George Engelmann, an expert on U.S. oaks, claimed in 1878 that tanoak wood was "brittle and worthless."[55] Tanoak was judged unfit for use due to "its supposed perishable nature . . . based largely on the observations of the bark men, who strip it in the early summer and leave the naked trunks on the mountain slopes to harden and check with the seasons, and then to rot."[56]

The misperception that the wood is inferior persists, in part due to unskilled producers using milling practices and drying schedules suited for easier-to-process softwoods (conifers). Consumers developed a negative attitude toward tanoak wood and other California hardwoods because poorly manufactured products were of inferior quality.[57] That was the fault not of the tree but rather of the inexperienced producers. In 1910, Jepson described the wood as "close-grained, hard and strong, and . . . highly valuable if taken care of when cut and subjected to proper treatment."[58] According to the authors of the Hoopa Valley Reservation Hardwood Study Report released in 1968, "A major reason for failure to harvest and manufacture western hardwoods profitably has been a general reluctance to recognize fundamental differences between softwoods and hardwoods requiring the use of different equipment and techniques."[59]

Domestic competition factored into the anemic interest in tanoak wood. During the early twentieth century, wood engineers conducted strength tests of various conifers, demonstrating that many, including Douglas-fir, formerly considered a weed, were strong enough for structural uses. Indeed their superior strength-to-weight ratio made them preferable to most hardwoods. Balloon framing, often with Douglas-fir, became the dominant form of single-family home construction in the United States during the late nineteenth and twentieth centuries.[60] Old-growth coast redwood "earned the highest rating from the USDA's Forest Products Laboratory."[61] This information, coupled with high demand for dimensional lumber during and after World War II, resulted in significant increases in demand for West Coast softwood species. Hardwood extraction in the United States centered on eastern deciduous forests where oaks grew in greater numbers in a landscape with less topographic relief (e.g., less mountainous) and more extensive road systems. Hardwoods had increased in numbers through natural succession after early conifer logging, and the cost of intensive forestry to restore the pines and other softwoods species was generally uneconomical because conifers in the Southeast and Pacific Northwest presented significant commercial competition. At least two major U.S. softwood producers concentrated on both of these regions, based on the premise that they would alternate operations between the two and allow for forest restocking, hence, their company names—Georgia-Pacific and Louisiana-Pacific.

Most industrialists rejected commercial use of tanoak wood because of lower profit margins relative to softwoods. Hardwoods suffer higher loss rates during the seasoning and milling process.[62] The secondary xylem, or wood, of conifers is composed primarily of water-conducting cells called tracheids.[63] Because of the tissue's cellular uniformity, conifer wood dries more evenly and therefore checks and warps less. In contrast, the wood of flowering plants, like tanoak, is made up of a greater variety of cell types.[64] As a result of this cellular diversity, areas in the tissue dry at different rates, resulting in more checking, warping, collapse, and other forms of deformation. Oak wood just off the mill can have up to 80 percent moisture content,[65] and a lot of loss can occur during the process of drying the wood to the industry standard of 6-8 percent moisture. High-density hardwoods like oak and tanoak require slow drying in order to avoid excessive warping, shrinking, checking, honeycombing, and collapse. Although tanoak is considered a challenging species to dry, proper practices, especially early in the process, are critical to minimizing losses including those caused by drying-induced staining.[66] Six months of air-drying before kiln-drying reduced warping and collapse.[67] But that processing time is significantly longer than what softwoods require because softwoods can be dried in a kiln earlier. Trying to speed up the drying process of green tanoak wood in a kiln without air-drying first did not yield promising results.[68]

Harvesting, drying, and milling tanoak wood into lumber were time- and labor-intensive, which drove production costs up and profit margins down. Because hardwood production requires more skilled labor than softwood production, this, too, created a disincentive for tanoak production, as most lumber companies opted to minimize their dependency on laborers with rare and specialized skills. The rising influence of increasingly consolidated lumber companies in early Western boom-bust economies radicalized some workers who were negatively affected. Within the "redwood empire," however, labor organizing in the late 1880s fractured due in part to dispersed worksites in remote areas, transient workers, repression of unionizing efforts, and "bitter factionalism."[69] The tide began to shift in 1907 when more than 2,500 workers employed by Humboldt County's redwood industry struck over poor working conditions.[70] During the 1930s, the number of unionized workers in the United States increased rapidly due to federal pro-labor legislation.[71] California redwood lumber operations claimed "the dubious distinction of suffering the longest major strike in American industrial history."[72] The Sawmill and Timber Workers Union ended its strike in April 1948 after an unsuccessful twenty-seven-month effort to win a significant increase in compensation and obligatory union membership.[73] The instability of their early transient labor force stimulated industrial leaders to try to attract steadier, family men in order to ensure more efficient extraction and a return on their investments in new technologies. In this schema of efficiency, tanoak was too much of a risk.

During the period of prosperity following World War II, timber workers did gain better working conditions and compensation, but the effectiveness of unions waned "[w]hen the lumber market collapsed in the late 1970s and early 1980s."[74] Also unions failed to effectively influence the modes of production, which ultimately shaped the nature of timber industry work.[75] Even-aged conifer monocultures enabled increased mechanization, which allowed for the downsizing and deskilling of the labor force, and thus a reduction in its negotiating power in labor disputes (fig. 5.5). Furthermore, the gyppo logging system, in which independent contractors supplied mills with logs for a fixed rate, expanded. As opposed to logging railroads, cheaper road systems combined with "the truck's flexibility made it possible for operators to focus on high-value timber."[76] Ironically, timber workers helped to convert old-growth forests of the West into even-aged coniferous forests. This vegetation type conversion made it possible for industrialists to mechanize modes of production, thereby reducing their dependence on workers, by significantly reducing the overall number needed to produce greater and greater volumes of lumber.

Another factor that posed a challenge to forest managers was the prolific root crown sprouting to which injured tanoak trees are particularly prone. University of California botany professor Willis Linn Jepson claimed that "as many as 1,400 have been counted on one large stump." Although the abundance of sprouts declined "by natural processes in 30 years to from four to eight of the most vigorous poles," productivity was diminished by the competition.[77] The labor cost to thin this coppice growth in order to produce millable tanoak trunks, or boles, proved prohibitive. The tanoak's asexual reproductive powers allowed it to gain dominance when logging opened the forest canopy, particularly in forests dominated by Douglas-fir. Foresters and timbermen began using herbicides in the mid-twentieth century, which hastened the establishment and growth of conifers by shortening the early successional phase dominated by tanoak and other hardwoods.[78] In refer-

You don't pay the man who isn't there

Engineered to Cut Costs . . .

CORLEY SAWMILL MACHINERY

CORLEY MANUFACTURING CO. CHATTANOOGA, TENN.

FIGURE 5.5 Image of millworker as replaceable through mechanization of lumber production. From *Forest Industries* 90, no. 11 (October 1963): 104. Courtesy of Corley Manufacturing.

ence to this widespread practice, forester Douglass Roy confessed in 1962 that "[m]anagement of forest lands often begins with extensive practices based upon scanty information."[79] The forest supervisor for the Six Rivers National Forest noted around 1950 that tanoak and other hardwoods "have been considered a nuisance to the logger, yet they are eyed almost universally with the idea that there ought to be a use for them." He concluded, "There is a substantial market ready to be established."[80] Despite ample evidence of tanoak wood's merit, managing for softwood species like coast redwood and Douglas-fir continues to dominate on production-oriented private and public forest lands in the West.

TANOAK WOOD USE

Even in the late 1800s and early 1900s, tanoak advocates existed, but they enjoyed little influence regarding wood use. Referring to its wood, one optimist claimed in 1853 that "there is some tall and tough oak on the northern coast which probably will begin to come into the market next year."[81] J. B. Armstrong, an early resident of Cloverdale, California, claimed in 1891 that "[n]o other oak begins to vie with it for beauty of grain. . . . It will stay exactly where the workman puts it, and will stand the roughest knocks without flinching."[82] Armstrong used tanoak wood to beautify his home and wished the "unappreciative destroyers" would end their ignorant mishandling of the wood and recognize its worth.[83] According to Jepson, "wagon makers in the Coast Range" preferred tanoak "for repair work" as a "superior . . . wood for felloes," or the rims of wheels supported by spokes.[84]

George Sudworth, one of the founders of the Society of American Foresters, described tanoak favorably in 1908.

> Wood dense and fine-grained, very hard, firm, and somewhat brittle (though brittleness varies with age), light brown, faintly tinged with red. The quality is suitable for agricultural implements and for finishing and furniture lumber. It is employed more generally for firewood. Economically a tree of the greatest importance in Pacific forests, both for its valuable tanbark and for the promise it gives of furnishing good commercial timber in a region particularly lacking in hardwoods. The present extensive practice of destroying this oak for its bark alone, without utilizing the wood, calls for prompt conservative action.[85]

A federal forester for more than forty years and a published authority on North American trees, at the time he wrote this, Sudworth was serving as the chief dendrologist for the Bureau of Forestry, the agency that became the U.S. Forest Service.[86]

H. S. Betts, who conducted timber tests for the U.S. Forest Service, concluded in 1911 that "there seems to be no good reason why tanbark oak should not take its place in the Pacific coast hardwood market for many if not all the purposes for which eastern hardwoods are now imported." He continued, "All things considered, the seasoning of tanbark oak seems to offer little, if any, more difficulty than is experienced with eastern oaks." The wood, he believed, was particularly well suited for flooring because of its "pleasing grain and color, and the necessary hardness."[87] In fact, the Union Lumber Company in Fort Bragg, California, was successfully milling tanoak for flooring by 1910.[88]

California hardwood promoters continued to insist in mid-century that the technical ability existed for milling tanoak. One hardwood authority claimed that "western hardwoods are equally satisfactory as comparable eastern species . . . and we need not apologize for any of them where care is exercised in their manufacture."[89] A university researcher noted in 1958 that "[t]anoak . . . is the most abundant hardwood species in California" and "the State has over 2 billion board feet of standing tanoak timber of saw log size."[90] Because of its straight, long, branchless trunks, forest-grown tanoaks yielded desirable material for milling.[91] In 1956, U.S. Forest Service researcher Douglass Roy asserted, "The wood has good properties, a pleasing appearance, and although considerable care is required in seasoning, additional experiments should develop practicable drying schedules."[92] He claimed that, despite the early lack of interest in California, fourteen native hardwood trees have potential commercial value. He was most optimistic about tanoak, California black oak (*Quercus kelloggii*), and red alder (*Alnus rubra*). He noted,

> So far foresters' efforts concerning tanoak have been directed toward destroying it. . . . Bark harvesting operations destroyed many of the largest trees. . . . Besides growing well on deep soil, tanoak also thrives on stony and shallow soil phases where conifers thin out. Yet tanoak requires more moisture than many other hardwoods. It will grow well on the shallow and stony soils of north slopes, for example, but will be supplanted by Pacific madrone, Oregon white oak, or California black oak on the warmer, drier south slopes. These facts suggest the sites where foresters might begin to manage tanoak.[93]

The Northwest Hardwood Association, formed in 1955, collectively addressed issues of concern to producers and wholesalers, such as grading, freight rates, and marketing.[94] By 1958, a state-funded experiment station reported that there were newly tested methods for reducing loss during processing of California hardwoods.[95] In the same year, tanoak was "compared with 19 eastern and western hardwoods and ranked among the best in terms of strength, hardness, and resistance to compression bending and shock."[96] It also ranked among the densest and stiffest of North American woods.[97] Researchers at university-affiliated Forest Products Laboratories in Wisconsin, California, and Oregon completed research on the characteristics and processing techniques for tanoak.[98] Its strength qualities compared favorably to eastern white oak (*Quercus alba*) except when compression was applied perpendicular to the wood grain.[99] Numerous woodworkers confirmed that the West Coast tree generated beautiful and highly workable material for flooring, furniture, and cabinets. Nevertheless, commercial interest in tanoak wood continued to be anemic.

Beginning in 1963, Union Lumber Company again pioneered the commercial use of tanoak wood, processing boxcar flooring under the trade name Doweloc (fig. 5.6).[100] In a trade journal describing the laminated decking product, the author claimed, "Progress in the lumber industry has often been coupled with utilizing a new or formerly weed species. . . . One of the West's 'newest' species is tanoak. . . . Several firms have shown interest in tanoak, but so far only one has made any volume use of the wood, and that is in a specialized product."[101] Because of the hardness of tanoak wood, Doweloc was very durable. However, in 1969, the family who owned Union Lumber Company sold to Boise-Cascade.[102] The new corporate owner shortly thereafter judged "the supply of tan oak on company timberlands . . . insufficient to maintain a profitable operation and the Doweloc plant was closed."[103] Union Lumber Company overestimated the number of usable trees in the forest. Many of the old-growth tanoaks it cut had extensive heart rot resulting in much of the trunk being left in the forest. Furthermore, the wood from older tanoak trees is prone to degrade more during the drying process.[104] Mineral staining, commonly found in old-growth trees, caused more of the wood than expected to be downgraded or deemed waste. Staining likely increased in logs kept for more than a month.[105] Loss rates during milling and seasoning also contributed to discontinued production.[106] Union Lumber Company used a Swedish gang mill that wasted usable material because it didn't handle crooked trunks well.[107] The Fort Bragg mill obtained the most satisfactory results with a combination of air- and kiln-drying. Stacking the wood with an adequate number of spacers, called stickers, and limiting the lumber thickness to one inch also helped to reduce loss. Ultimately, "the concept of a one product, low end use, hardwood mill probably doomed the project. . . . The end came when Federal Government subsidies to box car makers ended."[108]

Ironically, in the same year that Doweloc production ended at the former Union Lumber Company, a trade magazine claimed, "Tanoak, a neglected West Coast hardwood, is winning a slice of commercial respectability among flooring manufacturers, paper-makers and even baseball players."[109] The author noted that two companies tried and failed "to peel tanoak for veneer several years ago" because "it warped and cracked" but then went on to list tanoak wood producers in addition to Union Lumber Company. Menasha Corporation in North Bend, Oregon, began producing pulp in 1965, consuming roughly 180 million board feet of tanoak harvested from the Chetco District of Siskiyou National Forest, according to a 1968 trade magazine. A company located in Brookings, Oregon, Tanoak Industries, Inc., began producing tanoak baseball bats in 1968. Also from Brookings, South Coast Lumber Co. expanded its operations at the cost of $1 million and added a

FIGURE 5.6 Doweloc laminated boxcar flooring produced at Union Lumber Company, Fort Bragg, California, ca. 1960s. Courtesy of Fort Bragg–Mendocino Coast Historical Society Archives, Georgia-Pacific Donations, Union Lumber Co. Collection.

96-inch chipper to supply the market with tanoak wood chips. For the fiscal year 1969, the Forest Service projected sales of tanoak from the Chetco District alone at 6 million board feet.[110]

In 1977, shifts in hardwood resource availability and production costs inspired Philip McDonald, a U.S. Forest Service researcher, to promote tanoak as "a promising species." High-quality eastern U.S. hardwood sawlogs were on the decline, while transportation costs were rising. He noted that "native California hardwoods, and specifically tanoak, which could provide a major opportunity for increased wood and fiber production, are scarcely utilized."[111] McDonald emphasized the many fine qualities of tanoak wood that made it desirable for furniture making: "Numerous tall rays give rotary-cut veneer and flat-grain surface lumber a striking appearance, resembling rift-sawed oak. The wood is tough and hard. It has outstanding strength, resists denting and abrasion, machines easily, and does not split when fasteners are used. In addition, it takes stains and finishes well, and forms strong joints with glues."[112] The barrier to using tanoak wood posed by seasoning no longer existed, because, McDonald explained, "reliable techniques are available now and are described extensively in the literature."[113] Deformation of the wood during the drying process could be minimized through

FIGURE 5.7 Greenwood ladderback rocker made from tanoak wood by Dan Stalzer, a graduate of the James Krenov Woodworking School, College of the Redwoods, Fort Bragg, California, ca. 1997. Photograph by and courtesy of Seth Janofsky.

skillful use of a kiln, which could also enhance the "strength and working properties" of the lumber.[114] Use of tanoak for pulp did increase but represented an undervaluing of its beautiful wood.

Inventories of the tanoak resource indicated that mid-century sawtimber volume was approximately "2,036 million board feet in California and 1,700 million board feet in Oregon."[115] Another estimate made around the mid-1980s put the volume of tanoak sawlogs at 3.66 billion board feet in just "the California counties of Del Norte, Humboldt, Mendocino and Sonoma."[116] Daniel Oswald claimed in 1972 that in the latter two counties alone nearly half the commercial forestlands, or 768,000 acres, supported hardwoods, much of which was tanoak.[117] Statewide, tanoak dominated 861,000 acres of California timberlands in 1988, 86 percent of which was privately owned. The same study found that tanoak occurred on 2.425 million acres in the state, not including national forests and parks.[118] The "non-industrial private forestlands of the northern California coast region" alone could potentially sustain extraction of roughly 50 million board feet of tanoak wood annually.[119] Based on experiences in the northeastern United States,

the U.S. Forest Service emphasized the importance to profitability of producing for multiple markets from hardwood stands, rather than just a single
market.[120] Following this diversification model, hardwood producers on the
West Coast explored various markets for tanoak, including veneer, flooring,
cabinetry, furniture, pulpwood, and firewood (fig. 5.7).

In a mid-1980s report focused on potential use of tanoak wood, William Sullivan, a Humboldt State University forestry professor, pointed out
that the timber industry had changed significantly. "In the past there was
little reason for harvesting and milling the hardwood because of the great
difference in value between it and old growth softwood." But with most
of the old-growth coast redwood and Douglas-fir logged, "now the comparison must be made between second growth softwood and the existing
hardwood."[121] Comparing Michigan's hardwood production in 1980 to the
potential for tanoak wood processing in California's North Coast region,
he concluded that tanoak was an underutilized resource because less than
20 million board feet of tanoak were harvested and most of that was for
low-value pulpwood. In contrast, Michigan cut more than 200 million board
feet of hardwoods. In total, the state produced $751 million worth of wood
and lumber products, more than 90 percent from hardwoods. In 1980, this
wood-based industry employed roughly 30,590 people. Sullivan cautioned
that Westerners couldn't expect to establish such a successful hardwood
industry quickly, since it took Michigan a century.[122] McDonald and another
U.S. Forest Service researcher, John Tappeiner II, recommended making "a
commitment to manage tanoak and designate a large area of land for its
management, preferably land already stocked with good-quality trees."[123]

Dramatic increases in U.S. hardwood exports to Europe and Asia during
the 1980s suggest that markets existed for California hardwoods.[124] The U.S.
Forest Service rereleased a guide to producing nursery stock of hardwood
species, claiming, "More hardwood seedlings are being planted because the
demand for hardwood timber has increased and foresters have been able to
establish successful hardwood plantations."[125] Researchers working in the
Midwest on the reforestation of abandoned farmland even experimented
with the use of herbicides to favor planted hardwoods.[126] However, a limited
number of species gained most of the attention, in particular, cottonwood
(such as the hybrid *Populus trichocarpa x P. deltoides*), black walnut (*Juglans
nigra*), and sweetgum (*Liquidambar styraciflua*).[127]

Most California oaks have not been seriously considered as potential
plantation hardwood species due in part to slow growth and frequently a

short, less-than-straight trunk. In the case of tanoak, annual fertilizer applications can at least increase seedling growth significantly.[128] Under the right growing conditions, tanoak can also produce a long enough branchless trunk to be desirable for lumber production. According to Jepson, tanoak plantations would be successful only "where conditions are similar to those of the natural range of the tree,"[129] but "attempts to establish a plantation of tanoak by artificial seeding on an exposed site, which had been prepared by removing vegetation and exposing mineral soil, were unsuccessful."[130] During the 1990s, the U.S. Forest Service continued to fund research into utilizing wood from tanoak established through natural recruitment. Two of its researchers, Dean Huber and Philip McDonald, asserted in 1992, "Now is the time to develop a philosophy for managing California hardwoods for wildlife, wood, water, and esthetics."[131] Significant opportunity for increased production persisted. In the same year, the Forest Service estimated that the amount of California-sourced hardwood lumber produced in the state amounted to only 0.5 percent of the total volume used annually by manufacturers.[132]

Despite its abundance, California's hardwood resource was "poorly managed and scarcely utilized," according to Huber and McDonald.[133] They emphasized the importance of manufacturing practices and marketing that reflected an appreciation for the differences between hardwoods and softwood. They also noted that profitable processing of hardwood sawlogs often depended on also producing "secondary products like bark, chips, and fuelwood."[134] Based on knowledge of hardwood anatomy, technological innovations in processing led in turn to "progress toward solving a major problem."[135] The authors conclude that in the future, tanoaks and other California hardwoods "will contribute significantly to the state's economy. . . . The art of hardwood silviculture in California should enjoy its finest hour."[136]

Despite the capacity to be "largely wood self-sufficient," by 1996, California was importing much of the softwood and hardwood products consumed in the state from "other people's forests," a practice foresters deemed unethical.[137] Californians were exploiting forests in countries with weaker environmental and human rights protections in order to avoid logging locally. Like the British in the 1700s and 1800s, Californians sourced wood from the hinterlands, but the hope persisted that California hardwoods would in the future provide a locally grown alternative to imported tropical and eastern U.S. hardwoods. Advocates of more local production in affluent countries like the United States suggest that making the impacts of resource extraction more visible could potentially inspire a reevaluation of heavy consumption patterns.[138]

A challenging period in rural northern California and southwestern Oregon began in the late twentieth century as numerous mills relocated to other regions after more than a century of timber extraction. Many timber towns experienced the disappearance of their economic base. Some communities worked proactively to shape their future by fostering locally owned forest products industries that were sustainable and more diversified. Large-scale logging operators in California's coniferous forests had hesitated to process tanoak because its scattered distribution and more complex wood required "handling on a different scale, and with more critical requirements than for softwood operations."[139] But profitable small-scale hardwood production in the eastern United States offered a hopeful vision for northern California. The Golden State's softwood mills typically were heavily capitalized and often largely mechanized operations producing "30 to 150 million BF [board feet] per year." In contrast, hardwood mills normally "cut 5 million BF or less per year."[140]

One of the barriers to commercial use of tanoak wood was the dearth of hardwood kilns on the West Coast and the limited number of people knowledgeable in processing it (fig. 5.8).[141] Common imperfections in the trees required more expertise from loggers and mill operators.[142] Community leaders worked to change that, hoping that a new hardwood industry could offset the impact of the downsizing softwood industry. The U.S. Forest Service awarded the City of Fort Bragg $39,000 in the 1990s to study the feasibility of marketing California hardwoods, including tanoak.[143] Under the direction of the Mendocino Forest Conservation Trust, the author of the resulting report concluded that the North Coast needed a training academy and a hardwood marketing association. The academy would train "men and women who want to learn how to mill, grade and dry native hardwood lumber." The intended outcome was to create "a native hardwood industry potentially employing hundreds of people in Northern California."[144]

In his report on tanoak's economic potential, Sullivan recommended that public institutions collaborate with "land owners, mill owners, and the furniture industry" to better utilize California's hardwoods, since "it is unrealistic to assume any single firm could have the resources to explore

FIGURE 5.8 Hardwood drier at a mill operated for more than thirty-five years by Whitethorn Hardwoods, Humboldt County, California, 2014. Photograph by and courtesy of Ken Forden.

the issues which must be studied."[145] For decades, a variety of public institutions have been doing just that, including colleges and universities, state and federal forestry programs, economic stimulus programs, and even low-security prisons. In Mendocino County, Jim Anderson established a hardwood demonstration mill in 1991 at the Parlin Fork Conservation Camp, a facility still operated by the California Department of Forestry and Fire Protection in collaboration with the California Department of Corrections and Rehabilitations.[146] Anderson objected to only chipping tanoak, because it didn't produce enough jobs for timber workers displaced when Georgia-Pacific purchased the Boise-Cascade mill in nearby Fort Bragg in 1974 and, after reducing the workforce, closed the mill in 2002. He promoted the more lucrative, less wasteful use of tanoak for furniture, cabinets, and other value-added products.[147] As of 2002, with the aid of a dehumidification dry kiln, the camp produced annually "about 150,000 board feet of grade hardwoods."[148] Parlin Fork Conservation Camp has continued to invest in hardwood training and recently purchased a new computerized hardwood mill.[149] It supplies quality hardwoods to Chamberlin Creek Conservation Camp, "where it is crafted into cabinets and office furniture" that is used in California government offices.[150]

Some tanoak advocates hoped to create more markets for the hard and durable wood by fostering a local furniture industry. Fort Bragg's community college, the College of the Redwoods, produced many fine woodworkers whose furniture is featured in art galleries and promoted by urban interior designers. Marketing proved critical because low consumer demand for native hardwoods had made past attempts to harvest and process them profitably challenging. Roughly 1 percent of Americans buy handmade wooden furniture.[151] Woodworker guilds have emerged to learn how to best serve this niche market. Despite low demand, in 1994, Greg Guisti, Mendocino County's University of California Extension farm adviser, predicted that, in the future, "hardwoods will be managed as part of a diverse forest ecosystem and not just as 'weeds' which compete with valuable conifers."[152]

In Humboldt County, the Institute for Sustainable Forestry formed in 1991 to promote "community-based, small-scale sustainable forestry," in part through establishing third-party certification under the international Smart Wood label. Its certification criteria included no synthetic chemical pesticide use. The U.S. Forest Service and the Mead Foundation funded the institute in 1995, to assess whether an adequate supply of certifiable timber existed in the region to support such an economic agenda. The institute concluded that "a small-scale sustainable industry could be developed around the harvesting and processing of approximately 2 million board feet of tanoak per year and between 0.8 and 2.6 million board feet of other species per year."[153] It hoped to increase the native hardwood supply by encouraging small landowners to sustainably thin "cut-over forest tracts where hardwoods have outpaced conifers."[154] Although premium hardwood sawlogs can be purchased at pulp prices from industrial softwood logging operations, many local woodworkers refuse to do so out of principle due their opposition to clear-cut logging practices.[155] In an effort to foster small-scale hardwood production, the Institute for Sustainable Forestry partnered with Wild Iris Mill to create a demonstration hardwood-processing facility.[156] In addition to providing technical assistance with the processing of tanoak flooring, the institute also advised on effective marketing.

Jude Wait of Wild Iris Mill claimed in 2000 that tanoak "could eventually become a key to creating a local certified forestry industry."[157] A U.S. Forest Service report indicated that tanoak made up roughly 18 percent of

FIGURE 5.9 Tanoak and madrone flooring at Whitethorn Hardwoods in Whitethorn, 2014. Photograph by and courtesy of Ken Forden.

FIGURE 5.10 Tanoak logs to be converted into wood chips, to be sold for $125/ton, at Eel River Sawmill in Humboldt County, California, ca. 1995. Photograph by the author.

the gross volume of living hardwood trees in California for the years 2001-2005.[158] Roughly a quarter of the 3.6 billion cubic feet of this tree in the state is suitable in size and quality for milling.[159] Once sawn into lumber, a mere 1 percent of this volume would meet roughly 10 percent of the California hardwood demand.[160] But by 2014, many producers of local hardwoods were defunct. Whitethorn Hardwoods in Humboldt County is unusual in having milled tanoak for more than thirty-five years (fig. 5.9).

Tanoak has been used for pulpwood and biofuel for decades. Due to depressed market demand for tanoak sawlogs, many beautiful logs suitable for milling have been chipped or converted into cogeneration hog fuel instead (fig. 5.10).[161] Some lumber mills use tanoak biomass as a carbon-based fuel to create electricity and heat for their operations in cogeneration facilities, which recover waste heat to produce thermal energy. Compared to black oak and madrone, tanoak has historically been favored as a source of paper pulp chips due in part to its "fiber qualities and color."[162] However, the chip market is volatile and heavily influenced by demand from Asian markets, particularly Japan. According to a 1980 Forest Service publication, in an attempt to reduce energy costs and disposal expenses for wood waste, an increasing number of California sawmills were beginning to use on-site wood boilers.[163] Oversupply in the pulp market in part triggered the shift in increased use of tanoak chips for electricity generation. By the mid- to late 1990s, market demand for chips had plummeted. In 1998, tanoak's reputation still allowed "forest land managers to log the species at a modest profit for chips."[164] Since then, the market for tanoak chips has fallen further.

Some environmentalists opposed to herbicide use claim that if more tanoak wood chips could be sold, at least for biofuel or paper pulp, the timber industry would be less inclined to poison tanoaks and leave the dead trees standing, creating a significant fire hazard.[165] Thus the closure in 2009 of a mill in the town of Samoa just south of Eureka, California, which had retooled and become the only chlorine- and dioxin-free toilet paper manufacturer in the United States, represented a significant setback. Representing ten thousand members of the Sierra Club, Greg Gold lamented the lack of federal and state economic stimulus funds for creating green jobs, arguing that the Samoa mill "had the potential to transform an entire industry" by creating a tanoak market.[166] Representatives from affected labor unions also "expressed their profound disappointment." Greg Pallesen, vice president of the Association of Western Pulp & Paper Workers, remarked that U.S.

policies have failed American workers while U.S. consumers are increasingly supplied with paper from overseas mills that lack the environmental safeguards of the closed Samoa mill.[167] Profitable production of high-grade tanoak lumber depends on a reliable market for the associated low-grade material, which is what the Samoa mill would have provided.

Woody biomass derived from tanoaks has been used to make paper and fuel, but to date the latter use has been through direct combustion. In the future, cellulose from the cell walls of tanoaks may become a feedstock for the production of liquid biofuel for vehicles.[168] Currently, "[e]thanol, a gasoline fuel additive, is typically produced from starches in corn, sorghum and sugar cane." However, research continues to develop new, more cost-effective ways of generating "liquid transportation fuel" from other plants, including woody species.[169] Cellulosic ethanol production offers one way of reducing dependency on foreign oil while decreasing fuel loads in forests that can lead to wildfires. However, increased use of woody biomass from U.S. forests as a source of bioenergy remains controversial. Common concerns include whether it can be done in a way that doesn't compromise forest and human health. In an effort to assess the feasibility of such use, multiple studies "to quantify the volume of biomass supplies that are available" have been conducted. One such study concluded that "at least 50 million dry tons of woody biomass may be available in the United States for evolving wood bioenergy markets."[170] In the late twentieth century, the Bureau of Land Management began a study to determine the "biomass of tanoak trees . . . [and forecast] effects of various land management scenarios on tanoak and Douglas-fir carbon pools in the Coos Bay District of BLM."[171] Since 2005, the U.S. Forest Service has provided more than $36 million "in grants to be used for wood-to-energy projects" that "create jobs and local revenue."[172]

CONCLUSIONS

Many forestry reformers envision tanoak as a key species in the effort to move away from clear-cutting and herbicide use in northern California's industrial forests. They argue that developing more markets for tanoak-wood products is critical if it is to be an economically viable product. But, to date, tanoak hasn't been successful in domestic or global timber markets. Faster-growing hardwoods (e.g., hybrid cottonwoods, acacia, and eucalyptus) can be produced more cheaply thorough mechanization or outsourcing, or both. Tropical-plantation-grown hardwoods and bamboo flooring are significant new sources of competition. Fortunately, in 2008, an alliance of environmentalists, labor unions, and forest products industries successfully lobbied for the passage of an amendment to the century-old Lacey Act, which is helping to curb the entrance of illegally obtained tropical hardwoods into the United States.[173]

With the emergence of a lethal tanoak disease in the mid-1990s and the subsequent quarantines, most of the tanoak wood currently being harvested is for local use as firewood. In an effort to prevent the spread of *Phytophthora*, the pathogen that causes sudden oak death, "[s]tate and federal regulations prohibit movement of firewood cut from [sudden oak death] hosts out of quarantined infested areas."[174] According to John Shelly, a University of California woody biomass adviser, and Stephen Quarles, a senior scientist for an insurance institute, even though tanoak trees infested by *P. ramorum* eventually become degraded in value by secondary attacks of insects and decay fungi, high-quality lumber can still be produced and many valuable products manufactured particularly if "milling [occurs] before major deterioration."[175] Third-generation timber industry entrepreneur Robert Simpson claims his research indicates that profitable veneer production is possible even with diseased trees when combined with lumber and chip production.[176]

Fear of catastrophic fire fostered by tanoaks killed by sudden oak death could drive liquidation if a large enough market for tanoak existed and would likely undermine conservation efforts. Shelly and Quarles asserted in 2013 that "a viable market for tanoak wood products could provide the incentive needed to responsibly remove diseased trees from the landscape."[177] Mechanical thinning propelled by the market could potentially help foster tanoak health in part by reducing vulnerability to diseases, pests, wildfire, and climate change. Without effective safeguards, however, the historical record suggests that market-driven solutions won't achieve ecologically sustainable or socially just outcomes.

PLAGUE

[R]esource crises are important for the renewal of
management institutions (because the crisis forces social learning
by the institution), just as dynamic ecosystem processes (including
such "crises" as fire) are important for the renewal of ecosystems.

—**FIKRET BERKES**

DISEASED AND DYING TANOAK TREES WERE FIRST NOTICED IN THE mid-1990s north of San Francisco, in Marin County, around Mount Tamalpais, with blemishes on their trunks that oozed sticky sap.[1] Plant pathologists ultimately concluded that a newly described species previously unknown outside of Europe caused the observed bleeding stem cankers. The novel lethal tanoak pathogen, *Phytophthora ramorum,* probably originated in eastern Asia, but no one knows when it arrived in North America. *Phytophthora* means "plant destroyer," aptly named given the devastating impact species in this genus have had historically, such as *P. infestans,* which contributed to the Irish Potato Famine. Also in the mid-1800s, the root rot pathogen *P. cinnamomi* caused American chestnut tree die-offs in the Piedmont region of the southern United States.[2]

By obstructing xylem cells, *P. ramorum* reduces water supply to individual branches or the entire crown, which can ultimately kill the host, particular during drought.[3] As of 2001, sudden oak death had "reached epidemic proportions in coastal California," from the Big Sur coast to Sonoma County.[4] The water mold has spread through commerce in garden plants.[5] Although tanoak has proved to be the most susceptible, many native California species and common nursery and landscape plants serve as carriers.[6] Of the ornamental hosts most prone to spread the disease, plant pathologists list *Rhododendron*, *Camellia*, *Viburnum*, *Pieris*, and *Kalmia* (mountain laurel).[7] While the pathogen is fatal to tanoak and some other related tree species, most of its hosts suffer only shoot dieback or leaf spots and blotches. (An updated list of host plants is available at www. suddenoakdeath.org.)

Researchers believe that *P. ramorum* was introduced on imported nursery stock for North American gardens. Indeed the worldwide spread of non-indigenous invasive species has accelerated and represents "one of the greatest global threats to native biodiversity in North America, second only to habitat loss."[8] According to senior plant pathologist Clive Brasier, "Movement of plants and plant products between biogeographical zones . . . is now generally accepted to be the primary mode of introduction of exotic pathogens and pests." He holds "horticulturalists, foresters, garden designers and landscape architects" in part responsible for contributing to disease outbreaks when they indulge "their desire for novel [plant] material or (these days) cheaper plants and instant trees." He appeals to them as professionals to conserve natural resources and avoid "long-term negative impacts on the environment, economy and cultural heritage" by not aiding pathogen movement through commerce.[9] Global trade in nursery plants has increased significantly, exacerbating existing exotic plant disease problems and causing new introductions.

Ecosystem change can occur relatively rapidly through novel pathogens.[10] The dramatic decline of American chestnut (*Castanea dentata*) is a reminder that even common plants can rapidly become threatened. A century ago in North America's eastern deciduous forests, the exotic plant disease chestnut blight began to spread after the inadvertent introduction of *Cryphonectria parasitica* on an infected imported Chinese chestnut (*Castanea mollissima*). Thirty years after horticulturalists accidentally introduced the causal pathogen from Asia to North America, American chestnuts were virtually destroyed "through most of their natural range."[11] Although it is unlikely that *P. ramorum* will cause tanoak extinction, it will likely cause "the rapid and extensive loss of overstorey trees . . . within 30 years of pathogen establishment in many forests."[12] Large tanoak trees will become much less abundant in California landscapes (fig. 6.1). In regions of San Mateo, Marin, and Sonoma Counties that have been heavily affected by sudden oak death for about twenty years, shrubby vegetation dominated by resprouting tanoaks has replaced many forests.[13]

FIGURE 6.1 Tanoak killed by *Phytophthora ramorum*, Joe Hall Creek, Curry County, Oregon, ca. 2001. This is one of the first confirmed sudden oak death sites in Oregon. Photograph by and courtesy of Everett Hansen.

Current understanding of tanoak resistance to *P. ramorum* is incomplete, but given observed levels of susceptibility, a "risk of extirpation" exists.[14] Along the Big Sur coast south of Monterey, some sites have already experienced 100 percent tanoak mortality aboveground after infestation.[15] Although resprouting is often common, it remains unknown how long regrowth from the base of affected trees will occur given high rates of reinfection. From the central California region of Big Sur, overstory tanoaks have declined and even disappeared from many forests and woodlands north through the Santa Cruz Mountains and Marin and Sonoma Counties (fig. 6.2).[16] Through its alteration of forest stand structure, *P. ramorum* is significantly transforming the California landscape.[17] In 2000, Steve Zack, with the Wildlife Conservation Society, said, "The cascading effect of losing these trees is going to be awesome. We're just waiting for the other shoe to drop."[18]

Protections against future importations have been weakened just as global trade in potted plants and other risky materials has increased significantly. During the Clinton Administration, the federal government repealed the Plant Quarantine Act of 1912, originally passed to prevent

FIGURE 6.2 Tanoak mortality caused by *Phytophthora ramorum*, Sonoma County, California, documented September 9, 2011. Photograph by Jeffrey A. Mai of Aerial Survey & Aviation Safety Manager, Forest Health Protection. Courtesy of the U.S. Forest Service, http://eol.org/data_objects/27170928 (accessed March 21, 2014).

another massive native tree die-off caused by an introduced pathogen. According to agricultural economist Edward A. Evans, the Plant Protection Act of 2000, which superseded it, mirrors more closely the less restrictive World Trade Organization's Sanitary and Phytosanitary Agreement, which was designed to foster international trade.[19]

Currently in North America, *P. ramorum* is reproducing only asexually, which limits its capacity to evolve and adapt to environmental conditions. However, this could change. Two mating types and several lineages exist in North America, with the NA1 (A2 mating type) predominating. The more virulent A1 mating type, a strain from Europe (EU1), is found in a few "nurseries in California, northern Oregon, Washington, and British Columbia, Canada."[20] It has also escaped to a waterway in Humboldt County California.[21] The EU1 (A1 mating type) occurs in United Kingdom forests and extensively in European nurseries, and genetic research supports the hypothesis that one or more introductions of EU1-contaminated European nursery plants occurred despite monitoring of international trade.[22] Based on efforts to mate EU1 (A1 mating type) and NA1 (A2 mating type) in the laboratory, it is unclear whether *P. ramorum* has a functional sexual breeding system.[23] If it does, the potential remains for greater disease vigor "if genetic exchange occurs between the European and American subpopulations."[24] Despite the high rates of abortion, viable oospores appear to form, which means that "coexistence of both mating types on adjacent plants increases the chances for sexual recombination between these two genetically divergent lineages."[25] Currently, the less aggressive genetic lineage is the more prevalent one in North America, meaning that the impact of sudden oak death on tanoak could worsen. Although rare, two other, "generally more virulent" lineages already occur in North America (EU, and NA2).[26]

Sudden oak death already poses a significant threat to efforts to restore tanoak groves for increased acorn production in northern California. Based on multiple computer models, the coastal counties of Mendocino, Humboldt, and Del Norte are at high risk for widespread *P. ramorum* infection (fig. 6.3). Multiple host plants grow in the region, including salal (*Gaultheria shallon*) and huckleberry (*Vaccinium* spp.). Although *P. ramorum* sporulates on a wide variety of host species, some species play more important roles in spreading the disease.[27] California bay (*Umbellularia californica*) significantly increases disease risk, leading some researchers to advocate for its removal in order to reduce risk to neighboring oaks.[28] Although its production of asexual spores isn't typically as prolific as with California bay, tanoak, too, can inoculate forests with *P. ramorum*, particularly through sporangia production on leaves and twigs (fig. 6.4).[29] These two native trees "are central to pathogen spread within stands and across landscapes" in California.[30] In affluent Marin County, north of San Francisco, some property owners are trying to protect the aesthetically more valued coast live oak, which can contribute significantly to property value, by targeting tanoak and California bay as disease vectors and killing them.

Loss of productive tanoak trees to sudden oak death is already having a negative impact on tribal communities. In Sonoma County, *P. ramorum* spread to Kashaya Pomo Indian lands, probably from infected rhododendrons planted by neighbors.[31] Thousands of trees died near the forty-acre Stewarts Point Rancheria, where families still harvest tanoak acorns.[32] Infestation of culturally important tanoak stands farther north is predicted, and experts advise "a proactive strategy to reduce disease impacts."[33] Computer models indicate that tanoaks, even large ones, can persist after *P. ramorum* infests a site if the trees are widely spaced and not growing in association with California bay.[34] According to a group of thirteen researchers, the pathogen "has, and will continue to alter the distribution, prevalence,

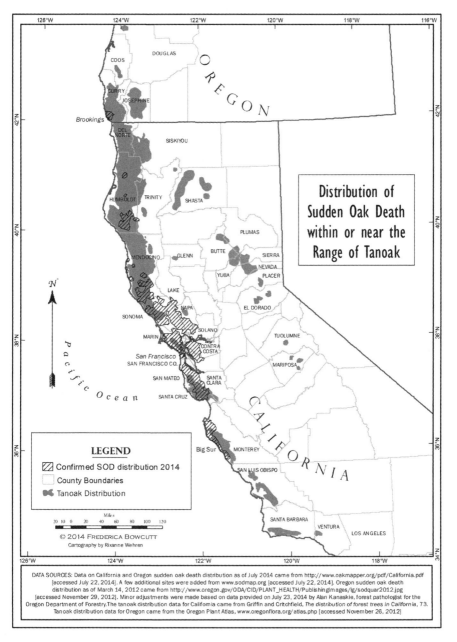

DATA SOURCES: Data on California and Oregon sudden oak death distribution as of July 2014 came from http://www.oakmapper.org/pdf/California.pdf [accessed July 22, 2014]. A few additional sites were added from www.sodmap.org [accessed July 22, 2014]. Oregon sudden oak death distribution as of March 14, 2012 came from http://www.oregon.gov/ODA/CID/PLANT_HEALTH/PublishingImages/lg/sodquar2012.jpg [accessed November 29, 2012]. Minor adjustments were made based on data provided on July 23, 2014 by Alan Kanaskie, forest pathologist for the Oregon Department of Forestry. The tanoak distribution data for California came from Griffin and Critchfield, *The distribution of forest trees in California*, 73. Tanoak distribution data for Oregon came from the Oregon Plant Atlas, www.oregonflora.org/atlas.php [accessed November 26, 2012]

FIGURE 6.3 Distribution of sudden oak death in relation to tanoak distribution. Cartography by Rixanne Wehren.

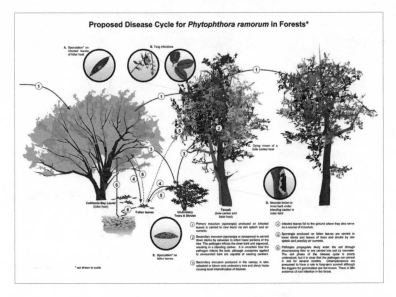

FIGURE 6.4 *Phytophthora ramorum* life cycle. Courtesy of Naoyuki Ochiai and Jennifer Parke.

and biomass of tanoak across California and Oregon . . . regardless of the amount and efficacy of management actions. However, the available management tools and current understanding of the disease may be sufficient to avoid the worst possible outcomes."[35] Their recommendations include manipulating culturally valuable tanoak stands before infestation, which would "increase the resiliency of these populations by reducing the potential for pathogen spread."[36]

Through regulation of interstate nursery trade, the U.S. Department of Agriculture's Animal and Plant Health Inspection Service (APHIS) strives to prevent the spread of sudden oak death pathogen "to noninfested areas of the United States."[37] In 2005, APHIS began requiring that California, Oregon, and Washington nurseries shipping "host plant nursery stock interstate be inspected and certified free of evidence of *P. ramorum*" after four West Coast nurseries "shipped potentially infected stock to over 1,200 nurseries in 39 states."[38] In regulated areas, growers must destroy or not ship infected plant material.[39] In 2001, only one California nursery tested positive for *P. ramorum*; by 2004, that number had jumped to 176 in multiple states.[40] The number dropped to 34 by 2010 after APHIS began regulating

the three states with known infected nurseries. But based on field investigations in 2009, *P. ramorum* spread to streams outside infested nurseries
in five states (Alabama, Florida, Georgia, Mississippi, and Washington).[41]
A number of southeastern U.S. forest species are vulnerable to *P. ramorum*,
including eighteen species of red oak (*Quercus* spp.); red oaks became dominant after the non-native, pathogen induced demise of American elm (*Ul-
mus americana*) and American chestnut.[42] Phytophthoras that can infect
forest plants are a biosecurity threat. As a result, in 2006, APHIS established
a protocol for responding to *P. ramorum* outbreaks in forest and wildland
environments, but as of 2011, there is "no Federal response protocol for
new wildland incursions."[43] "The continued spread of this and other new
Phytophthora species presents significant impetus for adjustments in the
management and regulation of forest pathogens and nursery stock."[44]

Due to the leaky federal quarantine administered by APHIS, various
states have attempted to protect their natural resources and industries by
establishing supplemental quarantines. However, APHIS has yet to approve
a special need request (SNR). A review of APHIS administration of the sudden oak death quarantine indicates that "the SNR process has not achieved
Congress' goal of allowing limited state regulation that is more restrictive
than federal requirements."[45] Read Porter, a senior attorney with the Environmental Law Institute, and Nina Robertson, a law clerk with the U.S.
District Court for the District of Columbia, defend states' rights to protect
against invasive species and call for an improved SNR process that would
aid in avoiding "the spread of pests into areas where they are not yet present
but are likely to cause substantial harm to the economy and environment."[46]
The interests of industry currently prevail, according to Porter and Robertson. "By focusing on facilitation of trade and reduction of risks rather than
prevention, Congress in effect created a preference for leaky quarantines
and for trade over environmental protection."[47] Nor have the courts upheld
a state's right to reduce *P. ramorum* infection risk. In 2004, the California
Association of Nurseries and Garden Centers sued to block Kentucky and
nine other states from enforcing their own sudden oak death quarantines
on horticultural products shipped from California, and won; the interstate
commerce was valued at roughly $500 million annually.[48] Justice James
McReynolds may prove prophetic when he warned in 1926, "It is a serious
thing to paralyze the efforts of a state to protect her people against impend-
ing calamity, and leave them to the slow charity of a far-off and perhaps
supine federal bureau."[49]

Quarantines and vigilance provide forests with some protection from exotic disease species, but their effectiveness is limited for a number of reasons. Current methods of testing are not sensitive enough to reliably and consistently detect pathogens. Furthermore, predicting destructive foreign organisms is not always possible because "most are unknown or innocuous in their native forests."[50] In the horticulture trade, widespread use of pesticides including fungicides masks symptoms of diseases that become apparent only after nursery plants are purchased by consumers who are often unfamiliar with plant diseases. Confirmation of *P. ramorum* requires culturing and microscopy or molecular analysis, which delays detection. Unfortunately, some nurseries are noncompliant with regulations and/or best practices, plus only a tiny fraction of the landscape plants produced for sale are tested. Because the detection of potential plant pathogens is difficult, Evans calls "the potential gains from [international] trade . . . questionable."[51] Susan Frankel, the U.S. Forest Service's research leader on sudden oak death, and Everett Hansen, an Oregon State University *P. ramorum* researcher, note that "tools designed to protect forests and nurseries need refinement."[52] Brasier more urgently calls for reform because global market influences have contributed to making "international plant biosecurity protocols . . . outmoded, flawed, institutionalized, and too ineffectual." He advocates that they "be fully scientifically reviewed and appropriately overhauled, taking full account of the underlying scientific weaknesses and of the many other causes of security failure."[53]

SUDDEN OAK DEATH RESPONSE

Once introduced to a landscape, *P. ramorum* can't be controlled in part because "no effective chemical treatment or biological control exists."[54] Many pesticides used on other species in the genus *Phytophthora* test effective against *P. ramorum* under experimental conditions.[55] However, pesticides cannot feasibly be used to control sudden oak death on a landscape scale due in part to the numerous potential hosts. In rugged areas with limited access, the labor costs for such intensive treatments are prohibitively expensive if commercial applicators are used, or the work is logistically impractical. Control of *P. ramorum* is further complicated because it often spreads over long distances unnoticed, and the expression of symptoms is delayed.[56]

Potassium phosphite (also known as potassium phosphonate or by the trade name Agri-Fos) has been used prophylactically, typically to protect large, specimen trees from infection. Although this chemical compound acts as a systemic fungicide, it "increases the tree's natural resistance response to infection" when used to prevent *P. ramorum* infection.[57] Phosphite can be sprayed on the trunk if a bark-penetrating surfactant is mixed with it, or tanoaks can be treated via injection. For injection, multiple shallow holes are drilled into the trunk along its circumference and a syringe is then inserted into each hole, into the sapwood directly under the bark. For maximum effectiveness, the phosphite is applied twice in the first year and then annually after that.[58] It is not cost-effective to treat tanoak seedlings and saplings, which instead are sometimes thinned in dense stands so that they will not infect larger, treated trees.[59]

Unfortunately, phosphite treatments are not always effective at preventing infection. "Based on results of field studies," spraying the bark "may not be adequate to protect large tanoaks,"[60] and injected applications also may not achieve intended outcomes. The San Francisco Public Utilities Commission hired Phytosphere Research to conduct a study on different treatment approaches to protect against *P. ramorum* at its Crystal Springs Reservoir in the Santa Cruz Mountains. According to Ted Swiecki, one of the principal plant pathologists for the consulting firm, "repeated injections at the . . . rate" recommended on the label proved to be "unsustainable over time" because of excessive tissue damage, "and the rate of recovery and wound closure associated with those injection holes [was] very slow. Repeated applications at that rate can lead to unacceptably high levels of damage."[61] These wounds could increase tanoak vulnerability to infection.[62] In addition, phosphite treatments can be toxic to tanoak, resulting in necrotic tissue "if applied at sufficiently high concentrations" either as a spray on the trunk or via injection.[63] However, phosphites, which are also used as chemical fertilizers, are generally considered relatively safe to plants and people.[64] Neither foliar nor aerial applications have showed promising results in controlling *P. ramorum*.[65]

Given our inability to prevent all plant disease introductions or to control them once they've spread, plant pathologists advise a quick response to early detections in order to limit their impact.[66] They emphasize "early detection, culling, and protection ahead of infection."[67] Based on computer modeling designed to predict where disease spread is most likely, the "[p]robability of invasion was positively related to precipitation and temperature in the wet season and the presence of the inoculum-producing foliar host *Umbellularia californica* and decreased exponentially with distance to inoculum sources."[68]

After *P. ramorum* was first detected in 2001 in Curry County, in the southwestern corner of the state, the Oregon Department of Agriculture adopted a management approach of "intensive control through extensive monitoring and removal of both infected host material and surrounding hosts as a buffer."[69] The state and federal governments aggressively attempted to protect ecosystems as well as the forest and horticulture industries. In an environmental assessment report on the use of glyphosate on tanoak, Bureau of Land Management staff summarized the eradication methods to be used on private and U.S. Forest Service (USFS) lands: "1) glyphosate (USFS) and imazapyr (private lands) injection (herbicide treatment) of tanoak prior to cutting to prevent resprouting; 2) mechanical removing (cutting) of infected host species (e.g. tanoak) and all other target hosts (evergreen huckleberry and Pacific rhododendron) within a defined treatment area; and 3) burning of all cut vegetation. . . . Sites may be retreated if the pathogen persists."[70] The treatments included herbicide use on tanoak and California bay stumps to limit additional *P. ramorum* spore production on regrowth. Although not eradicated, Oregon "prevented local intensification of the disease and minimized damage to the forest."[71]

Similar treatments have occurred at isolated outbreaks in Humboldt County in northern California, spurred by the concern they could catalyze landscape-scale infection in a high-risk area. Other infection sites, such as the one near the town of Redway, demonstrate how random, long-distance dispersal resulting in "unlikely outbreaks[,] . . . once established, can rapidly accelerate the spread of sudden oak death."[72] Currently containment of these outbreaks is possible, according to experts, because they are "geographically isolated from the wider epidemic in central California." Without intervention, they could catalyze "massive spread of *P. ramorum* . . . through the vast forest stretch that extends from Redway, southern Humboldt County, to Curry County, Oregon, due to favorable host and environmental conditions."[73] According to leading plant pathologists from the University of Cambridge, the University of California, and elsewhere:

> There is a consensus on the need to implement a systematic strategy
> to manage *P. ramorum* in Humboldt County in order to reduce the local

impacts (ecological, social, and economic) of the disease and to prevent further northward spread of the pathogen. While lessons can be learned from the extensive control efforts that have been implemented in Curry County, there is uncertainty as to which strategy to employ and as to what level of control is attainable in Humboldt County given the current size of the focus, limited resources available, and range of public opinion with regard to different options. . . . [Based on computer models,] the large size of the Redway focus and potential for long-distance dispersal of *P. ramorum* pose considerable challenges to containment, but . . . local control in this focus or early containment of new, smaller foci are attainable.[74]

A similar team of university scientists predicts "[i]n the absence of extensive control[,] . . . a ten-fold increase in disease spread between 2010 and 2030 with most infection concentrated along the north coast between San Francisco and Oregon." As a result, "substantial tree mortality, particularly of tanoak, is likely to follow." Based on their computer model, they predict "explosive growth in infection and disease . . . to occur around 2016."[75]

REFUGE IN DISEASED LANDSCAPES

In anticipation of *P. ramorum* range expansion in North America, some scientists and land managers advocate for tanoak refuges where infection risks can be reduced. Existing public lands provide opportunities for safeguarding tanoak, but many are already infested with the sudden oak death pathogen (table 4). Park visitors and neighboring gardeners have at times become unwitting disease vectors. Establishing management practices designed to reduce infection risk in uninfected parks on the north coast of California makes sense given that scientists predict explosive disease expansion in this region.

For years, Redwood National and State Parks (RNSP) have been identified as being at high risk of infection due to multiple vehicular entry points and high visitation rates combined with a favorable climate and an abundance of suitable hosts. The first and currently only infestation within RNSP was reported in August 2014, roughly eleven miles north of a preexisting sudden oak death outbreak in the Redwood Valley. Tanoaks are already succumbing at the thirty-four-acre disease site. In an effort to contain the infestation, removal of all tanoak and California bay is planned within the

TABLE 4. Partial List of Sudden-Oak-Death Pathogen-Infested Public Lands in the Range of Tanoak

State Lands	Federal Lands	County and Regional Lands*
Andrew Molero SP	Coos Bay District, Myrtlewood RA (Oregon BLM)	Anthony Chabot Regional Park
Angel Island SP	Golden Gate NRA	Bear Creek Redwoods OS
Annadel SP	Lacks Creek MA (California BLM)	Briones Regional Park
Armstrong Redwoods SR	Los Padres NF–Ventana W	Coal Creek OS
Austin Creek SRA	Muir Woods NM	Crystal Springs Watershed
Big Basin State Park	Presidio of San Francisco	El Sereno OS
Bothe–Napa Valley SP	Point Reyes NS	Huckleberry Botanic RP
Cape Sebastian State Park	Redwood National and SPs	Ignatio Valley OSP
Castle Rock SP	Rogue River–Siskiyou NF**	Jacobs Ranch OSP
China Camp SP		Jasper Ridge Reserve
Fort Ross SHP		Las Trampas Regional W
Hendy Woods SP		Long Ridge OSP
Henry Cowell Redwoods SP		Los Trancos OS
Humboldt Redwoods SP		Manzanita Regional Park
Jack London SHP		Marin Municipal Water District lands
John B. Dewitt Redwoods SR		Midpeninsula Regional OS
Julia Pfeiffer Burns SP		Mill Creek Redwood Preserve
MacKerricher SP		Monte Bello OS
Mailliard Redwoods SR		Mount Burdell OSP
Mount Tamalpais SP		Palo Corona Ranch
Navarro River Redwoods SP		Rancho San Antonio OS
Olompali SHP		Redwood Regional Park
Pfeiffer Big Sur SP		Roys Redwoods OSP
Salt Point SP		Russian Ridge OS
Samuel P. Taylor SP		Sierra Azul OS
Soquel Demonstration SF		Sobrante Ridge RP
Sugarloaf Ridge SP		Tilden Regional Park
The Forest of Nisene Marks SP		White's Hill OS
Tomales Bay SP		Wildcat Canyon Regional Park

Sources: Based primarily on data from Maggi Kelly and Sam Blanchard, Department of Environmental Sciences, Policy and Management, University of California, Berkeley.

Note: BLM = Bureau of Land Management, MA = Management Area, NF = National Forest, NM = National Monument, NRA = National Recreation Area, NS = National Seashore, OS = Open Space, OSP = Open Space Preserve, RA = Resource Area, RP = Regional Preserve, SF = State Forest, SHP = State Historic Park, SP = State Park, SR = State Recreation Area, W = Wilderness

*The list of county and regional public lands is significantly abbreviated. Infected city lands are not listed.

**Siskiyou National Forest is infected according to the California Oak Mortality Task Force Report, June 2012, http://www.suddenoakdeath.org/wp-content/uploads/2012/06/COMTF-Report-June-2012.pdf (accessed July 11, 2012).

affected area and a 328-foot buffer zone. Herbicide treatment of all stumps will follow to limit regrowth that could reinfect the site. Park managers plan to monitor closely for the pathogen and "initiate a rapid response for any new outbreaks identified in the park."[76]

In anticipation of "the inevitable arrival of *P. ramorum*," RNSP natural resources managers had identified measures intended to slow its spread once it arrived. Having already recognized tanoak as a valuable ecological component of the coast redwood forests, they expressed particular concern about the "important cultural legacy of large stands of old tanoak trees that have been managed by Native American families for many generations."[77] Park managers considered "creating tanoak refuges (defined as tanoak groves that are least likely to become infected due to spatial or temporal factors) and protecting them through the creation of no-host buffers."[78] Wide stretches of grasslands could function as no-host buffers around islands of vulnerable tanoaks. The risk of infection is heightened when "tanoak stands are denser and more continuous."[79] Based on epidemiological modeling, widely spaced tanoaks associated with plants that are immune to *P. ramorum* infection "resulted in slow-enough transmission to retain overstorey tanoak."[80] Creating conditions unfavorable to the pathogen by manipulating vegetation before the disease arrives could radically reduce risk.

FIRE AND FOREST PATHOGENS

The health status of a particular tree may not be a significant factor in the sudden oak death epidemic because *P. ramorum* is a novel pathogen in North America and tanoak currently exhibits little resistance. However, other forest insect and disease epidemics often link to "environmental stresses that predispose trees to being attacked and killed by secondary agents."[81] In Yosemite National Park, termination of natural and Native American fire regimes caused colonization of oak woodlands by conifers, which increased competition for light, water, and nutrients. "As oaks have become stressed due to suppression by encroaching conifers, they have succumbed to several canker rots."[82] Before Euro-American settlement, Native peoples burned Yosemite Valley to control black oak diseases and pests and to release oaks from conifer competition.

In regions with tanoak, fire suppression and the termination of indigenous burning shifted vegetation structure by allowing fire-sensitive species, such as California bay, to succeed. A 2005 study by Max Moritz and Dennis Odion suggests that "areas burned in recent decades" experienced decreased vulnerability to sudden oak death relative to unburned areas.[83] However, these results have been challenged given the limitations of sudden oak death distribution and fire history maps, which make studying the relationship between "pathogen invasion and persistence" and burning difficult.[84] Fires don't appear to immunize forests, and prescribed burning and catastrophic wildfires do not eliminate *P. ramorum* from a site, although they can reduce its spread.[85] Preliminary results from experimental treatments in southwestern Oregon and northern California forests suggest "that burning can be a valuable tool in cleaning up small infectious material in infested sites" even when it does not eliminate the pest.[86] Moritz and Odion acknowledge that "a much deeper understanding is necessary before fire can be actively used as a tool in slowing the epidemic."[87] Thus far, frequent, low-intensity fires that mimic traditional ecological practices of indigenous peoples experienced with managing tanoak have not yet been tested as a prophylactic measure or as treatment for an infected site.

Using aerial photographs taken in 1942 and 2000, researchers studied the impact of human-caused changes on land use in northern California as related to sudden oak death disease expression. The study area, located forty-four miles north of San Francisco, encompassed nearly 70,000 acres.[88] The researchers found that the acreage covered by woodlands increased significantly at the expense of grasslands and chaparral over nearly six decades. They "conclude[d] that enlargement of woodlands and closure of canopy gaps, likely due largely to years of fire suppression, facilitated establishment of *P. ramorum* by increasing the area occupied by inoculum-production foliar hosts and enhancing forest microclimate conditions" conducive to *P. ramorum*.[89] The increase particularly of California bay, a major foliar host responsible for generating significant amounts of inoculum, fostered the spread of sudden oak death. Thus, "decades of land-use change and associated increases in host abundance may have set the stage for this pathogen's rapid rate of spread."[90]

CLIMATE CHANGE AND SUDDEN OAK DEATH

Current trends in global climate change indicate that "day-to-day weather has grown increasingly erratic and extreme," which "could have consequences for ecosystem stability and the control of pests and diseases."[91] Wetter and warmer conditions will radically increase tanoak's vulnerability to sudden oak death by favoring *P. ramorum* spore production.[92] Spore production begins with winter rains or shortly thereafter. Sporulation peaks with warm spring rains and drops off to zero with hot, dry summer weather. However, in coastal areas with summer fog, inoculum persists year-round.[93] Windblown rain is the dominant mode by which spores spread over a distance of roughly three miles.

As a climatic relict of a wetter, more temperate period in North America's past, tanoak may be vulnerable to periods of increased drought and erratic frost events, which are both predicted to occur more frequently with global climate change. Frost can compromise tanoak's sexual reproduction, and drought stress can reduce its resistance to pathogens and insect pests. Multiple disturbances linked to climate change affect tanoak's resilience. Drought negatively affects *P. ramorum* populations, but they recover quickly once rainfall resumes.[94] Although snags don't significantly elevate fire risk, areas with many recently killed tanoaks still standing with dead leaves may increase wildfire severity.[95] Indeed, in areas with high rates of tanoak mortality, sudden oak death can result in elevated "fire hazard for a number of years."[96]

CONSERVATION OF GENETIC DIVERSITY

Retaining large tracts of undeveloped land in northern California where extensive tanoak die-off can occur without intervention may be important so that disease resistance might develop and/or have a chance to express itself. According to one forest biodiversity expert, "Maintaining large, relatively natural populations of all native tree species will allow natural selection to operate with sufficient intensity to ensure different mechanisms and levels of resistance and tolerance can develop over time, without catastrophic losses of genetic diversity."[97] Unfortunately, preemptive and salvage logging in anticipation of or after disease spread has historically accelerated American tree declines.[98] Liquidating American chestnut trees for lumber, firewood, and tanbark during the chestnut blight crisis contributed to their loss because it did not allow the populations to express and/or develop disease resistance.[99] Economic incentives to log combined with limited understanding of pathogen biology contributed to failed attempts to curb disease spread. "In pathogen-invaded landscapes, disease may be a useful force to select for more resistant tanoak. . . . In highly disease impacted stands, treatments which remove surviving trees would clearly exacerbate the loss of tanoak and may reduce genetic resources important for developing molecular markers of resistance and restoration planting stock."[100] The current low economic value of tanoak provides little incentive to harvest large trees, and if this condition persists, it could de facto assist tanoak conservation efforts. Alternatively, if tanoak becomes a viable source of marketable products again, it will be important to retain extensive acreage of tanoak that is unavailable for harvesting so that genetic resistance is allowed to express itself and emerge.

Seed saving may be a successful strategy, as "reintroduction of material stored ex situ has made the difference between extinction in the wild and continued survival" for some plant species.[101] Global efforts to protect threatened plant species prioritize seed banks that store dried seeds at low temperatures because they provide valuable insurance against extinction "at the lowest cost."[102] However, multiple challenges to this kind of off-site conservation approach exist, not the least of which are "growing threats that are difficult to predict and mitigate."[103] Unfortunately, saving tanoak seeds beyond a year is not a viable option at this time because the embryo inside acorns is short-lived. Viability plummets with desiccation of the nuts, making them unsuitable for "standard drying and frozen storage, used on species with orthodox seed storage behavior."[104] Cryogenic storage of recalcitrant (desiccation-resistant) seeds like tanoak may offer an alternative. However, this approach is labor-intensive and more expensive, requiring seed storage at liquid nitrogen temperatures.[105] Despite the challenges, researchers have succeeded in developing protocols for the use of in vitro propagation and cryopreservation for several species of oaks in the related genus *Quercus* and conclude that further research is needed, as this approach could be an important complement to living collections.[106]

The creation of living collections through plantings could also safeguard tanoak genetic diversity. American chestnut breeding programs for creating individuals resistant to chestnut blight relied in part on plantings that survived outside the tree's natural range. In Australia, rare native plant species threatened by *Phytophthora cinnamomi* were introduced into areas beyond their natural distribution in an effort to conserve the species.[107] Suitable planting areas outside the natural range of tanoak will likely experience summer drought. Tanoak is already being successfully grown in numerous arboreta and botanic gardens in Australia, Canada, Europe, and the United States (table 5). To truly be a meaningful conservation effort, living collections need to be grown from well-documented wild collected material, reflect sufficient genetic diversity, and be grown in numerous sites that are at low risk for sudden oak death.[108] Currently, those criteria have not been adequately met for most living tanoak collections worldwide.

For the purpose of conserving tanoak's genetic diversity and reintroducing it into infested areas, efforts to identify "suitable seed sources will be critical."[109] Seed exchanges could be a means of distributing acorns as long as safeguards ensure that the acorns are disease free. Distribution of infected acorns could worsen the current problem. According to a 1990 Forest Service report, propagation via cuttings and grafting were unreported.[110] Recent attempts with cuttings have been successful, leading researchers to conclude that grafting tanoak might also work.[111] Tanoak has also been propagated via layering, whereby sucker tips are bent to contact soil and forced to root while still attached to the parent plant.[112] Clonal reproduction of vegetative offshoots of individuals resistant to *P. ramorum* may be useful in future restoration efforts.

EDUCATIONAL OUTREACH

One of the biggest challenges to rallying concern for tanoak is the widespread perception that the plant is a nuisance with little value and that it competes with economically important species, like coast redwood and Douglas-fir. Public agencies and private institutions could contribute to an educational campaign designed to counter this misperception. Botanic gardens, arboreta, parks, natural history museums, and societies dedicated to conserving California's native plants could provide venues for educational outreach about this indigenous nut tree. Better interpretation of tanoaks is recommended, especially in *P. ramorum*–infected parks with high visitation rates. Efforts to raise awareness of the value of tanoak might include the creation of commemorative U.S. Postal Service stamps similar to its vanishing wildlife species program. Permits for collecting non-timber forest products could be developed modeled on the Federal Migratory Bird Hunting and Conservation Stamps issued by the U.S. Fish and Wildlife Service, which have functioned as hunting licenses and a source of revenue for the creation of wildlife refuges. Duck stamps also helped to educate the public

TABLE 5. Partial List of Arboreta and Botanic Gardens with Living Tanoak

Country	Specific Location
Australia	Blue Mountains Botanic Garden, Mount Tomah
	Royal Botanic Gardens, Melbourne
Canada	University of British Columbia Botanical Garden
	VanDusen Botanical Garden
France	Arboretum National des Barres (et Fruticetum Vilmorinianum)
Germany	Forstbotanischer Garten der Technischen Universität Dresden
United Kingdom	Oxford University Botanic Garden
	Royal Botanic Garden Edinburgh
	Royal Botanic Gardens, Kew (London)
	Royal Botanic Gardens, Kew (Wakehurst Place in Sussex)
	The Sir Harold Hillier Gardens
United States	Brooklyn Botanic Garden
	C. M. Goethe Arboretum
	The Charles R. Keith Arboretum
	Hoyt Arboretum
	Huntington Botanical Gardens
	Kruckeberg Botanic Garden
	Mendocino Coast Botanical Gardens
	Peavy Arboretum
	Rancho Santa Ana Botanic Garden
	San Francisco Botanical Garden (formerly Strybing Arboretum)
	San Luis Obispo Botanical Garden
	The Santa Barbara Botanic Garden
	University of California (UC) Davis Arboretum
	University of California Botanical Garden at Berkeley
	University of Washington Botanic Gardens

Source: Data © copyright Botanic Gardens Conservation International PlantSearch Database (May 7, 2014).

about the plight of waterfowl and the importance of defending wetland habitats and flyways.[113] An educational effort to counter the widespread perception that tanoak is a pest could be launched.

CONCLUSIONS

We need more effective ways of tempering the negative influences of the market on human communities and ecosystems. The solution that addresses the root cause of the tanoak plague problem—restrictions on global and domestic trade that reflect environmental limits and the limits of science to mitigate negative consequences—currently appears to be politically unattainable. Despite the recognition that limiting global trade would reduce the spread of diseases, "it is very unlikely that trade will be significantly reduced in the near future."[114] Consumers could press for reforms in horticulture through third-party certification of sustainability. Judging from the impact of similar programs for coffee and chocolate, the effort will likely not affect more than a small percentage of the market, at least initially. However, it is a way to educate the public, horticulturalists, and policy makers. Sustainable forestry certifications could be modified for systems with tanoak to require practices that do not diminish this threatened tree's future. Current domestic and international trade policies undermine the efforts of tribal people, plant pathologists, botanists, environmentalists, and others to conserve tanoak. With P. ramorum already spreading in much of tanoak's range, collaborative efforts are already occurring that include tribes with a vested interest in tanoak's future. The use of frequent, low-intensity fires for treating infested sites and reducing infection risk remains worthy of further investigation.[115] Timely intervention is important because of tanoak's ecological and cultural significance.

7

LANDSCAPES

As a nation—as foresters, land managers, tribal members,
environmentalists, ecologists, farmers, ranchers, and loggers—
we are trying to figure out new ways of working with the western
lands. Yet before we can come up with sustainable ways of managing
ecosystems, we need to understand how we ended up in the current
mess. Without a historical and ecological perspective on what has
happened to the landscape, there is little chance that current
restoration efforts will avoid repeating past mistakes.

—NANCY LANGSTON

INDIGENOUS PEOPLES MANIPULATED VEGETATION WITH FIRE FOR
thousands of years to maximize tanoak acorn production. They engaged in
a kind of permaculture and agroforestry using native species. By design,
Native people created cultural landscapes with fire where grasslands and
tanoak groves thrived in a region naturally dominated by coniferous forests.
Many tribes in California used frequent, low-intensity fires for clearing
understory vegetation, removing grass thatch, increasing food production,
and reducing insect pest populations and plant diseases. Evidence for in-
tentional burning exists in microfossil research results, the ethnographic
record, ecological response to fire, and the historical record, including serial
photographs documenting vegetation change over time.[1]

Burning practices developed in response to climate change. Research
based on microfossils shows that vegetation has shifted in relation to
changing climate and fire frequency over the past fifteen thousand years.
Pollen cores extracted from wetlands in the Siskiyou Mountains of Oregon

indicate that during the late glacial period (more than 10,900 years before present [BP]), subalpine forest extended to lower elevations and latitudes than they do today. During the early Holocene (ca. 10,900-4,500 cal yr BP), the climate shifted to "warmer-and-drier-than-present summer conditions" favoring xerophytic species such as oaks and chinquapin.[2] Xerophytic vegetation contracted when the climate became cooler and wetter during the late Holocene period (ca. 4,500 cal yr BP–present), except where burned regularly by Native peoples. Fossilized pollen of tanoak resembles chinquapin pollen, making fine-grained vegetation reconstruction difficult;[3] however, pollen evidence indicates indigenous burning changed vegetation elsewhere in the West. For example, in Yosemite Valley, *Quercus* pollen begins to increase at about 700 years BP despite climatic conditions that favored fir (*Abies*). Archaeological evidence indicates indigenous peoples of Yosemite Valley became more dependent on oak acorns between 650 to 750 BP, thus giving them an incentive to burn frequently and thus kill pines and fir. "At contact [with Euro-Americans], much of the valley was an open oak-grassland with few conifers. However, after nearly three-quarters of a century of fire suppression or exclusion, the valley was choked with shrubs and young conifers."[4]

Paleobotanical research based on phytoliths, another kind of microfossil, indicates that coniferous forests and coastal scrub have expanded with fire suppression over the past century on the northern coast of California. Humboldt State University professor Susan Bicknell and others found an abundance of phytoliths unique to grasses in areas now dominated by conifers in Sinkyone Wilderness State Park on the northwestern Mendocino coast.[5] These silica deposits originate between and inside plant cells and can persist in the soil for millions of years. Researchers use phytoliths to study vegetation change over time. Bicknell and her graduate students also found Douglas-fir seedlings, saplings, and trees in nearly all their grassland and scrub plots, which led them to conclude that this conifer could naturally occupy most sites in the park. Photographs taken over the past century corroborate their findings, documenting an increase in Douglas-fir and coastal scrub in Sinkyone Wilderness State Park at the expense of coastal prairies.[6]

The anthropological literature documents indigenous burning to favor tanoaks and associated prairies on the North Coast of California. Ethnographer Llewellyn Loud claimed in 1918 that prairies would have produced forests if the Wiyot Indians did not annually burn "so as to gather various seeds, especially a species of sunflower." The location of these food oases was well known by the Wiyot, and they "maintained regular trails between them."[7] In addition to making human travel easier, burning cleared the ground before acorn harvesting.[8] Various indigenous groups burned so as to facilitate *Quercus* and *Notholithocarpus* nut gathering.[9] After completing their acorn harvest, the Tolowa burned the inland tanoak groves of high value to them before returning each year to their coastal villages.[10] Ethnographer Gladys Nomland noted that Sinkyone "[m]en fired grassy meadows" to foster food production.[11]

Myths point to burning as a cultural practice. Alfred Kroeber, Nomland's anthropology professor at the University of California, Berkeley, recorded a Sinkyone story that features a buzzard flying "over the dry grass. Wherever he went, he fired the grass, and the flames spread."[12] In the 1930s, both Kroeber and Gifford noted indigenous burning specifically in mixed evergreen forests.[13] Kroeber recorded in his 1939 field notebook that the Yurok burned under tanoaks about every three years in order to clear competing brush. They burned when the grass was dry, but near villages, this was done after the first heavy rains. According to Kroeber, they cleared firebreaks and used green boughs of Douglas-fir or other fresh branches to "beat the fire out" when it threatened to get out of control. In prairies, they set the edge on fire first, then the center.[14] Fred Kniffen, also from the University of California, wrote in 1939 that the Pomo Indians of Redwood Valley burned annually in order to maintain widely spaced oaks with a grassy understory. In their "beautiful park landscape," burning controlled the brush while leaving "the larger trees . . . uninjured."[15]

Mamie Offield, a Karuk Indian woman, explained that annual burning of tanoak controlled disease and insect pests.[16] During their development, trees abort acorns infested with weevil and moth larvae; thus a surface fire set after initial acorn drop kills the pests inside as well as any already in the leaf litter, reducing insect populations.[17] Without frequent fires, filbert weevils (*Curculio uniformis*), filbertworm moth larvae (*Cydia latiferreana*), and other insects can destroy more than half of the acorn crop.[18]

By decreasing fuel loads, regular burning by tribal peoples reduced the risk of catastrophic wildfire that would destroy mature tanoak trees.[19] Frequent burns also minimized loss of tanoak acorns caused by unfavorable climatic conditions. Tanoak acorns ripen in their second autumn.[20] As a result, late frost during the late winter or early spring after pollination can destroy reproductive organs and thus radically reduce acorn productivity. By clearing underbrush, Indian people maintained good airflow around harvested tanoaks, which reduced loss of flowers and developing acorns to cold temperatures.[21] During unfavorable climatic conditions, the southwestern Pomo would also pray for acorns "when hail comes from the north."[22]

Ecological evidence bolsters the argument that Indian people burned to foster wildlife, including species they hunted. Repeated low-intensity fires favor tanoak over species like Douglas-fir that don't resprout.[23] The coppice growth that develops from tanoak's basal burl after burning provided basket materials and browse for deer and elk. Regular burning in the summer by the Yuroks would "give the deer and elk better grass."[24] Studies based on tree rings and associated fire scars suggest that fires occurred more frequently in mixed evergreen forests with tanoaks than would be expected given the probability of lightning ignition, leading multiple researchers to conclude that Native peoples also set fires.[25]

Based on the accounts of early explorers, botanists, anthropologists, and settlers, indigenous peoples from Washington to California burned for a variety of reasons including to maintain prairie systems with a variety of associated oak species.[26] Prairies in the Puget Sound region and the Willamette Valley were once more abundant along with their frequently affiliated Oregon white oaks (*Quercus garryana*). In part based on historical records, researchers in Washington concluded that "people began setting fires to create and maintain an open prairie landscape within at least the last 2,300 years" on Whidbey Island west of Seattle.[27] They claimed that use of fire maintained these food-producing cultural landscapes, which "were once a relatively common component of the Northwest landscape mosaic."[28] Willis Linn Jepson noted this practice in California's Central Valley, possibly under valley oaks (*Quercus lobata*), where "dense growth was usually burned each year by the native tribes, making a quick hot fire sufficiently destructive to kill seedlings, although doing little injury to established or even quite young trees."[29]

In his 1911 tanoak monograph commissioned by Gifford Pinchot's Forest Service, Jepson specifically addressed fire ecology. He claimed that "fires rarely kill tanbark oak trees, but make long vertical wounds," which usually heal on young trees and spread on trees older than a century.[30] Jepson noted that fire injury is most common among trees growing on slopes, and the unhealed wounds often become sites of fungal decay, which can weaken the tree and make it vulnerable to toppling in heavy snowstorms.[31] Mature ridgeline tanoaks suffered the least damage from burning. According to Jepson, "about 80 per cent are comparatively free from fire hollows, because a fire traveling up a slope is either running high or going out when it reaches the top."[32] In addition to recognizing tanoak acorns as an indigenous food source, he noted that Indian-set fires improved deer forage in wooded areas with tanoak.[33] Jepson recognized tanoak's great capacity to recover, by resprouting from burls at the base of the trunk, even if it dies down to the ground.[34] This vegetative reproductive response to fire led later researchers to dub tanoak an "endurer."[35] Although fire can kill individual trees outright or lead to their ultimate demise, "it is essential for continuation of oak stands," as the taller conifers otherwise outcompete them.[36]

AGRARIAN LANDSCAPES

From the nineteenth century and into the early twentieth century, white communities usurped occupied land. Instead of recognizing a cultural landscape shaped by fire, settlers judged the indigenous population to be primitive and unskilled people who were wasting the true potential of the land. Drawing from social Darwinist ideology, whites saw themselves as better stewards of nature with superior food systems. Settlers took a different approach to manipulating landscapes, believing in their capacity to improve California through labor and the control of nature. "By the sweat of their brow," they established their moral superiority as Christians and their power to shape the land's future. Landscapes increasingly linked to distant markets replaced the acorn landscapes depended on by Native people.

American migration to northern California beginning in the mid-nineteenth century relegated Native survivors to a relatively small land base of poorer environmental quality. Dependence on pinole in the indigenous diet dropped significantly with American settlement, due to the rapid changes caused by livestock grazing, repression of periodic burning, and conversion of native grasslands to non-native weedy species, row crops, and towns.[37] In response to diminishing access to pinole, dependency on tanoak acorns likely increased. Cattle, sheep, and horses consumed grassland seeds and clover that Native people relied on, while quasi-feral hogs in particular fattened on tanoak acorns. Displacement of indigenous survivors still dependent on groomed tanoak populations was justified in part by the fiction that Native people lived as passive gatherers and hunters.

Tensions mounted between indigenous peoples and settlers over land use. Indigenous people killed the settlers' livestock in order to subsist;[38] settlers threatened or retaliated with lethal results. In response, Congress authorized the establishment of five Indian reservations in 1852, intended to facilitate the assimilation of Native people to an agrarian lifestyle.[39] However, the early reservations were notorious for being unable to reliably feed, shelter, and clothe Indians, who continued to depend on wild foods for sustenance. During the 1850s, even when Indian men could enter the wage economy, women remained critically important to the Indian economy as they continued to procure wild foods like tanoak acorns that provided a buffer "against the lean winter months."[40] In a letter to the local Indian agent, dated May 1, 1855, Mendocino Coast settlers complained of Indians pilfering potatoes, flour, and livestock because "the acorn crop failed." The settlers stated that a "war of extermination" would begin if the government did not intervene with "a schooner-load of potatoes."[41] Genocide as a means of clearing Humboldt and Mendocino Counties for American settlers is well documented.[42]

Estimates of indigenous peoples killed in the California Coast Range during a four-month period in 1860 exceed the number of Indians killed during the century of Spanish and Mexican domination.[43] Some California state senators blamed the violence in part on the federal government for not giving the Indians adequate means to grow, hunt, or gather food and argued that the "Mendocino Wars" could have been avoided "had the United States government recognized" the legitimate land claims of the remaining indigenous northern Californians.[44] The California senate majority in 1860 commented that "Indians continue to kill cattle and horses as a means of subsistence, and the settlers in retaliation punish with death."[45] Ross Browne, a San Franciscan reflecting in 1862 on his eleven years of experience with northern California tribes, noted that "wherever they attempted to procure a subsistence they were hunted down; . . . the result . . . of the inefficient and discreditable manner in which public affairs were administered by the Federal authorities in Washington. It was the natural consequence of a corrupt political system . . . so far as the Indians are concerned. They have no voice in public affairs."[46]

The Homestead Act of 1862 facilitated the dispossession of Native peoples by making legitimate land claims dependent on improving the land through human labor, with improvement being defined as European-style agriculture. Tanoaks tended for acorn production were seen by settlers as natural, not part of a cultural landscape. White settlers never seriously considered acorns as a human food source. Instead, regional boosters like Lyman Palmer supported European-style agriculture over an indigenous

*Pour ceste tempeste cuiter
et eulz hors du pais getter*

*Comment les gens du temps passe
Nauoient tresor amasse
fors tout commun par Bonnefoy*

FIGURE 7.1 European handmade books of the Early Modern era illustrated widespread cultural attitudes regarding acorn use. In the image on the left, pre-Christians collecting *Quercus* acorns in Europe for human food are presumed primitive, Flanders, Bruges, ca. 1490-1500. Wheat became the preferred European staple, which also came to represent the body of Christ during communion. From Backhouse, *The Illuminated Page*, 215.

agroforestry system. Palmer wrote in his 1880 biography of an early Mendocino County settler, "Mr. Sherman has passed through all the stages of frontier life, ranging from savage occupation of the forest to civilized occupation, by white people, of smiling fields, yielding abundant harvests—all within a quarter of a century."[47] Palmer's comments reflect Eurocentric food preferences and ignorance about the preexisting cultural landscape created by indigenous peoples. Clinton Hart Merriam, first executive chief of the U.S. Biological Survey, from 1886 to 1910, defended acorns from *Notholithocarpus* and *Quercus* as good human food, claiming "that a food of such genuine worth should be disregarded . . . is one of many illustrations of the reluctance of the white man to avail himself of sources of subsistence long utilized by the aborigines. We seem to prefer crops that require laborious preparation of the soil, followed by costly planting and cultivation."[48] But most Euro-Americans saw acorns as an inferior food of primitive peoples, which would be replaced by wheat and other grains deemed superior staple food plants (fig. 7.1). American settlers remade the land using European and American ideas about how best to order the world. By privileging Euro-American cultural biases around food preferences and landownership, settlers radically changed land use within decades.

FIRE SUPPRESSION

A prohibition on burning "to increase the productivity of wild foods" in California occurred as early as 1793 under the Spanish governor José Joaquín de Arrillaga.[49] In 1858, shortly after Alta California became a U.S. state, the Euro-American settlers of the Mattole Valley of Humboldt County passed a resolution that the Indians "not set fire to the grass."[50] The valley lies in a region of northern California with an abundance of tanoaks. A collector of wild lily bulbs for the horticulture trade watched as beds he sustainably harvested over multiple years ultimately became overgrown and shaded out during the 1870s due to suppression of indigenous burning.[51]

John Wesley Powell, as director of the Bureau of Ethnology at the Smithsonian Institution, noted in an 1879 report on the arid West that removal of Native peoples from the land would significantly reduce frequent fires by eliminating a common cause of ignition.[52] Yet in 1890, he defended the indigenous practice of "[r]egular surface firing" because it made "forests virtually immune to crown fires" by controlling fuel loads.[53] This idea clashed with scientific forestry doctrine of the time, which called for aggressive firefighting to protect timber as well as forested watersheds critical to white settlements that depended on irrigation to farm arid valleys.[54] In 1910, *Sunset*, the iconic home and garden magazine of the West, "revived Powell's appeal for the 'Indian fires' that relied on frequent light burning to prevent large fires."[55]

Jepson noted in the same year that coniferous forests dominated more acreage in the West than when whites first began arriving.[56] He attributed this in part to "an increasing control of the annual fires."[57] The consequences of fewer human-set fires became apparent within decades of American settlement. Speaking in general about California forests, Jepson noted that annual burning favored "under certain conditions the development of large individual trees." In contrast, even five to ten years of fire suppression resulted in fuel accumulation that could lead to destructive fires that "injure more severely or even consume large trees." In his 1909 treatise on California trees, Jepson concluded that, based on their skillful use of fire as a management tool, "some credit must be given to the native tribes as foresters."[58] He blamed modern forest fires for unnecessary losses and recommended state intervention in collaboration with "coast counties, the redwood companies, the tanbark companies, and cattle-range owners to reduce the danger of fire." He advocated burning slash in the winter after bark peeling in order to "prevent the destruction of young growth and of passed [tanoak] trees by wild forest fires."[59] Jepson believed that conservation efforts that included the wise use of fire in coast redwood forests would result in "a continuous crop" of lumber while benefiting tanoak.[60]

But the still nascent Forest Service fought the idea of using frequent burning as a tool, including, initially, Aldo Leopold, who was serving as a forest supervisor in 1920. Leopold claimed that "the Forest policy of absolutely preventing forest fires insofar as humanly possible is directly threatened by the light-burning propaganda."[61] Based on his field observations in the Southwest and California, he concluded in his article "'Piute Forestry' vs. Forest Fire Prevention" that Native American burning damaged the soil and destroyed the reproductive capacity of desirable plants including timber species. He concluded that "[i]t is, of course, absurd to assume that the Indians fired the forests with any idea of forest conservation in mind."[62] Later in his career, Leopold began to question widespread arguments against using fire as a tool.[63] However, in 1923, a special research panel charged with studying light burning denounced it as a forest management tool, calling it "nonsense and heresy."[64]

Fire-suppression policies dominated through most of the twentieth century, negatively affecting a variety of culturally important resources used by Native peoples. In Mendocino County, the resulting overgrowth of brush caused a shortage of suitable basket-making materials, which was noted by a basket dealer in 1923.[65] Limited access and reduced productivity made acorns more difficult to obtain. The Lassik kept "much of their territory . . . completely clear of underbrush" through frequent low-intensity surface fires, particularly along the Eel and Mad Rivers. According to one Lassik informant, probably Lucy Young, "much of Trinity County" was "almost open prairie," but by 1938, it was "choked with thick brush."[66] Acorns served as a Lassik staple, so the inability to burn to favor mature trees reduced productivity, prompting the comment, "If the Indians ain't got acorns, it seem like he ain't got nothing."[67] Members of the Karuk, Yurok, and other tribes noted that less burning caused a decrease in diversity

FIGURE 7.2 Smokey the Bear's message "Thou Shalt Not Destroy Thy Forests" and other Christianity-influenced U.S. Forest Service messages about fire prevention, 1958. Courtesy of the Forest History Society, Durham, North Carolina.

and quantities of edible mushroom as well as access.[68] LaVerne Glaze, a Karuk-Yurok woman, recalled that "[h]er grandmother, Catherine Ferris, talked about burning specifically under the tanoaks where the American matsutakes grow in late October or November."[69]

Initially, fire suppression on a landscape scale was not feasible. But the political will to prevent and control forest fires steadily grew in the United States between 1910 and the 1960s, aided by the advent of various technological innovations such as helicopters and bulldozers combined with an increased labor force (fig. 7.2).[70] Plant ecologist Frederic Clements (1874–1945) lent further credibility to the goals of fire suppression with his ideas about succession as a linear process leading to a climatic climax community, such as coast redwood forest. This ideology legitimated the idea that disclimax communities caused by disturbance were not nature's intention for the land. In climatic zones dominated by conifers, grasslands in a mosaic with tanoak containing woodlands existed in part due to the frequent disturbance caused by regular burning by Native Americans. Seen in the worst light, indigenous peoples were characterized as destructive arsonists incapable of wise land stewardship.[71] Alternatively, one might argue, people make choices about what is best for the land and, if able, work to bring into being the kind of world they want.

Despite numerous setbacks in the effort to suppress fires in the West, critics continued to be ignored, but the pro-suppression rhetoric began to unravel in the 1960s.[72] A. Starker Leopold, son of Aldo Leopold, chaired a commission on revising the land management directives for the National Park Service. In 1963, it released "The Leopold Report," which asserted that fire needed to be reintroduced in order to create "vignette[s] of Primitive America" in the parks.[73] The commissioners recognized that early successional vegetation provided important wildlife habitat and required active management. On this point they were forward-thinking for the times, although they failed to recognize the significance of burning by Native people. Decades of fire suppression not only resulted in accelerated loss of early successional vegetation but increased fuel loads and thus the risk of uncontrollable wildfires. In addition, evidence mounted that many ecosystems in the West are fire-dependent. Foresters and forest ecologists increasingly recognized "the need to continue to use fire to sustain ecosystem health."[74]

Fire ecology emerged as a distinct area of research, and academic institutions increasingly trained professionals in the field. In 1994, indigenous people organized to form the California Indian Forest and Fire Management Council (CIFFMC), to "promote California Indian forest and fire management issues and concerns."[75] Their stated purpose included "promoting prescribed fire management with an emphasis on cultural burning" and "encouraging the training and development of Indian natural resource professionals."[76] According to ethnobotanists Ann Garibaldi and Nancy Turner, "We need to restore not only landscapes but also the diversity-enhancing capabilities of the human communities inhabiting those landscapes."[77]

PARTNERSHIPS

The people of this state do not yield their sovereignty
to the agencies which serve them. The people, in delegating
authority, do not give their public servants the right to decide
what is good for the people to know and what is not good for them to
know. The people insist on remaining informed so that they may
retain control over the instruments they have created.

—STATE OF CALIFORNIA GOVERNMENT
CODE SECTION 54950

MANY CALIFORNIA INDIANS ARE DEEPLY COMMITTED TO CONTIN-
ued use of tanoak acorns and seek partners in addressing the *P. ramorum*
threat.[1] A growing number of people, Native and non-Native alike, are ques-
tioning exclusive reliance on Western scientific expertise at the expense of
other forms of knowledge when making decisions about environmental
issues that affect stakeholders. They advocate for "partnerships between
experts, policy advisers and stakeholders" that embrace "participatory approaches."[2]

Native peoples rely on tanoak acorns and are proactively seeking ways
of fostering this important food source. Unfortunately, the possibilities
for reestablishing managed tanoak acorn trees are limited. Privatization of
land has already reduced or eliminated the ability to manipulate vegetation
through the use of fire. The densest stands of tanoak occur in northwestern
California and southwestern Oregon, and most are not on existing reservations or rancherias. The Yurok and Hoopa Valley Tribes have reintroduced
burning on their tribal lands in an effort to foster tanoak acorn production.

INDIAN LAND FOR SALE

GET A HOME | | PERFECT TITLE
OF | | ❋
YOUR OWN |  | POSSESSION
❋ | | WITHIN
EASY PAYMENTS | | THIRTY DAYS

FINE LANDS IN THE WEST

IRRIGATED
IRRIGABLE   GRAZING   AGRICULTURAL
DRY FARMING

IN 1910 THE DEPARTMENT OF THE INTERIOR SOLD UNDER SEALED BIDS ALLOTTED INDIAN LAND AS FOLLOWS:

Location.	Acres.	Average Price per Acre.	Location.	Acres.	Average Price per Acre.
Colorado	5,211.21	$7.27	Oklahoma	34,664.00	$19.14
Idaho	17,013.00	24.85	Oregon	1,020.00	15.43
Kansas	1,684.50	33.45	South Dakota	120,445.00	16.53
Montana	11,034.00	9.86	Washington	4,879.00	41.37
Nebraska	5,641.00	36.65	Wisconsin	1,069.00	17.00
North Dakota	22,610.70	9.93	Wyoming	865.00	20.64

FOR THE YEAR 1911 IT IS ESTIMATED THAT **350,000** ACRES WILL BE OFFERED FOR SALE

For information as to the character of the land write for booklet, "INDIAN LANDS FOR SALE," to the Superintendent U. S. Indian School at any one of the following places:

CALIFORNIA:
  Hoopa.
COLORADO:
  Ignacio.
IDAHO:
  Lapwai.
KANSAS:
  Horton.
  Nadeau.

MINNESOTA:
  Onigum.
MONTANA:
  Crow Agency.
NEBRASKA:
  Macy.
  Santee.
  Winnebago.

NORTH DAKOTA:
  Fort Totten.
  Fort Yates.
OKLAHOMA:
  Anadarko.
  Cantonment.
  Colony.
  Darlington.
  Muskogee,
  Pawnee.

OKLAHOMA—Con.
  Sac and Fox Agency.
  Shawnee.
  Wyandotte.
OREGON:
  Klamath Agency.
  Pendleton.
  Roseburg.
  Siletz.

SOUTH DAKOTA:
  Cheyenne Agency.
  Crow Creek.
  Greenwood.
  Lower Brule.
  Pine Ridge.
  Rosebud.
  Sisseton.

WASHINGTON:
  Fort Simcoe.
  Fort Spokane.
  Tekoa.
  Tulalip.
WISCONSIN:
  Oneida.

WALTER L. FISHER,
Secretary of the Interior.

ROBERT G. VALENTINE,
Commissioner of Indian Affairs.

FIGURE 8.1 U.S. enclosure and tribal dispossession of land, 1910. "Indian Land for Sale" poster, Broadside Portfolio 240, no. 24. Note the listing of Hoopa lands projected to be on sale in 1911. Courtesy of the Rare Book Division of the Library of Congress.

The Hoopa also thin manually on some of their lands to encourage broad canopies composed of wide tanoak crowns for increased acorn production.[3] Foresters recommend thinning lightly over a period of time to avoid damaging trees by sudden exposure to sunlight after logging.[4] Many tribal groups aspire to reestablish traditional stewardship of native species, such as tanoak, and reintroduce culturally informed prescriptive firing of coastal prairies and tanoak groves in the interests of improving ecosystem health. This approach is consistent with contemporary ecological restoration of *Quercus*-dominated woodlands, which often combines manual removal and prescribed fire "to reduce conifer density."[5] One study involving removal of all Douglas-fir overtopping Oregon white oak resulted in increased acorn production, which was attributed to greater canopy exposure to sunlight.[6] Given that the ethnographic record indicates the effectiveness of annual, low-intensity surface fires against other kinds of tanoak diseases, it is worth investigating whether this traditional knowledge could help address the current sudden oak death crisis.

Contemporary efforts to foster tanoak acorn consumption is part of a worldwide movement of indigenous peoples uniting around issues of "cultural survival, ownership of knowledge or intellectual property rights, empowerment, local control of land and resources, cultural revitalization, and self-determination."[7] Many tribal peoples lost access to productive tanoak trees through government land appropriation and relocation policies as well as prohibitions on burning (fig. 8.1). Traditional California Native people feel that plants thrive in positive relationships with people.[8] Tribal elders contend that "plants want to be used"; otherwise, their quality deteriorates and their numbers diminish.[9] For tanoak to thrive, human intervention with good intentions and skillful means may be required.

Indigenous people partnered with environmental groups and land trusts to acquire a large tract of undeveloped land with tanoak on the Mendocino coast. They established conservation easements as a safeguard against exploitive resource extraction and enclosure of more northern California land into forested ranchettes, typically for second homes or retirement property.[10] This kind of privatization and fragmentation limits or eliminates the ability to use burning as a management tool while simultaneously often increasing wildfire risk. In an effort to reassert "a presence on their aboriginal lands," more tribes are using conservation trust tools grounded in the belief that "[t]he wisdom, spiritual will, and traditional ecological knowledge of

FIGURE 8.2 Yurok Tribe member and Yurok Tribal Forestry employee Tinman Gist (right) conducting research on tanoak resistance to *P. ramorum* in collaboration with plant pathologists from the University of California, Davis, including Heather Mehl (left), 2014. Photograph by Richard Cobb. Courtesy of Richard Cobb, Tinman Gist, and Heather Mehl.

Native trustees may indeed be necessary to guide this country during a time of climate crisis."[11]

Multiple tanoak conservation strategies are emerging due to the threat posed by *P. ramorum.* One of the tribes that has already felt the impact of sudden oak death, the Kashaya Pomo, collaborated with academics from two nearby public institutions: the University of California, Davis, and the University of California, Berkeley. They hosted forums where members could learn about the disease and express their concerns to researchers, as well as learn about treating uninfected heritage tanoaks with potassium phosphonate prophylactically, to reduce further loss of large trees. With a small land base of only forty acres that are heavily infested, management options remain limited. Also, this Stewarts Point Rancheria is located in Sonoma County, which has already been significantly affected by the pathogen. Multiple tribes in northern California are working with academics to monitor for *P. ramorum* and research tanoak resistance (fig. 8.2). The Hoopa and Yurok tribes both have larger land bases farther north in Humboldt County. Their tribal forestry departments actively manage for softwood species, primarily coast redwood and Douglas-fir, but they also have a history of favoring tanoaks in smaller portions of their land base. With their active forestry departments, the Hoopa and Yurok have the resources to manage the land, including manually thin to reduce *P. ramorum* hosts and competition from conifers. Traditionalist tribal members typically object to chemical intervention. Not only are the potassium phosphonate treatments expensive, time-consuming, and of questionable effectiveness; some oppose drilling into living trees and injecting them, which they see as a violation of tanoak's sovereignty.

After more than a century of suppression, the natural resource management skills of indigenous peoples are becoming more widely recognized. Collaborative relationships are beginning to emerge between various northern California tribes and public agencies including the U.S. Forest Service, the Bureau of Indian Affairs (BIA), the National Park Service, and the California Department of Parks and Recreation. Within the Six Rivers National Forest, Yurok, Hoopa, and Karuk elders advised on "a series of experimental burns to enhance the quality and quantity of . . . beargrass," which is used for basket making.[12] On the Hoopa Valley Indian Reservation, the BIA ceded power in the late twentieth century to a tribal governing body, which approved a forest management plan in 1994 that ended decades of intensive timber extraction practices and instead prioritized management for culturally useful plants like tanoak.[13] Traditional ecological knowledge is experiencing a revival in California and elsewhere, driven in part by renewed interest in traditional food systems and basket making. However, activities off of tribal lands threaten continued tribal use of tanoak and renewal of cultural practices that foster the health of people and places. According to Winona LaDuke, "At stake is nothing less than the ecological integrity of the land base and the physical and social health of Native Americans throughout the continent."[14]

Some scholars in tribal law claim that the federal and state agencies that prevailed over indigenous peoples and their land rights failed to steward nature over the past 150 years and instead "opened Native territorial lands to consumption by private interests."[15] Widespread criticism in the late twentieth century that the Forest Service discriminated against ethnic and racial minorities informed efforts by the agency to hire more tribal members. Hoopa tribal member Merv George currently serves as the deputy forest supervisor for the Six Rivers National Forest, assuming the role in 2011 after beginning his career in the Forest Service in 2008. He describes his purpose as "to build collaborative bridges that result in positive land management practices" and observes that the criticism he receives most frequently from the native community is that there are not enough prescribed fires.[16]

Frank Lake, of Karuk ancestry, works as a restoration ecologist for the Forest Service. He earned his PhD in traditional ecological knowledge at Oregon State University. In his words, "The federal government has a trust responsibility to manage public lands for tribal nations that ceded territories under treaties or executive orders or lands that have otherwise been removed from tribal control. . . . Additional research cooperatively conducted with tribes or tribal organizations are needed to properly identify their issues on their terms, as well as having partners honor and respect tribal approaches to management."[17] According to researchers at the University of California, more inclusive accounts of the factors shaping "the original working landscapes of the West's original inhabitants" can lead to better understanding of "the historically and culturally dynamic nature of ecosystems." These new insights can lead to "new management alternatives and practices" for contemporary ecosystem managers "as well as the opportunity to establish mutually beneficial relationships with American Indian tribes."[18] With the support of multiple partnerships, the Karuk began burning again in the late twentieth century within tanoak stands and other culturally important sites in northwestern California to reduce wild-fire hazard and foster ecosystem health inspired by traditional ecological knowledge. In addition to co-managing sites with the Forest Service, the tribe partners with community-based Fire Safe Councils supported by a nonprofit organization funded through grants.[19] The work includes collabo-ration with private landowners. The Happy Camp and Orleans-Somes Bar Fire Safe Councils assist local communities with their fire preparedness work, including mechanical thinning and prescribed burning (fig. 8.3). In-creasingly, tribes and local communities are proactively reducing wildfire risk, often despite reactive federal agencies that continue to emphasize fire suppression.[20] "Building the Tribe's capacity to play an appropriate role in ecosystem management is the only means by which ecosystem restoration, cultural survival and community prosperity will be achieved," according to the tribe's Department of Natural Resources.[21] The Karuk and the other tribes on the Klamath River believe that "[o]ur responsibility for partici-pating in the 'recreation of the world' . . . is never finished."[22]

The National Park Service and the California Department of Parks and Recreation also collaborate with local tribes to use burning for the restora-tion of tanoak stands and other cultural landscapes. Redwood National and State Parks annexed the Bald Hills, an area of 4,200 acres between the Klamath River and Redwood Creek, in 1978. Restoration efforts began in the 1990s and focused on removing conifers and reintroducing regular burning to favor prairie and oak woodland vegetation.[23] In 2008, Redwood National and State Parks staff hoped to complete additional work with local tribes to underburn Gann's Prairie and associated mature tanoaks, a cultural land-scape that had deteriorated due to fire suppression.[24] They claimed that with further restoration work, the cultural landscape would be eligible for listing on the National Register of Historic Places. In their effort to build better working relationships with local tribes, the parks contracted with the Yurok Tribe Culture Department to document their past management of prairies and oak woodlands in the area in part through oral history work with tribal elders.[25] Given significant changes to forest systems, reintroduc-ing fire alone won't address the challenges facing tanoak. Any potential benefits should be weighed against the risks, but that analysis needs to occur in ways that involve Native people with a stake in tanoak wellness. Although often marginalized, traditional ecological knowledge is increas-ingly being recognized as important to collaborative restoration work with community members who depend on cultural landscapes.[26]

FIGURE 8.3 Underburning in a tanoak stand in Humboldt County, California, near the town of Orleans, October 2010. Orleans–Somes Bar Fire Safe Council implemented the prescribed burn. Workers tending to the fire are Ben Beaver (left) and Will Harling (center). Photograph by and courtesy of Frank Lake, Karuk descendant, private landowner working with Orleans–Somes Bar Fire Safe Council on neighbor's property.

FOOD SOVEREIGNTY

Tribal people are working to reimagine and recreate secure food systems that revitalize their cultures and heal and nourish their bodies. The National Institute of Food and Agriculture sponsored the University and Jepson Herbaria at the University of California, Berkeley, to work collaboratively with the Karuk, Yurok, and Klamath tribes on enhancing "tribal health and food security in the Klamath Basin of Oregon and California by building a sustainable regional food system" that includes "culturally relevant foods."[27] The five-year, multimillion-dollar project is using a "participatory action research approach" with "stakeholders from all parts of the food system" being "involved in project development, implementation and evaluation."[28] In their proposal, they argued that despite being able to sustain themselves from the land for millennia, they now live in a food desert. Their access to fresh produce declined, while availability of processed foods high in carbohydrates and unhealthful fats increased. Rates of diabetes and other diseases associated with a poor diet are at historic highs. Fostering the long-term health of tanoaks for acorn production is a priority in crafting a more stable source of traditional, local, and native foods.

Tanoak remains a culturally significant tree despite reduced access and productivity (fig. 8.4). This is evident from the continuation of ceremonies linked to the phenology of the plant.[29] For example, the biannual Hupa Jump Dance occurs when acorns are ripe. The dance serves to "put the world in balance and to drive all of the bad things away. During the Jump Dance the female medicine woman prays (makes medicine) as she cooks the acorns" (fig. 8.5).[30] The Kashaya Pomo also still pray, sing, dance, and feast to honor tanoak at their annual Acorn Festival, which is held over four nights.[31] Ceremonies such as these "strengthen cultural cohesiveness" and "facilitate the cultural continuity of landscape use and management."[32] Dishes made with tanoak acorns are still served at celebrations and tribal gatherings and as a healing food for the sick and elderly.[33] Unfortunately, many examples exist of indigenous people losing access to "cultural keystone species."[34] This raises the issue of environmental racism and social injustice.

According to ethnobotanists Ann Garibaldi and Nancy Turner, "The concept of cultural keystone species provides us with a focus for considering the impacts of economic and environmental change on a particular group of people and their life ways."[35] Many health practitioners argue that adoption of a Western-style diet has contributed to the high rates of diabetes among indigenous people. According to the Centers for Disease Control and Prevention, "American Indian and Alaska Native adults are twice as likely to have diagnosed diabetes as non-Hispanic whites."[36] Despite being identified as "a significant public health problem" among Native Americans since the 1960s, a study published in 2002 found diagnosis of the disease in children, adolescents, and young adults increased 71 percent between 1990 and 1998.[37] Native Americans with diabetes also suffer a higher rate of "serious complications associated with the disease including heart disease, kidney failure, blindness and limb amputations."[38] Medical research links diabetes with diets high in simple carbohydrates and low in healthful fats, which are prevalent in the Western diet, particularly among the poorest populations. "The potential for foods to protect against chronic and degenerative diseases has prompted a reevaluation of the modern diet with an emphasis on increasing consump-

FIGURE 8.4 Harvest of tanoak acorns and California bay nuts over two years drying near a wood stove, in Kathy McCovey's home, Happy Camp, California, ca. 2010. Photograph by and courtesy of Kathy McCovey, Karuk tribal member and traditional gatherer.

FIGURE 8.5 Cooking tanoak acorns for the Hupa biannual Jump Dance, fall 2010. The dance is meant to "put the world in balance and to drive all of the bad things away. During the Jump Dance the female medicine woman prays (makes medicine) as she cooks the acorns." Left to right: Kayla Carpenter, Gina Nulph, and Melodie George-Moore, all Hupa tribal members. Quote and photograph by Laura Lee George of the Hupa tribe, both used with her permission.

tion of foods rich in micronutrients and bioactive phytochemicals. Many of these compounds are thought to have been higher in native diets."[39] The Cultural Conservancy, the Center for Disease Control and Prevention, and many other organizations working to address contemporary Native American health issues advocate for increased use of native foods.[40]

Responses to the crisis of sudden oak death and climate change need to account for continued use of tanoak acorns as human food. To do otherwise is in conflict with the United Nations Declaration of the Rights of Indigenous Peoples and its emphasis on the "free, prior, and informed consent" of Native peoples.[41] For federal agencies, to do so is also a violation of Executive Order 13175, signed by President Bill Clinton in 2000 and subsequently reaffirmed by President Barack Obama, which "requires tribal consultation and coordination on policies that have substantial direct effects on tribes."[42] "Environmental Justice laws require that federal agencies identify and address adverse affects to human health or the environment of their actions on minorities and low-income populations."[43] Decision-making needs to incorporate the use of both Western science and traditional ecological knowledge by tribes on their own terms and embrace participatory approaches that empower communities to determine their future, including the right to maintain their cultural identity. Fostering alternatives to industrial food systems is recognized as a right of sovereign nations.

Climate change is forcing the need to adopt food plants that are better adapted to place (e.g., drought-tolerant species and varieties in regions with a Mediterranean or desert climate). Agriculture dependent on irrigation will become increasingly unsustainable, including in many areas of the world that are currently important food-producing regions. Efforts at fostering food sovereignty globally need to include native plants. More research is needed on the nutritional value of native foods that goes beyond protein, fat, and carbohydrate content to include minerals and phytonutrients. Common assumptions about the inferiority of native foods are ironic, given the growing evidence that the modern Western diet is a significant factor in current high diabetes rates and hypertension. To judge Native American diets as inadequate based on consumption patterns after colonization is ahistorical. Many food resources had been damaged by early livestock grazing, row cropping, and the fur trade by the time Europeans and Euro-Americans arrived in the West in significant numbers.

Adaptability will be critical to maintaining food sovereignty as climate change and other negative environmental realities compromise food production and access worldwide. Solutions to food insecurity more often promoted in developing countries, such as agroforestry that incorporates diverse native food plants, could reduce vulnerability to a variety of threats to important, industrially produced crops even in developed countries. Maximizing our ability to adapt requires being flexible about what we eat. Speaking in 1984, Hoopa tribal woman Winnie Marshall warned that in the future "everyone might have to rely on native foods" to survive.[44] Some Native people see the current sudden oak death epidemic as a consequence of disregarding tanoak, of treating it as worthless. Some traditionalists in California are increasing their harvesting of tanoak as a way of showing gratitude to the plant for the gift of its acorns.

CONCLUSIONS

Ecology's most profound insights call for far-reaching
modifications of long-standing social arrangements.
—GARRETT HARDIN

BY HIGHLIGHTING THE DYNAMIC RELATIONSHIP BETWEEN HU-
mans and tanoak, this case study puts into stark relief the effects on nature
of our cultural biases and economic organization. Mass migration and rapid
industrialization transformed the California landscape. The early American
history of tanoak use began a volatile and nonsustainable pattern of forest
product use involving the exploitation of one commodity after another.
Centers of economic power reshaped hinterlands like northern California.

Most Americans summarily rejected tanoak acorns as human food, even
though tanoak can be grown without supplemental irrigation and large
labor inputs. Not even the first executive chief of the U.S. Biological Survey
could change the attitude of dismissal of this source of human nutrition.
More recent evidence indicates that tanoak acorns contain valuable fatty
acids and phytonutrients in addition to protein and carbohydrates. But during early American settlement, a white majority imposed its worldview on
surviving ethnic minorities, repurposing one of their favored plant-based
foods, plants as livestock fodder, particularly for hogs.

Tanoak fostered early industrialization in the West. As fodder, the
acorns helped establish a pork industry by the late 1800s. In addition to
meeting local needs, tanoak acorns enabled excess pork production for
sale particularly to gold-mining boomtowns. Initially, many settlers used
a grazing commons on which to fatten pigs on the acorn mast. But as the

land became enclosed and privatized, that free resource and unregulated commons evaporated. Also grains produced in abundance through mono-cultures facilitated a radical increase in enclosed pork production as opposed to open-range-based production. Despite its early contributions to industrialization, commercial use of tanoak ended in part because it defied efforts to domesticate it and make it conform to industrial production.

Tanoak's tannin-rich bark fueled a lucrative tanning industry until the 1920s. As with dominant food preferences, European tanning practices replaced preexisting cultural practices. Because manufacturers exported much of the leather produced with tanoak bark, the local vegetable tannin resource was quickly depleted. Replacing it with foreign vegetable tannin sources failed to save the tanoak-dependent industry in part because of rising U.S. labor costs. Increasingly, domestic leather producers struggled to compete with South Africa, South America, and other leather-producing regions with lower wages and standards of living. Despite strong objections from foresters, botanists, and environmentalists, the tanning industry liquidated old-growth tanoak except for a small percentage, much of it in coast redwood parks.

Botanists, foresters, wood scientists, and local communities have all advocated for producing wood from tanoak. More than a century of data has been generated on how to work skillfully to produce beautiful and durable objects from it, including flooring, furniture, cabinets, and even baseball bats. Yet the myth persists that hardwood from tanoak is worthless except as firewood or wood chips. Even the physical objects that attest to the falseness of that claim do not appear to sway this widespread sentiment. Competition from plantation-grown and wild-forest extracted eastern U.S. and tropical hardwoods further erodes serious consideration of tanoak's value. Indeed the influence of global trade has been felt within the range of tanoak since at least the mid-1800s.

Conservationists failed to end unsustainable use of tanoak because this tree did not lend itself to efficient, mechanized, or centralized production of acorns, bark, or wood. Nor could it compete with the higher profit margins generated by coast redwood and Douglas-fir, particularly old growth. With pork, tanbark, and hardwood production centralized in other locales on the globe, foresters aided the creation of softwood mono-cultures over multispecies forests and diversified production in California and southwestern Oregon. The timber industry embraced large-scale vegetation-type conversion from old-growth forests with tanoak to younger, more homogeneous, even-aged conifer stands. With the end of tanoak's utility as a cash crop in an emerging industrialized landscape, the focus shifted to killing it in favor of conifers that lent themselves to efficient and mechanized production.

As a result of decades of overharvesting bark for industrial tanning, beginning with American settlement and cut-and-run logging of old-growth conifers, large, mature, and widely spaced tanoaks were replaced with higher densities of younger tanoak sprouts stressed by excess competition. In response, by the mid-1900s, a tanoak eradication campaign combined with twentieth-century fire suppression was favoring conifers over tanoak. In a mere century, from 1850 to 1950, this nut tree was transformed from a major indigenous food source to a weed species. Given the totemic significance of tanoak to indigenous peoples, this change exemplifies the cultural bias implicit in American forest use and the selective use of science by industry and governmental agencies. The reputedly objective approach to scientific forest management that entails killing tanoaks was advanced through government-funded research. Governmental regulations to date have proved insufficient to reverse devastating assaults on tanoak due to a complex interplay of economic, ecological, and cultural factors.

We need to be pragmatic about the necessity of using forests while limiting that use based on the values of social justice, democratic process, and sustainability. Indigenous practices of forest use may be a source of new ideas about methods and, more important, alternative narratives. What if some wild plants need people if they are to thrive, as some traditional tribal members contend? What if once-abundant native plants can become rare or threatened through an absence of human care? Exotic diseases don't just threaten foods favored by a relatively small population. The movement of invasive species via global trade in combination with environmental degradation is putting at risk many plant species that a majority of people rely on for food, fodder, medicine, and fiber. For example, anthropogenic climate change threatens to create conditions favorable to wheat leaf rust (*Puccinia triticina*) in several major areas of production worldwide.[1] If this devastating disease expands its current range, it could reduce food security and increase food costs.

We need to proactively safeguard and cultivate local food sovereignty, including through the use of perennial native plants. Tanoak could also help to shrink our dependency on foreign wood, leather, and oil, thereby mitigating U.S. contributions to the global climate change crisis. Viewed in this way, tanoak might more accurately be called by its other common name: sovereign oak. Building diverse, multicultural partnerships to address issues of food security, global climate change, and other environmental challenges requires understanding and acknowledging the ways in which colonization and American expansion have worked for and against social equality and inclusive governance. Such partnerships will increase in effectiveness if state and federal regulators become more responsive to citizens and less beholden to commercial interests. The insights of scientists within academia, government, and communities need more serious consideration when their research exposes and challenges various ecologically unmaintainable business practices. Our efforts to find sustainable ways to coexist with tanoak and the rest of nature will depend on finding ways to benefit nature in the process of producing or otherwise obtaining the goods we need and the gardens we desire.

NOTES

INTRODUCTION

Epigraph: Schiebinger, *Plants and Empire*, 3.
1 Nomland, "Sinkyone Notes," 169.
2 Freinkel, *American Chestnut*.

1. THE BEAUTIFUL TREE

Epigraph: Jacob, *The Scientific Revolution*, 34.
1 For more accurate spelling of Pomo names with an alternate alphabet, see Gifford, "Ethnographic Notes," 12.
2 Greene, *Illustrations of West American Oaks*, 42.
3 Armstrong, "New Uses for Tan-bark Oak," 213.
4 Sargent, *The Silva of North America*, 185.
5 Ibid.
6 Anonymous, "Resources of Mendocino," in *California As It Is* (San Francisco: San Francisco Call, 1882), 11.
7 Sudworth, *Forest Trees*, 320–321.
8 For a more detailed description of range, see Munz, *A California Flora*, 902, and Tucker, "Fagaceae," 803.
9 Nixon, "Fagaceae," 443.
10 Dodd et al., "Genetic Structure of *Notholithocarpus densiflorus* (Fagaceae)," 131.
11 Tucker, Sundahl, and Hall, "A Mutant of *Lithocarpus densiflorus*," 221–225.
12 Schniewind, "The Strength and Related Properties of Tanoak."
13 Fryer, "*Lithocarpus densiflorus* in Fire Effects Information System."
14 Tappeiner, McDonald, and Roy, "*Lithocarpus densiflorus* (Hook. & Arn.) Rehd. Tanoak," 422.
15 Peattie, *A Natural History of Western Trees*, 414.
16 Fryer, "*Lithocarpus densiflorus* in Fire Effects Information System."
17 Tappeiner, McDonald, and Roy, "*Lithocarpus densiflorus*," 422.
18 Ibid.
19 Ibid.
20 Jepson, *The Silva of California*, 238.
21 Nixon, "Fagaceae," 443.
22 Brush, "Knowing Your Trees," 126.
23 Peattie, *A Natural History of Western Trees*, 414.
24 Roy, "Silvical Characteristics of Tanoak," 443.
25 Tappeiner, McDonald, and Roy, "*Lithocarpus densiflorus*," 419.

26 Nixon, "Fagaceae," 442.
27 Harlow and Harrar, *Textbook of Dendrology*, 290.
28 Fryer, "*Lithocarpus densiflorus* in Fire Effects Information System,"
29 Wright and Dodd, "Could Tanoak Mortality Affect Insect Biodiversity?" 87.
30 Ibid., 92.
31 Fryer, "*Lithocarpus densiflorus* in Fire Effects Information System." See also Roy, "A Record," 4.
32 Martin G. Raphael, "Wildlife-Tanoak Associations," 187.
33 Storer and Usinger, *Sierra Nevada Natural History*, 30.
34 Fryer, "*Lithocarpus densiflorus* in Fire Effects Information System."
35 Ibid.
36 Martin G. Raphael, "Wildlife-Tanoak Associations," 187.
37 North et al., "Forest Stand Structure," 520–521.
38 Block and Morrison, "Conceptual Framework and Ecological Considerations," 170.
39 Ehrlich, Dobkin, and Wheye, *The Birder's Handbook*, 434.
40 Bergemann and Garbelotto, "High Diversity of Fungi," 1389.
41 Bergemann et al., "Implications of Tanoak Decline," 95.
42 Bergemann and Garbelotto, "High Diversity of Fungi," 1393.
43 Fryer, "*Lithocarpus densiflorus* in Fire Effects Information System."
44 Anderson and Lake, "California Indian Ethnomycology," 37, 38, 48, 50, 55.
45 Ibid., 54.
46 Ibid., 38, 50, 62.
47 Ibid., 62.
48 Donoghue and Denison, "Commercial Production of Shiitake," 272.
49 Hooker and Arnott, *Botany of Captain Beechey's Voyage*, 391.
50 Jepson, *The Trees of California*, 175.
51 Sargent, *Manual of the Trees of North America*, 236.
52 Manos, Cannon, and Oh, "Phylogenetic Relationships and Taxonomic Status," 181.
53 Kevin C. Nixon, professor and director, L. H. Bailey Hortorium, Department of Plant Biology, Cornell University Ithaca, New York, e-mail to the author, October 10, 2010.
54 Graham, *Late Cretaceous and Cenozoic History*, 123.
55 Diane M. Erwin, museum scientist, University of California Museum of Paleontology, interview with the author, September 10, 2010.
56 Diane M. Erwin, e-mail to the author, May 6, 2013.
57 Diane M. Erwin, interview with the author, September 10, 2010. For the currently accepted geologic time scale, see International Commission on Stratigraphy, "International Chronostratigraphic Chart," http://www.stratigraphy.org/index.php/ics-chart-timescale (accessed October 9, 2014), and University of California Museum of Paleontology, "Geologic Time Scale," http://www.ucmp.berkeley.edu/help/timeform.php (accessed October 9, 2014).
58 Briles, Whitlock, and Bartlein, "Postglacial Vegetation, Fire, and Climate History," 47.
59 Denk and Grimm, "Significance of Pollen Characteristics."
60 Thomas Denk, senior curator, Swedish Museum of Natural History, Stockholm, e-mail to the author, April 8, 2013.
61 Crepet, "History and Implications," 55.

62 Thomas Denk, senior curator, Swedish Museum of Natural History, Stockholm, e-mail to the author, April 8, 2013. See also Nixon, "Origins of Fagaceae."
63 Manos and Stanford, "Historical Biogeography of Fagaceae," S77.
64 Ibid., S79, S88.
65 Graham (*Late Cretaceous and Cenozoic History*, 254) placed this uplift as beginning roughly 4.5 million years ago. However, more recent research indicates it began much earlier. See DeCelles, "Late Jurassic to Eocene," and Henry, "Uplift of the Sierra Nevada."
66 Schorn, Myers, and Erwin, "Navigating the Neogene," 143.
67 Ibid., 143. Graham, *Late Cretaceous and Cenozoic History*, 254, placed this shift as occurring in the late Pliocene and Pleistocene, but it is now known to have occurred much earlier.
68 Manos, Cannon, and Oh, "Phylogenetic Relationships and Taxonomic Status," 187.
69 Bowcutt, "Tanoak Landscapes." For a history of past threats due to economic activity, see Bowcutt, "Tanoak Target."

2. ACORNS

Epigraph: Ham, *Environmental Interpretation*, xviii.

1   Vander Wall, "The Evolutionary Ecology of Nut Dispersal," 98.
2   Roy, "California Hardwoods," 185.
3   Ibid., 185.
4   Baumhoff, "Ecological Determinants," 164–165. See also Radtke, "The Tan Oak," 10. Note that many oaks in the genus *Quercus* also produce large amounts of acorns in good years.
5   Gifford, "Californian Balanophagy," 90. See also Heizer and Elsasser, *The Natural World*, 91, 100; and Chestnut, "Plants Used by the Indians," 342.
6   Gifford, "Californian Balanophagy," 90.
7   Baumhoff, "Environmental Background," 16.
8   Gould, "Ecology and Adaptive Response," 62.
9   Goodrich, Lawson, and Lawson, *Kashaya Pomo Plants*, 84.
10 Bocek, "Ethnobotany of Costanoan Indians," 248.
11 Sherrie Smith-Ferri, director, Grace Hudson Museum and Sun House, interview with the author, Ukiah, Calif., September 14, 2011.
12 Nomland, "Sinkyone Notes," 169.
13 Heizer and Elsasser, *The Natural World*, 100. Wolf, *California Wild Tree Crops*, 51.
14 Hendryx and Davis, *Plants and the People*, 78.
15 Baumhoff, "Ecological Determinants," 162–163.
16 Gilliland, *Proximate Analysis*, 41–43, 67.
17 Meyers, Swiecki, and Mitchell, "An Exploratory Study," 6188.
18 Ibid.
19 Fattore and Fanelli, "Palm Oil and Palmitic Acid."
20 Séquin, *The Chemistry of Plants*, 59.
21 Ibid., 109. Tanoak acorns have more tannins than *Quercus* acorns according to Essene, "Cultural Element Distributions," 56.
22 Schenck and Gifford, "Karok Ethnobotany," 382.
23 Ibid.

24 Curtin, "Some Plants Used by the Yuki Indians," 15.
25 Hosten et al., "Oak Woodlands and Savannas," 64.
26 Gould, "Ecology and Adaptive Response," 60.
27 Kniffen, "Pomo Geography," 379.
28 Gifford, "Ethnographic Notes," 12.
29 Shanks and Shanks, *Indian Baskets*, 50, 63–64, 127, 146.
30 Wallace, "Hupa, Chilula, and Whilkut," 174.
31 Nomland, "Sinkyone Notes," 154–155.
32 Kroeber and Gifford, "World Renewal," 57–59.
33 Baumhoff, "Ecological Determinants," 167.
34 Essene, "Cultural Element Distributions," 56.
35 Driver, "The Acorn," 56.
36 Schenck and Gifford, "Karok Ethnobotany," 382.
37 For discussions on granaries for *Quercus* acorns, see Bates, "Acorn Storehouses"; and Barrett and Gifford, "Miwok Houses," 283–284.
38 Series of photographs taken by Josepha Haveman in 1960 titled "Essie Parrish Building Acorn Cache," archived at the Phoebe A. Hearst Museum of Anthropology, University of California, Berkeley, and accessible through the California Digital Library, http://content.cdlib.org/ark:/13030/kt2r29n62h/?query=acorn&brand= calisphere (accessed June 23, 2011).
39 Gifford, "Californian Balanophagy," 87. Note that Hupa refers to a native northern California ethnic group and its indigenous language. Members of the Hoopa Valley Tribe are referred to as Hoopa and may or may not be of Hupa ancestry.
40 Hendryx and Davis, *Plants and the People*, 78.
41 Gifford, "Ethnographic Notes," 12.
42 Ibid.
43 Driver, "The Acorn," 57.
44 Gifford, "Californian Balanophagy," 87.
45 Basgall, "Resource Intensification among Hunter-Gatherers," 34.
46 Ibid., 32.
47 Chartkoff and Chartkoff, *The Archaeology of California*, 131. See also Basgall, "Resource Intensification among Hunter-Gatherers," 30.
48 Driver, "The Acorn," 56.
49 Sherrie Smith-Ferri, director, Grace Hudson Museum and Sun House, interview with the author, Ukiah, Calif., September 14, 2011.
50 Chartkoff and Chartkoff, *The Archaeology of California*, 116.
51 Schenck and Gifford, "Karok Ethnobotany," 382.
52 Essene, "Cultural Element Distributions," 55–56. Round Valley Reservation is located inland near the small town of Covelo. A variety of northern California tribes are represented at Round Valley Reservation, including descendants of the Sinkyone people.
53 Ibid., 56. Note that the author's use of the word "traditional" refers primarily to those cultural beliefs and practices whose origins predate white settlement. The use of the term does not preclude modification over time, but it does imply resistance to assimilation into non-Native society.
54 Descriptions of acorn preparation in this paragraph are based on Driver, "The Acorn," 57–60; and Gifford, "Californian Balanophagy," 90–96.
55 Gifford, "Californian Balanophagy," 93.

56 Driver, "The Acorn," 58–60.
57 Sherrie Smith-Ferri, director, Grace Hudson Museum and Sun House, interview with the author, Ukiah, Calif., September 14, 2011.
58 Baker, *The Ethnobotany of the Yurok, Tolowa, and Karok Indians*, 36.
59 Ibid., 36.
60 Sherrie Smith-Ferri, director, Grace Hudson Museum and Sun House, interview with the author, Ukiah, Calif., September 14, 2011.
61 Chartkoff and Chartkoff, *The Archaeology of California*, 228.
62 Heizer and Elsasser, *The Natural World*, 95.
63 Ray Raphael, *An Everyday History of Somewhere*, 79.
64 *History of Humboldt County, California*, 137, 146.
65 *California As It Is*.
66 California Department of Parks and Recreation, "Sinkyone Wilderness State Park Unit History," 1–3. McKee's homestead dated back to 1871.
67 Radtke, "The Tan Oak," 11; and Radtke, "Notes," 13–14.
68 Radtke, "The Tan Oak," 9–10.; and Radtke, "Notes," 1–2, 13–14.
69 Wolf, *California Wild Tree Crops*, 68.
70 Curtin, "Some Plants," 15.
71 Barrett, *The Beautiful Tree—Chishkale*. This 16 mm film was funded by the National Science Foundation and was made in collaboration with the University of California.
72 Jacknis, *Food in California Indian Culture*, 385.
73 Ibid., 4.

3. BARK

Epigraph: Greene, *Illustrations of West American Oaks*, 42.
1 Farmer, *Trees in Paradise*, 58.
2 Hittell, "Autobiography and Reminiscence."
3 Hittell, *Commerce and Industries*, 490.
4 Bauer, "The Beginnings of Tanning," 61.
5 Ibid.
6 Hittell, *Commerce and Industries*, 488.
7 Knapp, "Nature and Essential Character," 659.
8 Bauer, "The Beginnings of Tanning," 63–64.
9 Ibid., 63.
10 Hittell, *Commerce and Industries*, 490.
11 Baker, *Ethnobotany*, 108.
12 Tanoak bark was being used in 1958 as a fishnet preservative according to Schniewind, "Strength and Related Properties."
13 Bocek, "Ethnobotany of Costanoan Indians," 248.
14 The Wappo used bark from various species of *Quercus* "for curing hides," according to Beard, *The Wappo*, 53. Based on interviews conducted by M. Kat Anderson, the Salinan and the Wintu tanned hides with oak bark. M. Kat Anderson, e-mail to the author, August 18, 2007.
15 Jepson, "Tanbark Oak," 14.
16 Finlay, *Growing American Rubber*, 3.
17 "California Made Leather."

18 Ibid.
19 Séquin, *The Chemistry of Plants*, 109.
20 Margareta Séquin, San Francisco State University, e-mail to the author, December 13, 2005.
21 Séquin, *The Chemistry of Plants*, 126–127.
22 Ibid., 127.
23 California State Board of Forestry, "Wattles," 37.
24 Teague, *From Buckskin to Teambells*, 74.
25 Ibid., 74.
26 "Tanbark Industry on the Coast," 3.
27 Bauer, "The Beginnings of Tanning," 60.
28 Ibid., 59.
29 Ibid., 63–64.
30 Ibid.
31 Ibid., 66.
32 Ibid., 65–66.
33 Cronise, *The Natural Wealth of California*, 131, 619.
34 Carranco and Carranco, "Briceland," 1.
35 Carr, "Shoe Trees," 8–9.
36 Bauer, "The Beginnings of Tanning," 69.
37 "California Made Leather."
38 Ibid.
39 Carpenter, "Tan Bark," 6.
40 *History of Humboldt County*, 146.
41 California State Board of Forestry, "Wattles," 38.
42 Hittell, *Commerce and Industries*, 486.
43 Hough, *Report on Forestry*, 105.
44 U.S. Forest Service, "Consumption of Tanbark," 4. In 1905, hemlock provided the United States with 73 percent of its tanbark, or 799,755 cords for the 477 tanneries surveyed, according to Hale, "Consumption of Tanbark," 1.
45 "California Oak Tan Bark."
46 Griffin and Critchfield, "Distribution of Forest Trees," 73.
47 "Tanbark Oak of California." Pacific Oak Extract Works began operations in 1902.
48 "Stockton."
49 Jepson, "Tanbark Oak," 5–6.
50 "Tanbark Oak of California."
51 Bauer, "The Beginnings of Tanning," 60.
52 Miller, "The Pivotal Decade," 7–8.
53 Schofield, *Forest Laws of California*, 5.
54 California State Board of Forestry, *First Biennial Report*, 9, 63.
55 Ibid., 180.
56 Ibid., 9.
57 California State Board of Forestry, *Third Biennial Report*, 9.
58 California State Board of Forestry, "Wattles," 38.
59 Ibid., 37–38.
60 California State Board of Forestry, *First Biennial Report*, 6. Note that from 1833 to 1948, Ceylon was considered part of the British East Indian colony. The dried

bark of *Cinchona ledgeriana* (Rubiaceae) contains the alkaloid quinine, used for the treatment of malaria.

61 Hittell, *Commerce and Industries*, 491. Note that the common name "chestnut oak" was sometimes used for tanoak.

62 California State Board of Forestry, *First Biennial Report*, 5.

63 California State Board of Forestry, "Wattles," 38.

64 Hough, *Report on Forestry*, 106.

65 California State Board of Forestry, "Wattles," 39.

66 Clark, "Forestry; Redwoods," 325.

67 Bauer, "The Beginnings of Tanning," 60–61.

68 Muir, *The Mountains of California*, 172.

69 Jepson, *The Silva of California*, 238.

70 Carpenter and Millberry, *History of Mendocino and Lake Counties*, 24.

71 Harris, Harris, and James, *Oak*, 92.

72 "California Oak Tan Bark."

73 Carranco and Carranco, "Briceland," 4.

74 Bandekow, "Present and Potential Sources," 729.

75 Description of the A. K. Salz Tannery Collection archived at the Santa Cruz Museum of Art & History, California, http://www.santacruzmah.org/2011/a-k-salz-tannery-collection/ (accessed October 21, 2012).

76 Bandekow, "Present and Potential Sources," 729.

77 "Ancient Industry Thrives," 86.

78 Bandekow, "Present and Potential Sources," 732.

79 Ibid., 732–733.

80 Hilgard, "The Canaigre," 2–9. Hilgard had tested a number of other substitutes for tanoak bark ten years earlier and discussed his findings in Bulletin no. 4, published in January 1884. In addition to tanners dock, he tested "three varieties of wattles or acacias; sumac (*Rhus coriaria*); and California tall sumac (*R. integrifolia*)," according to Bauer, "The Beginnings of Tanning," 60.

81 Jepson, "Tanbark Oak," 16.

82 "Tanbark Oak of California."

83 Bandekow, "Present and Potential Sources," 729.

84 Sherry, *The Black Wattle*, 108; and Christopher, *Colonial Africa*, 101.

85 Christopher, *Colonial Africa*, 101.

86 "The Mark of the Range."

87 "Famous Saddle Leather." The California Saddle Leather line was developed in the 1930s by A. K. Salz, who decided not to erase scars and branding iron marks but to leave them as "historical evidence of life on the range." See "The Mark of the Range."

88 Marston, "Leather with Personality."

89 "New Ways to Cure Leather."

90 Lehmann, "Industrial Development: Tanneries."

91 Description of the A.K. Salz Tannery Collection archived at the Santa Cruz Museum of Art & History, California. http://www.santacruzmah.org/2011/a-k-salz-tannery-collection/ (accessed October 12, 2012).

4. WEED

Epigraph: Dizard, *Going Wild*, 147–148.

1 Emerson, "The Fortune of the Republic," 396.
2 Huber and McDonald, "California's Hardwood Resource," 5.
3 Radosevich, Passof, and Leonard, "Douglas Fir Release," 144.
4 Harrington and Tappeiner, "Growth Responses," 1.
5 Ibid., 10.
6 Bowcutt, "Resistance to Logging"; Carranco and Labbe, *Logging the Redwoods*; and Cornford, *Workers and Dissent*.
7 Michael Williams, *Americans and Their Forests*, 351.
8 Tyrrell, *True Gardens of the Gods*, 78. Note Douglas-fir is also called Oregon pine.
9 Farmer, *Trees in Paradise*, 154.
10 Ibid., 154.
11 Michael Williams, *Americans and Their Forests*, 350.
12 Tyrrell, *True Gardens of the Gods*, 74, 80–82.
13 Bunting, *The Pacific Raincoast*, 142, 147–148.
14 Jepson, "Tanbark Oak," 19.
15 Buckley, "A Factory without a Roof," 77.
16 Michael Williams, *Americans and Their Forests*, 317–318.
17 Jepson, *The Silva of California*, 238.
18 Harlow and Harrar, *Textbook of Dendrology*, 290.
19 Emanuel Fritz, memo addressed to Ben S. Allen of the Pacific Lumber Company in San Francisco, May 16, 1949, Union Lumber Company Records, 1854–1960, 68/21 c carton 14 in ctn 14:18 Reforestation file, 3. Bancroft Library, University of California, Berkeley. The subject line on the memo reads "Reforestation in Redwood. Historical notes and basic principles."
20 Harrington and Tappeiner, "Growth Responses," 2. See also Harrington, "Stand Development."
21 Tappeiner, McDonald, and Roy, "*Lithocarpus densiflorus*," 421.
22 Tappeiner and McDonald, "Development of Tanoak Understories," 271. See also Radosevich, Passof, and Leonard, "Douglas Fir Release."
23 Tappeiner and McDonald, "Development of Tanoak Understories," 271–272.
24 Harrington and Tappeiner, "Growth Responses," 2.
25 Ibid., 9.
26 Harrington, Tappeiner, and Hughes, "Predicting Average Growth," 127.
27 Harrington and Tappeiner, "Growth Responses," 10.
28 Ibid., 9.
29 Tappeiner and McDonald, "Development of Tanoak Understories," 274.
30 Tappeiner, Harrington, and Walstad, "Predicting Recovery of Tanoak," 415–416.
31 Tappeiner and McDonald, "Development of Tanoak Understories," 274.
32 Ibid., 276.
33 Ibid., 273.
34 Ibid., 276–277.
35 Schubert, "Control of Sprouting."
36 Ibid., 2.
37 Kay, Leonard, and Street, "Control of Madrone and Tanoak," 372–373.
38 Tim Harrington, research forester, U.S. Forest Service Pacific Northwest Research

Station, Olympia, Washington, e-mail to the author, February 4, 2013.
39 Kay, Leonard, and Street, "Control of Madrone and Tanoak," 372.
40 Ibid., 373.
41 Piirto et al., "Efficacy of Herbicide Application Methods."
42 Kay, Leonard, and Street, "Control of Madrone and Tanoak," 369.
43 Dahms, "Chemical Control of Brush."
44 Estes and Blakeman, "Foliar Spraying of Sprouting Tanoak," 1.
45 Ibid., 4.
46 McDonald and Fiddler, "Development of a Mixed Shrub-Tanoak-Douglas-fir Community," 3.
47 Ibid., 5–7.
48 *FIR Report*, 1.
49 Walstad, "History," 42.
50 Radosevich, Passof, and Leonard, "Douglas Fir Release," 144.
51 Ibid.
52 Roy, "Killing Tanoak," 3.
53 Ibid.
54 Radosevich, Passof, and Leonard, "Douglas Fir Release," 144.
55 Ibid.
56 Helgerson, "Response of Underplanted Douglas-fir."
57 Ibid., 89.
58 David Bakke, pesticide use specialist, USDA Forest Service, Vallejo, Calif., e-mails to the author, December 21, 2012, and May 10, 2013. See also California Department of Pesticide Regulation, "Search for Products by Chemical," http://www.cdpr.ca.gov/docs/label/chemcode.htm (accessed May 16, 2013).
59 David L. Priebe, state registration specialist, Pesticides Division, Oregon Department of Agriculture, Salem, e-mail to the author, December 20, 2012.
60 Oregon Department of Agriculture, "Search Pesticide Products Information," http://oda.state.or.us/dbs/pest_productsL2K/search.lasso (accessed September 27, 2014).
61 California Department of Pesticide Regulation, "DPR Registers 17 New Pesticides."
62 Sarah Billig, Mendocino Redwood Company, California, e-mail to the author, October 29, 2012.
63 Mendocino Redwood Company and Humboldt Redwood Company, "Tanoak."
64 Lavy et al., "Exposure of Forestry Ground Workers."
65 Durkin, "Imazapyr Human Health," xii.
66 Yahnke et al., "Effects of the Herbicide Imazapyr."
67 Mendocino Redwood Company and Humboldt Redwood Company, "Tanoak."
68 Ibid.
69 Ibid.
70 Ibid.
71 California Department of Pesticide Regulation, "Annual Statewide Pesticide Use Report," indexed by Commodity Mendocino County, http://www.cdpr.ca.gov/docs/pur/pur09rep/comcnty/mendoc09_site.pdf and http://www.cdpr.ca.gov/docs/pur/pur10rep/comcnty/mendoc10_site.pdf (accessed May 10, 2014).
72 Roy, "Killing Tanoak.," 1.
73 Roy, "California Hardwoods," 1.

74 McDonald and Tappeiner, "Silviculture, Ecology, and Management," 68.

75 Carson, *Silent Spring*, 68–69.

76 Ibid., 67.

77 Ibid., 63.

78 Van Strum, *A Bitter Fog*, 94–106.

79 Whiteside, *The Pendulum and the Toxic Cloud*, 1–4, 60.

80 Van Strum, *A Bitter Fog*, 94–106.

81 Whiteside, *The Pendulum and the Toxic Cloud*.

82 Merchant, *Earthcare*, 159.

83 Ibid.

84 Brown, *In Timber Country*, 24.

85 Bureau of Land Management, "Applying Glyphosate on Tanoak," Scoping Document, 2.

86 Walstad and Dost, "All the King's Horses," 28.

87 Ball, "'Hack and Squirt.'"

88 Philp, "Poison Programs."

89 "Staff Evaluation of the 1994 Aerial Application of Herbicides on Private Timberlands on the North Coast," produced by Christine Wright-Shacklett, February 27, 1995, for an Executive Officer's Report for the State of California Regional Water Quality Control Board's North Coast Region.

90 Gale and Randolph, "Lower Klamath River Sub-basin Watershed Restoration Plan," 1.

91 Snyder, "Yuroks Fear Cancer," A1.

92 Wilkinson, McDonald, and Morgan, "Tanoak Sprout Development," 21.

93 Merv George, Deputy Forest Supervisor, Six Rivers National Forest, e-mail to the author, January 31, 2013.

94 Resolution of the Yurok Tribe regarding "Opposition to the Use of Pesticides on the Yurok Reservation," Klamath, California. Resolution 96–23 was unanimously approved at a regular meeting of the Yurok Tribal Council on April 25, 1996, and signed by Susie L. Long, Chairperson of the Yurok Tribal Council.

95 California Oaks, a project of California Wildlife Foundation, letter from Thomas N. Lippe, dated February 6, 2006, regarding "Comments of the California Oak Foundation on the Draft Programmatic Environmental Impact Statement [PEIS] for Vegetation Treatments Using Herbicides on Bureau of Land Management Lands in 17 Western States," addressed to Brian Amme, PEIS Project Manager, Reno, Nevada, http://www.californiaoaks.org/ExtAssets/FinalCommentsDrftPEIS.pdf (accessed October 9, 2012).

96 Bureau of Land Management, "Applying Glyphosate on Tanoak," Scoping Document, 2.

97 Jim Kirkpatrick, silviculturalist, Bureau of Land Management, North Bend, Oregon, e-mail to the author, December 31, 2012.

98 Van Strum, *A Bitter Fog*, 17.

99 Oppmann, "Spray Areas Detailed."

100 Lowry, *Gardening with a Wild Heart*, 87.

101 Walstad and Dost, "All the King's Horses."

102 David Bakke, Pesticide Use Specialist and Invasive Plants Program Manager, U.S. Forest Service, Vallejo, California, e-mail to the author, December 21, 2012.

103 See U.S. Forest Service, "National Pesticide Risk Assessments," http://www.fs.fed.us/foresthealth/pesticide/risk.shtml.

104 For these pesticide fact sheets, see Oregon Department of Forestry, "Private For-

ests Program," http://www.oregon.gov/odf/privateforests/pages/pesticides.aspx (accessed April 20, 2013).

105 Carson, *Silent Spring*, 297.

106 Holling and Meffe, "Command and Control," 328.

107 Wilkinson, McDonald, and Morgan, "Tanoak Sprout Development," 25.

108 Harrington and Tappeiner, "Long-Term Effects of Tanoak Competition," 774.

109 Perry, "The Scientific Basis of Forestry," 454.

110 Hobbs, "Reforestation without Herbicides," 14. See also Westport Municipal Advisory Council, "Summary minutes for meeting on April 5, 2011, Westport, California," http://www.westportmac.org/2011_Meetings/WMAC_Minutes_4-5-11.pdf (accessed September 28, 2012).

111 Wilkinson, McDonald, and Morgan, "Tanoak Sprout Development," 21–22.

112 McDonald, Fiddler, and Harrison, "Repeated Manual Release," 4.

113 Jaramillo, "Growth of Douglas-fir," 8.

114 McDonald, Vogler, and Mayhew, "Unusual Decline of Tanoak Sprouts," 1.

115 Wilkinson, McDonald, and Morgan, "Tanoak Sprout Development," 22.

116 McDonald and Fiddler, "Feasibility of Alternatives to Herbicides," 2015.

117 Anonymous interview on the Sherwood Rancheria in Willets, California, April 18, 1995.

118 Hawk Rosales, executive director, InterTribal Sinkyone Wilderness Council, Coyote Valley Rancheria, Ukiah, California, e-mail to the author, February 24, 2011.

119 Wilkinson, McDonald, and Morgan, "Tanoak Sprout Development," 24.

120 Westport Municipal Advisory Council, "Summary minutes for meeting on April 5, 2011, Westport, California," http://www.westportmac.org/2011_Meetings/WMAC_Minutes_4-5-11.pdf (accessed September 28, 2012).

121 McDonald, Vogler, and Mayhew, "Unusual Decline of Tanoak Sprouts," 3.

122 Ibid., 1.

123 U.S. Census Bureau, "Median and Average Square Feet of Floor Area in New Single-Family Houses Completed by Location," 1973–2013, Characteristics of New Single-Family Houses Completed, U.S. Department of Commerce, https://www.census.gov/construction/chars/pdf/medavgsqft.pdf (accessed October 3, 2014). The U.S. Census Bureau did not collect data on home size in 1950. For statistics on 1950, see National Association of Home Builders (NAHB), "Housing Facts, Figures and Trends," March 2006, p. 14, http://www.soflo.fau.edu/report/NAHBhousingfacts-March2006.pdf (accessed April 3, 2014). NAHB also describes the typical new home in 1950 as being 1,000 square feet or less in its 2003 report *A Century of Progress: America's Housing 1900–2000*, 3.

5. HARDWOOD

Epigraph: Brown, *In Timber Country*, 281.

1 Bacon, "New Atlantis," 471.

2 Merriman, "The Demoiselles of the Ariège, 88.

3 Sahlins, *Forest Rites*.

4 Peluso, *Rich Forests, Poor People*, 45.

5 Michael Williams, *Deforesting the Earth*, 193–196.

6 Harris, Harris, and James, *Oak*, 92.

7 Wade, *Quercus; or Oaks*. This translation of André Michaux's 1801 book integrates

subsequently gathered information from his son François and others "who have traveled in search of vegetable treasures to the remotest parts of the globe" (vi).

8 Harvey, *Douglas of the Fir*, 182.

9 Mitchell and House, *David Douglas*, 176–177.

10 Hooker and Arnott, *The Botany of Captain Beechey's Voyage*, title page, 391.

11 Hooker, *Icones Plantarum*, tab. 380, which fails to capture the recurved acorn cap scales.

12 Brockway, *Science and Colonial Expansion*, 3, 80.

13 Herbarium specimen records at the Kew Royal Botanic Gardens, http://apps.kew.org/ herbcat/getHomePageResults.do?homePageSearchText=lithocarpus+densiflora&x =14&y=7&homePageSearchOption=scientific_name&nameOfSearchPage=home_ page (accessed April 17, 2014).

14 Hooker and Arnott, *The Botany of Captain Beechey's Voyage*, 315–316. The specimens were not collected by anyone on the voyage; rather, they are discussed in a "California Supplement" at the end of the treatise based on Douglas's specimens. Clarification regarding type specimen status from Heather Lindon, Royal Botanic Gardens, Kew, e-mail to the author, April 11, 2014.

15 Findlen, *Possessing Nature*, 4.

16 Michaux, *The North American Sylva*.

17 Mitchell and House, *David Douglas*, 181.

18 Hooker and Arnott, *The Botany of Captain Beechey's Voyage*, title page, 391.

19 Ørsted, "Bidrag til Egeslægtens Systematik," 83.

20 Jepson, *The Silva of California*, 238.

21 Common name used in Carr, "Shoe Trees," 8, and Marston, "Leather with Personality."

22 Tanoak is referred to as chestnut oak in multiple late nineteenth- and early twentieth-century sources, including "California Made Leather"; Greene, *Illustrations of West American Oaks*, 42; and Jepson, *The Silva of California*, 238. Note that this same common name is also used to refer to *Quercus montana* and the now unaccepted taxon *Quercus prinus*.

23 California State Board of Forestry, "Wattles," 37.

24 California State Board of Forestry, *First Biennial Report*, 179.

25 Bolander, "Remarks on California Trees," 231.

26 Ørsted, "Bidrag til Egeslægtens Systematik," 22, 26, 60, 80–81.

27 Munz, *A California Flora*, 902, 1553. See also Rehder, *Manual of Cultivated Trees and Shrubs*, 152.

28 Munz, *A California Flora*, 902.

29 Bailey, *The Standard Cyclopedia of Horticulture*, 6:3569.

30 Ibid.

31 Koidzumi, "Classification of Castaneaceae."

32 Manos, Cannon, and Oh, "Phylogenetic Relationships and Taxonomic Status," 181.

33 Harris, Harris, and James, *Oak*, 77.

34 Jackson, *Crabgrass Frontier*, 125.

35 Harris, Harris, and James, *Oak*, 64.

36 Logan, *Oak*, 250–253. See also Harris, Harris, and James, *Oak*, 125.

37 Marsh, *Nature and Man*, 260.

38 Miller, "The Pivotal Decade," 8–9.

39 Langston, *Forest Dreams, Forest Nightmares*, 104.

40 *Noyo Chief*, June 1960, 4.

41   Michael Williams, *Americans and Their Forests*, 357.
42   Ibid., 349.
43   Wiemann, "Characteristics and Availability" 2–9–2–10.
44   Schniewind, "Strength and Related Properties of Tanoak," no page numbers.
45   "Tanbark Oak of California."
46   Jepson, *The Trees of California*, 177.
47   Jepson, "Tanbark Oak," 23.
48   Ellwood, "Problems and Prospects."
49   "Californians Pioneer Tanoak," 67.
50   Cronise, *The Natural Wealth of California*, 131, and Rowland, "Early Santa Cruz Industry," 1.
51   Roy, "California Hardwoods," 185.
52   Huber and McDonald, "California's Hardwood Resource," 6.
53   Bolander, "Remarks on California Trees," 231.
54   Mast, "Tanoak Utilization Story," 31.
55   Engelmann, "About the Oaks," 380.
56   Armstrong, "New Uses for Tan-bark Oak."
57   Huber and McDonald, "California's Hardwood Resource," 5.
58   Jepson, *The Silva of California*, 237.
59   Economic Development Administration, "Hoopa Valley Reservation Hardwood Study Report," 13.
60   Jackson, *Crabgrass Frontier*, 124–128, 292.
61   Farmer, *Trees in Paradise*, 46–47.
62   Fearing, "An Engineering Study, 7.
63   Conifers lack vessel elements and have relatively little axial parenchyma. Parenchyma cells are the most common cell type in plants. They occur in many types of tissue including the rays of wood that radiate outward from the core of a tree trunk like the spokes of a wheel.
64   Tanoak wood contains two different water-conducting cells (tracheids and vessel elements of different diameters), several types of fibers, and parenchyma cells.
65   Boone et al., "Quality Drying of Hardwood Lumber," 6.
66   Shelly and Quarles, "The Past, Present, and Future," 122.
67   Shelly, "Does It Make 'Cents'?"
68   Espenas, "The Seasoning of One-Inch Tanoak Lumber," 15.
69   Cornford, *Workers and Dissent*, 94–98.
70   Buckley, "A Factory without a Roof," 79.
71   Schwantes, *The Pacific Northwest*, 390.
72   "This Sort of Thing."
73   Cornford, *Workers and Dissent*, 215.
74   Ibid., 216.
75   Rajala, *Clearcutting the Pacific Rain Forest*, 30.
76   Ibid., 38.
77   Jepson, "Tanbark Oak," 16.
78   Roy, "Killing Tanoak," 1–9.
79   Roy, "California Hardwoods," 184.
80   Fisher "Humboldt County Hardwoods," 1, 7.
81   Huber and McDonald, "California's Hardwood Resource," 1.
82   Armstrong, "New Uses for Tan-bark Oak."

83 Ibid.

84 Jepson, "Tanbark Oak," 23.

85 Sudworth, *Forest Trees*, 320–321.

86 Gerald W. Williams, *The Forest Service*, 298–299.

87 Betts, "Utilization," 32, 29, 31.

88 Huber and McDonald, "California's Hardwood Resource," 1, 3; and Betts, "Utilization," plate VII.

89 Pfeiffer, "The Case for Northwest Hardwoods," 10.

90 Schniewind, "Strength and Related Properties of Tanoak," no page numbers.

91 Ibid.

92 Roy, "Killing Tanoak," 1.

93 Roy, "California Hardwoods," 185.

94 The organization later changed its name to the Western Hardwood Association.

95 Ellwood, "Problems and Prospects," no page numbers.

96 McDonald and Tappeiner, "Silviculture, Ecology, and Management of Tanoak," 65. See also G. H. Sander, "Oregon Hardwoods."

97 Shelly and Quarles, "The Past, Present, and Future," 120.

98 Sullivan, "Economic Potential," 21. See also E. M. Davis, "Machining Madrone"; and Olson, "Gluing Characteristics."

99 Wiemann, "Characteristics and Availability," 2–9.

100 "Californians Pioneer Tanoak," 66–67.

101 Ibid., 67.

102 Levene and Miklose, *Fort Bragg Remembered*, 154.

103 Barth, "A New Look at Coast Hardwoods," 3–4.

104 Shelly, "Does It Make 'Cents'?"

105 Ibid.

106 Allan Holmes, retired Union Lumber Company mill worker, telephone conversation with the author, July 26, 1996.

107 Transcript of Doweloc panel discussion, December 11, 1993, at College of the Redwoods, Fort Bragg, California. Hosted by the Mendocino Forest Conservation Trust and facilitated by Don Nelson. Excerpts from tape 1, side 1 (Disk-Hardwood/File-1DL1293). Copies of the transcript were deposited at the Mendocino County Museum in Willets, California, and the Guest House Museum in Fort Bragg, California.

108 Ibid.

109 Mast, "Tanoak Utilization Story," 31.

110 Ibid.

111 McDonald, introduction to "Tanoak . . . a Bibliography."

112 Ibid.

113 Ibid.

114 Sander and Rosen, "Oak," 10.

115 Roy, "Silvical Characteristics of Tanoak," 13.

116 Sullivan, "Economic Potential," 2.

117 Oswald, "Timber Resources," 7–8.

118 Bolsinger, "Hardwoods of California's Timberlands," 51.

119 Shelly, "Does it Make 'Cents'?"

120 Carpenter, Sonderman, and Rast, "Defects in Hardwood Timber," 1.

121 Sullivan, "Economic Potential," 1.

122 Ibid., 5.

123 McDonald and Tappeiner, "Silviculture, Ecology, and Management of Tanoak," 69.
124 Luppold and Thomas, "New Estimates of Hardwood Lumber Exports," 1.
125 Williams and Hanks, *Hardwood Nursery Guide*, 1.
126 Ponder and Bey, "Effects of Calcium Cyanamide," 1.
127 Williams and Hanks, *Hardwood Nursery Guide*, 1.
128 Burns, *Silvicultural Systems*, 30.
129 Jepson, "Tanbark Oak," 17.
130 Tappeiner, McDonald, and Roy, "*Lithocarpus densiflorus*," 420.
131 Huber and McDonald, "California's Hardwood Resource," 12.
132 Shelly, "An Examination of the Oak Woodland," 445.
133 McDonald and Huber, "California's Hardwood Resource: Status," 1.
134 Ibid.
135 Ibid., ii.
136 Ibid.
137 Libby, "Ecology and Management of Coast Redwood."
138 Berlik, Kittredge, and Foster, *The Illusion of Preservation*, 3.
139 Ellwood, "Problems and Prospects," no page numbers.
140 Sullivan, "Economic Potential," 22.
141 Huber and McDonald, "California's Hardwood Resource," 8.
142 Ibid., ii.
143 Barth, "A New Look at Coast Hardwoods," 18.
144 Donald Nelson, "A Hardwood Training Academy for California?," 3. Prepared for the Mendocino Forest Conservation Trust, Fort Bragg, California, in 1995. Unpublished manuscript in the author's possession.
145 Sullivan, "Economic Potential," 23.
146 Jim Anderson, retired from California Department of Forestry and Fire Protection, telephone interview with the author, September 19, 2012. Anderson then became a private consultant on tanoak wood processing.
147 Peterson, "One Man's Trash . . . ," 11, 15–16.
148 Clayton, "Tools of the Future," 27.
149 Anderson, phone interview with the author, September 19, 2012.
150 Peterson, "One Man's Trash . . . ," 15–16.
151 Hight, "Value Added," no page numbers.
152 Barth, "A New Look at Coast Hardwoods," 18.
153 Harper, Metz, and Hrubes, "An Analysis," 20.
154 Hight, "Value Added," no page numbers.
155 Ibid.
156 Harper, Metz, and Hrubes, "An Analysis," synopsis, no page number.
157 Holschuh, "The New Face of Forestry," no page numbers.
158 Christensen, Campbell, and Fried, technical eds., "California's Forest Resources, 2001–2005," 170.
159 Shelly and Quarles, "The Past, Present, and Future," 119.
160 Ibid.
161 Hall, *Management, Manufacture, Marketing*, 151.
162 Ibid., 150.
163 Stine, "Economics of Utilizing Oak," 349.
164 Hall, *Management, Manufacture, Marketing*, 151.
165 Sims, "Pulp Mill Closes for Good."

166 Ibid.
167 Ibid.
168 Shelly and Quarles, "The Past, Present, and Future," 123.
169 Mendell and Lang, *Wood for Bioenergy*, 27.
170 Ibid., 41–42.
171 Tim Harrington, U.S. Forest Service, e-mail to the author, April 4, 2014.
172 "Woody Biomass," University of California Forest Research and Outreach, http://ucanr.edu/sites/forestry/?blogstart=22&blogasset=56962 (accessed May 3, 2014).
173 Hawk, "Branching Out."
174 Swiecki and Bernhardt, "A Reference Manual," 67.
175 Shelly and Quarles, "The Past, Present, and Future," 123.
176 Robert Simpson, timber industry entrepreneur, telephone conversation with the author, July 11, 2014.
177 Shelly and Quarles, "The Past, Present, and Future," 119.

6. PLAGUE

Epigraph: Berkes, *Sacred Ecology*, 75.
1 McPherson et al., "Sudden Oak Death in California," 72.
2 Freinkel, *American Chestnut*, 198.
3 Parke et al., "*Phytophthora ramorum* Colonizes Tanoak Xylem," 1566.
4 Rizzo et al., "*Phytophthora ramorum* as the Cause of Extensive Mortality," 211. See also Rizzo and Garbelotto, "Sudden Oak Death," 197–198.
5 Mascheretti et al., "Reconstruction of the Sudden Oak Death Epidemic," 2756, 2765–2767; and Ivors et al., "Microsatellite Markers," 1493, 1503–1504. See also Rizzo, Garbelotto, and Hansen, "*Phytophthora ramorum*," 311, 315, 327.
6 Rizzo et al., "*Phytophthora ramorum* and Sudden Oak Death," 733, 738–739.
7 Frankel, "Sudden Oak Death," 21. For an updated list of host plants, see Animal and Plant Health Inspection Service (APHIS), "APHIS List of Regulated Hosts."
8 Loo, "Ecological Impacts," 81. See also Vitousek et al., "Biological Invasions."
9 Brasier, "The Biosecurity Threat," 792, 803.
10 Pamela K. Anderson et al., "Emerging Infectious Diseases of Plants," 538. See also Brasier, "The Biosecurity Threat"; Desprez-Loustau et al., "Fungal Dimension of Biological Invasions"; Kluza et al., "Sudden Oak Death," 584; and Loo, "Ecological Impacts."
11 Brasier, "The Biosecurity Threat," 792.
12 Cobb et al., "Ecosystem Transformation," 717.
13 Richard Cobb, University of California, Davis, e-mail to the author, May 29, 2014.
14 Hayden et al., "Will All the Trees Fall?" 1781.
15 Davis et al., "Pre-impact Forest Composition," 2350.
16 Cobb et al., "Biodiversity Conservation," 155.
17 Fichtner, Lynch, and Rizzo, "Detection, Distribution, Survival, and Sporulation," 1366.
18 Yoon, "Puzzling Disease Devastating California Oaks."
19 Evans, "Potential Problems."
20 Kliejunas, "Sudden Oak Death and *Phytophthora ramorum*," 10–11.
21 Susan Frankel, sudden oak death research leader, U.S. Forest Service, interview

with the author, Albany, California, January 19, 2012. See also Frankel, "Sudden Oak Death," 22.

22 Goss et al., "*Phytophthora ramorum* in Canada," 170.
23 Brasier and Kirk, "Production of Gametangia," 826–827.
24 Ibid., 826.
25 Garbelotto et al., "Potential for Sexual Reproduction," 129.
26 Kliejunas, "Sudden Oak Death and *Phytophthora ramorum*," 10–11.
27 Cobb et al., "Biodiversity Conservation," 152.
28 Kliejunas, "Sudden Oak Death and *Phytophthora ramorum*," 37. See also Swiecki and Bernhardt, "A Reference Manual," 71.
29 Cobb et al., "Biodiversity Conservation," 152.
30 Ibid.
31 David M. Rizzo, plant pathology professor and sudden oak death researcher, University of California, Davis, interview with the author, Davis, September 9, 2011.
32 Ortiz, "Contemporary California Indian Uses for Food," 420.
33 Cobb et al., "Biodiversity Conservation," 153.
34 Ibid., 157.
35 Ibid., 158.
36 Ibid., 161.
37 Knighten and Redding, "USDA Takes Action."
38 Kliejunas, "Sudden Oak Death and *Phytophthora ramorum*," 6.
39 Animal and Plant Health Inspection Service (APHIS), United States Department of Agriculture, Confirmed Nursery Protocol.
40 Frankel and Hansen, "Forest *Phytophthora* Diseases," S162.
41 Ibid., S161.
42 Kluza et al., "Sudden Oak Death," 584.
43 Frankel and Hansen, "Forest *Phytophthora* Diseases," S163–164.
44 Frankel, "Sudden Oak Death," 19.
45 Porter and Robertson, "Tracking," 11018.
46 Ibid.
47 Ibid., 11013.
48 Hirsch, "Nursery Group Wins Dispute."
49 Oregon Washington Railroad & Navigation Company v. Washington.
50 Schowalter et al., "Integrating the Ecological Roles," 182.
51 Evans, "Potential Problems.".
52 Frankel and Hansen, "Forest *Phytophthora* Diseases," S159.
53 Brasier, "The Biosecurity Threat," 805.
54 Filipe et al., "Landscape Epidemiology," 2.
55 Kliejunas, "Sudden Oak Death and *Phytophthora ramorum*," 86.
56 Filipe et al., "Landscape Epidemiology," 2.
57 Swiecki et al., "Management of *Phytophthora ramorum*."
58 Kliejunas, "Sudden Oak Death and *Phytophthora ramorum*," 87.
59 Swiecki and Bernhardt, "A Reference Manual," 83.
60 Ibid., 91.
61 Tedmund J. Swiecki, principal at Phytosphere Research, Vacaville, Calif., e-mail to the author, April 4, 2014.
62 Swiecki and Bernhardt, "A Reference Manual," 70.

63 Ibid., 86.

64 Ibid.

65 Ibid., 87.

66 Meentemeyer et al., "Mapping the Risk," 195, 197, 213–214.

67 Filipe et al., "Strategies for Control," 124.

68 Meentemeyer et al., "Early Detection," 377.

69 Filipe et al., "Landscape Epidemiology," 3.

70 Bureau of Land Management, "Applying Glyphosate on Tanoak," Environmental Assessment, 3.

71 Filipe et al., "Landscape Epidemiology," 3.

72 Meentemeyer et al., "Epidemiological Modeling of Invasion," 16.

73 Filipe et al., "Strategies for Control," 122.

74 Ibid.

75 Meentemeyer et al., "Epidemiological Modeling of Invasion," 1, 12, 16.

76 California Oak Mortality Task Force, "California Oak Mortality Task Force Report," August 2014, Newsletter Archive, http://www.suddenoakdeath.org/wp-content/uploads/2014/08/COMTF-Report-August-2014.pdf (accessed October 8, 2014).

77 Bueno, Deshais, and Arguello, "Waiting for SOD," 297.

78 Ibid., 298–299.

79 Swiecki and Bernhardt, "A Reference Manual," 43.

80 Cobb et al., "Ecosystem Transformation," 712.

81 Oak Mortality Task Force, "Ecology of Tree Diseases."

82 Rizzo and Slaughter, "Root Disease and Canopy Gaps," 160.

83 Moritz and Odion, "Examining the Strength and Possible Causes," 112.

84 Lee, "Sudden Oak Death and Fire," 1, 6.

85 Ibid.

86 Ibid., 4.

87 Moritz and Odion, "Examining the Strength and Possible Causes," 106.

88 Meentemeyer et al., "Influence of Land-Cover Change," 160.

89 Ibid., 159.

90 Ibid., 160.

91 Kelly, "Erratic, Extreme Day-to-Day Weather." See also Medvigy and Beaulieu, "Trends."

92 Meentemeyer et al., "Epidemiological Modeling of Invasion," 11.

93 Kliejunas, "Sudden Oak Death and *Phytophthora ramorum*," 40.

94 Eyre, Kozanitas, and Garbelotto, "Population Dynamics," 1148.

95 Metz et al., "Interacting Disturbances," 318.

96 Swiecki and Bernhardt, "A Reference Manual," 51.

97 Loo, "Ecological Impacts," 93.

98 Cobb et al., "Biodiversity Conservation," 154.

99 Freinkel, *American Chestnut*, 139.

100 Cobb et al., "Biodiversity Conservation," 160. See also Rizzo, Garbelotto, and Hansen, "*Phytophthora ramorum*," 327.

101 Guerrant, "Characterizing Two Decades," 9.

102 Kramer and Pence, "The Challenges of *Ex-Situ*," 94–95.

103 Ibid., 91.

104 Ed Guerrant, Jr., director, Rae Selling Berry Seed Bank & Plant Conservation Program, Portland State University, Ore., e-mail to the author, January 26, 2014.

105 Ibid.

106 Kramer and Pence, "The Challenges of Ex-Situ," 95–96, 100–101.
107 Guerrant, "Characterizing Two Decades," 18.
108 Kramer and Pence, "The Challenges of Ex-Situ," 95.
109 Dodd et al., "Genetic Structure of Notholithocarpus densiflorus," 131.
110 Tappeiner et al., "Lithocarpus densiflorus," 422.
111 Katherine Hayden, former research associate, Environmental Science, Policy, and Management, University of California, Berkeley (now a postdoctoral fellow at Tree-Microbe Interactions, INRA, University of Lorraine, Nancy, France), e-mail to the author, June 23, 2014.
112 Frank Lake, research ecologist, U.S. Forest Service, Orleans, Calif., e-mail to the author, February 21, 2014.
113 Bowcutt, "Tanoak Conservation," 106–107.
114 MacLeod et al., "Evolution," 60.
115 Bowcutt, "Tanoak Landscapes."

7. LANDSCAPES

Epigraph: Langston, Forest Dreams, Forest Nightmares, 10.
1 Bicknell et al., "Sinkyone Wilderness State Park." Unpublished report in author's possession. See also Bowcutt, "A Floristic Study"; and Bowcutt, "Tanoak Target."
2 Briles, Whitlock, and Bartlein, "Postglacial Vegetation, Fire, and Climate History," 53. The authors provide their time spans in calibrated years BP. Note that BP means "before present," which is set at before 1950.
3 Ibid., 47. This claim is further supported by the fact that extant tanoak and chinquapin pollen appear to be indistinguishable based on light microscopic study of Estella Leopold's reference collection at the University of Washington, Seattle.
4 Anderson and Carpenter, "Vegetation Change," 11.
5 Bicknell et al., "Sinkyone Wilderness State Park."
6 Bowcutt, "A Floristic Study," 90.
7 Loud, "Ethnography and Archaeology," 230–231.
8 Schenck and Gifford, "Karok Ethnobotany," 382. See also Beard, The Wappo, 52; Harold E. Driver, "Culture Element Distributions," 314, 381; and Stewart, Forgotten Fires, 278, 282–283.
9 Beard, The Wappo, 52. See also Driver, "Culture Element Distributions," 314, 381.
10 Gould, "Ecology and Adaptive Response," 60.
11 Nomland, "Sinkyone Notes," 153.
12 Kroeber, "Sinkyone Tales," 347.
13 Anderson and Lake, "California Indian Ethnomycology," 69.
14 Stewart, Forgotten Fires, 277–278.
15 Kniffen, "Pomo Geography," 373.
16 Schenck and Gifford, "Karok Ethnobotany," 382.
17 Vander Wall, "Evolutionary Ecology," 88. See also Roy, "A Record," 2–3; and Warburton and Endert, Indian Lore, 104–105.
18 Roy, "A Record," 2.
19 M. Kat Anderson, Tending the Wild, 288–289.
20 Jepson, A Manual, 278.
21 Low spring temperatures commonly kill oak (Quercus) flowers in Michigan and West Virginia. See Gysel, "Measurement of Acorn Crops," 306.

22 Gifford, "Ethnographic Notes," 45.
23 Henry T. Lewis, "Patterns of Indian Burning," 74.
24 Stewart, *Forgotten Fires*, 277–278.
25 Anderson and Lake, "California Indian Ethnomycology," 69–70.
26 Boyd, *Indians, Fire and the Land*, 94–163; and Stewart, *Forgotten Fires*, 251–259, 272–283.
27 Weiser and Lepofsky, "Ancient Land Use," 188.
28 Ibid., 185.
29 Jepson, *The Silva of California*, 11.
30 Jepson, "Tanbark Oak," 19.
31 Ibid., 19–20.
32 Ibid., 20.
33 Ibid. See also Stewart, *Forgotten Fires*, 277–278.
34 Ibid., 23
35 Agee, *Fire Ecology of Pacific Northwest Forests*, 190, 199.
36 Plumb and McDonald, "Oak Management in California," 10.
37 Preston, "Serpent in the Garden," 272–273.
38 Cook, *The Conflict* , 289.
39 Carranco and Beard, *Genocide and Vendetta*, 42.
40 Hurtado, *Indian Survival*, 167.
41 Residents of Mendocino to Robert White, May 1, 1855. Letters Received by the Office of Indian Affairs, 1824–81. National Archives Mf., record group 75, series microcopy no. 234, roll 34.
42 Coy, *The Humboldt Bay Region*, 152–154. See also Carranco and Beard, *Genocide and Vendetta*.
43 California Senate, "Majority and Minority Reports of the Special Joint Committee on the Mendocino War," *Appendix to the Journal of the California Senate*, 11th session, 4.
44 California Senate, "Majority and Minority Reports," 3–5, 54.
45 Ibid., 4.
46 Browne, *The Coast Rangers*, 43.
47 Palmer, *History of Mendocino County*, 590.
48 Merriam, "The Acorn," 136.
49 Lightfoot, *Indians, Missionaries, and Merchants*, 86–87.
50 Bledsoe, *Indian Wars*, 286.
51 M. Kat Anderson, *Tending the Wild*, 349.
52 Powell, *Report*, 17–18.
53 Pyne, *America's Fires*, 23.
54 Pyne, *Fire in America*, 192–193.
55 Pyne, *America's Fires*, 28.
56 Jepson, *The Silva of California*, 16.
57 Ibid.
58 Jepson, *The Trees of California*, 31.
59 Jepson, "Tanbark Oak," 23.
60 Ibid.
61 Leopold, "'Piute Forestry' vs. Forest Fire Prevention," 69. This essay was originally published in 1920.
62 Ibid., 70.

63 Ibid., 68.
64 Pyne, *America's Fires*, 30.
65 M. Kat Anderson, *Tending the Wild*, 221.
66 Essene, "Cultural Element Distributions," vii, 55.
67 Ibid., 55.
68 Lake, *Traditional Ecological Knowledge*, 68, 463, 468, 666.
69 Anderson and Lake, "California Indian Ethnomycology," 70.
70 Pyne, *Fire in America*, 424–449.
71 Lake, *Traditional Ecological Knowledge*, 296–297.
72 For an accessible historical summary, see Pyne, *America's Fires*, ch. 5.
73 Pyne, *Fire in America*, 300–302.
74 Pyne, *America's Fires*, x.
75 California Indian Forest and Fire Management Council, "History," http://ciffmc. stormloader.com/History.html (accessed April 19, 2014).
76 California Indian Forest and Fire Management Council, "Purpose," http://ciffmc. stormloader.com/Purposes.html (accessed April 19, 2014).
77 Garibaldi and Turner, "Cultural Keystone Species," 13.

8. PARTNERSHIPS

Epigraph: State of California Government Code Section 54950, http://www.leginfo. ca.gov/cgi-bin/displaycode?section=gov&group=54001–55000&file=54950-54963 (accessed May 17, 2014).
1   Ortiz, "Contemporary California Indian Uses," 421, 425.
2   MacLeod et al., "Evolution," 58.
3   Wilkinson, McDonald, and Morgan, "Tanoak Sprout Development," 21. Although the Hoopa Valley Tribe does manage against tanoak in other areas of the reservation in favor of conifers for timber, they do not use herbicides, which was prohibited in 1978 by tribal ordinance.
4   McDonald and Huber, "California's Hardwood Resource: Managing," 8. See also McDonald and Tappeiner, "Silviculture, Ecology, and Management," 68.
5   Hosten et al., "Oak Woodlands and Savannas," 83. See also Reed and Sugihara, "Northern Oak Woodlands," 59–63.
6   Devine and Harrington, "Restoration Release," 93.
7   Berkes, *Sacred Ecology*, 23.
8   Kat Anderson, "Native Californians," 173.
9   Ibid., 155.
10 Middleton, *Trust in the Land*, 49–50, 52–57.
11 Wood and Welcker, "Tribes as Trustees Again (Part I)," 432.
12 Kat Anderson, "Native Californians," 173.
13 Colegrove, "The Forest."
14 Wood and Welcker, "Tribes as Trustees Again (Part I)," 375.
15 Ibid, 374.
16 Merv George interview, "Faces of the Forest Service," U.S. Forest Service Office of Communication, http://www.fs.fed.us/news/2012/faces/george/index.shtml (accessed April 19, 2014).
17 Lake, *Traditional Ecological Knowledge*, 337, 309, respectively
18 Diekmann, Panich, and Striplen, "Native American Management," 49.

19 Senos et al., "Traditional Ecological Knowledge," 402–404.
20 Lake, *Traditional Ecological Knowledge*, 297.
21 Senos et al., "Traditional Ecological Knowledge," 402.
22 Ibid., 397.
23 Arguello, "Case Study."
24 National Parks Conservation Association, "Redwood National and State Parks."
25 Ibid. and Arguello, "Case Study."
26 Senos et al., "Traditional Ecological Knowledge."
27 U.S. Department of Agriculture, Research, Education, and Economics Information System, "Enhancing Tribal Health and Food Security."
28 Ibid.
29 Garibaldi and Turner, "Cultural Keystone Species."
30 Laura Lee George, Hoopa, California, e-mail to the author, April 18, 2014.
31 Ortiz, "Contemporary California Indian Uses," 421.
32 Garibaldi and Turner, "Cultural Keystone Species."
33 McCarthy, "Managing Oaks," 213. See also Ortiz, "Contemporary California Indian Uses," 421.
34 Garibaldi and Turner, "Cultural Keystone Species."
35 Ibid.
36 Centers for Disease Control and Prevention, "Traditional Foods Project."
37 Acton et al., "Trends in Diabetes Prevalence," 1485.
38 Norgaard, "The Effects of Altered Diet," 6.
39 Meyers, Swiecki, and Mitchell, "Understanding the Native Californian Diet," 7686.
40 The Cultural Conservancy, "Indigenous Health/Native Circle of Food," 2010, http://www.nativeland.org/native_circle.html (accessed September 18, 2014); California Rural Indian Health Board, "Advancing California Opportunities to Renew Native health systems (ACORNS)," http://www.crihbacorns.org (January 22, 2015).
41 United Nations, "Declaration of the Rights of Indigenous Peoples," 2008, 6, 8, 10, 12, http://www.un.org/esa/socdev/unpfii/documents/DRIPS_en.pdf (accessed September 18, 2014).
42 Romero, "Tribal Consultation."
43 Norgaard, "The Effects of Altered Diet," 1.
44 Winnie Marshall, "The Art of Making Acorn Soup," reproduced in newsletter for Phoebe A. Hearst Museum of Anthropology, University of California, 2008, http://hearstmuseum.berkeley.edu/community/newsletter/2008-fall (accessed September 17, 2014).

CONCLUSIONS

Epigraph: Hardin, *Filters against Folly*, v.

1   Legrève and Duveiller, "Preventing Potential Disease and Pest Epidemics," 56.

GLOSSARY

aggregate. A cluster of individual units, such as an aggregation of flowers.

barrel staves. Boards of wood joined along their vertical edges that make up a barrel.

basal area. The cross-sectional area occupied by each tree trunk measured at 4.5 feet aboveground. Often used in forestry to measure tree density based on an approximation of the sum of the basal areas of all tree trunks within a specified geographic area.

binomial. The scientific name or genus and species names of a plant, animal, or other living organism; "bi" means "two," "nomen" means "name." For example, *Notholithocarpus densiflorus* is the binomial for tanoak.

biofuel. A fuel derived from plants or other living organisms.

biogeography. The study of distribution patterns of biological organisms.

biological control. An approach to pest management that involves the use of parasites, predators, or diseases of pest species.

biomass. The total mass of organic material derived from plants or other organisms in a particular area or volume. Also such materials that are used as fuel.

board feet. A unit of volume for lumber equal to twelve inches by twelve inches by one inch.

bole. A tree trunk; typically refers to a straight trunk useful for making lumber.

bract. A modified leaf, often with a specialized function, such as protection of a reproductive organ.

burl. A knotty or lumpy outgrowth on a tree that typically is hemispheric in shape.

canker. An open sore in plant tissue caused by infection or injury.

catkin. A kind of flowering cluster, usually a spike, that is unisexual, either male or female. The clusters bear scaly bracts and usually petal-less flowers. Examples of trees with catkins include tanoak, alder, and willow. Also known as an ament.

chipping. The process of grinding up wood and woody debris into small chunks.

chrome tanning. The process of converting animal hides to leather that uses chromium salts instead of tannic acid. It requires open-pit mining of chromium; tannic acid derived from plants, in contrast, is a renewable resource.

clear-cutting. An approach to logging that involves removal of all the trees.

commodity. A material object or service that is bought and sold in a marketplace.

conifer. A cone-bearing plant in the phylum Coniferophyta; usually a tree with needles or scales for leaves, occasionally a shrub. Examples include Douglas-fir and redwood.

cooper. Someone who makes barrels.

coppice. Group of trees or shrubs periodically cut at ground level in order to stimulate new growth that typically is straight and, as a result, suitable when green for making baskets, wattle fences, and other woven items. Older coppice growth may be used for firewood or even timber.

corvid. A group of smarter-than-average birds that includes jays, crows, and ravens.

Cretaceous. The last period of the Mesozoic era occurring roughly between 146 million to 65 million years ago.

creosote. A dark brown oil distilled from coal tar that is used to prevent rotting of wood. Commonly used for railroad ties, telephone poles, and pier pilings.

cryogenics. The science and application of using very low temperatures, in the case of seeds to suspend growth and extend embryo viability for long-term storage and future use.

cryopreservation. A conservation method that slows degradation using sub-zero temperatures with limited damage to tissues during the freezing process. A method used to extend the life of seeds, extracted plant embryos, and other plant material to protect them for future use.

cultural landscape. A landscape that is shaped intentionally by people to meet particular cultural needs.

cupule. A small cuplike structure, for example, an acorn cup.

deciduous. A plant that loses its leaves during a period of dormancy, typically during the winter.

decoction. A strong tea made by boiling bark, roots, or other hard plant parts in water for the purpose of extracting active chemical constituents.

demoiselles. French for "young women."

dendrology. The study of trees.

defoliant. A toxic substance that causes plants to drop their leaves.

drip tip. The end of a leaf that tapers narrowly to a point, allowing rain to drip off easily. A common feature in tropical and semitropical ecosystems with high rainfall.

dimensional lumber. A board of wood cut to particular measurements, such as a two-by-four-foot board.

dog-hole. A small shipping port between southern Oregon and central California that served small schooners during the late nineteenth and early twentieth centuries. With the exception of Coos Bay, Monterey Bay, and San Francisco Bay, the rugged topography of this coastline restricted access to only the more maneuverable boats.

Druid. A priest of the ancient Celtic religion practiced by people who revered oaks as sacred in parts of Europe including the British Isles.

economic botany. The study of the plants that people use for food, fiber, medicine, or recreation, or for aesthetic reasons such as gardens; the study of economically important plants.

ecosystem. A community of organisms functioning as a unit, interacting with one another and their physical environment.

ectomycorrhizae. A kind of mutually beneficial relationship between a fungus and various plants. The fungal partner grows around the roots and between cell walls and allows for increased water and mineral uptake by the plant in exchange for some of the carbohydrates the plant produces through photosynthesis.

Eocene. An epoch that occurred between the Paleocene and Oligocene and lasted from roughly 55.8 million to 33.9 million years ago.

epicormic buds. Dormant buds that can rapidly generate sprouts after injury, such as on a stump after logging or on a burl at the base of a tree after a fire.

epidemiology. The study of diseases and how they affect their host populations.

ethnobotany. The study of the relationships between plants and people. Term often used to refer to the practices of indigenous peoples.

ethnography. A research method that involves interviewing and recording information gleaned from members of a definable social group, such as people in a particular tribe or occupation; used in anthropology and oral history.

evolution. The biological process by which organisms change over time to adapt to their environment through natural selection or survival of the fittest.

extant. Still living, not extinct.

fissure. A crack.

fodder. Plant material used to feed livestock.

forage. Plant material used to feed livestock in the field.

fossil. The remains, imprints, or traces of prehistoric organisms conserved in petrified form or as a rock mold or a stone cast.

foundation species. A species that significantly affects community structure through its impact on ecosystem function. Its demise would thus result in significant ecosystem change.

friable or friability. Easily crumbled; a characteristic of healthy soil.

genus, genera (plural). A category in the nested classification used by taxonomists to cluster closely related plants, animals, and other living organisms. It is the first name of a binomial or scientific name, for example, tanoak (*Notholithocarpus densiflorus*) is in the genus *Notholithocarpus*.

germinate. The process of a spore or a seed beginning to grow after a period of dormancy.

glaciation. The effect on the land when a glacier moves across it.

glacier. A large sheet of ice that moves slowly down a mountain slope, across a valley, or over a wide swath of land.

granary. A place to store grain such as corn. Also used for acorn string structures.

grazing commons. A shared pasture or other community-owned place for grazing livestock.

girdle. Removal of bark in a complete circle around the trunk of a tree. This removes the vascular tissue that conducts the carbohydrates made through photosynthesis that the plant needs for root functioning; thus the tree usually dies after being girdled.

glyphosate. A synthetic herbicide that travels throughout the plant body via the vascular system. It is more effective on perennial plants than on annuals.

growth ring. Layers of secondary xylem, or woody water-conducting tissue, laid down annually in temperate regions that are used for gauging the age of trees and some shrubs.

hardwood. A tree with flowers, such as alder, beech, dogwood, maple, and tanoak. Also the wood produced by hardwood trees. Contrast with softwood trees, which are conifers.

heart rot. Decomposition of the wood in the center of a tree; interferes with accurately determining the age of the tree.

heartwood. Older wood in the center of a tree or shrub that has stored secondary metabolites, or biochemical compounds produced by the plant. Tannins found in heartwood typically darken it relative to the younger sapwood that surrounds it.

herbs or herbaceous. Plants that live for one year (annuals) or for multiple years (perennial herbs), in which case they usually die to the ground each winter in regions with frost.

herbarium. A repository or research facility dedicated to maintaining specimens that typically are dried, pressed plant material glued and/or taped to archival paper with a label listing when and where they were collected and by whom.

herbicide. A substance that is toxic to plants or a group of plants and is used to weed chemically, with lower labor costs than for manual removal.

hinterland. An area, typically remote, that is exploited for resources by a distant town, city, or port.

Holocene. The current epoch in the Cenozoic era and the Quaternary period. It follows the Pleistocene and spans from about 11,700 years ago to the present.

hopper basket. A bowl-like woven object with a hole in the bottom that is placed on top of a mortar to keep the meal that is being ground or pounded from spilling out.

horticulture. The study and practice of growing garden plants for food and as ornamentals.

hulling. The process of removing the outer covering of a fruit or seed.

inflorescence. An aggregation or cluster of flowers.

inoculate. To introduce a disease-causing microorganism into a suitable host.

in vitro. Occurring in a test tube, a petri dish, or other location outside of a living organism.

irrigation. Supplemental water for growing plants beyond what is naturally available through rain, groundwater, and the like. Often delivered via hoses, sprinklers, ditches, and similar means of conveyance.

laissez-faire capitalism. An economic system unregulated by governments.

leach. The process of removing a chemical constituent using water or another liquid.

macrofossil. Preserved prehistoric organic remains that are visible without a microscope.

Manifest Destiny. The widespread belief in the nineteenth century that Euro-Americans were destined to colonize western North America.

margin. The edge of a plant structure, such as a leaf or petal.

mast. A bumper crop of seeds produced by plants that vary the volume of seeds they produce annually in part to limit the ability of herbivores such as squirrels to build up their populations.

mating type. A strain found in sexually reproducing plants, animals, fungi, water molds, and other eukaryotes that can mate and produce offspring only with the other strain or strains of the same species. Compatibility is regulated on a genetic level.

microfossil. Preserved prehistoric organic remains that require microscopy for study.

micromorphology. The study of microscopic external form, for example, the shape or external patterning of a pollen grain.

mineral staining. Discoloration of hardwood attributed to a variety of causes and not well understood. It typically is considered a defect that diminishes the value of the wood.

Miocene. A prehistoric block of time occurring between the Oligocene and Pliocene, roughly from 23 million to 5.3 million years ago.

monoculture. A system of agricultural or silvicultural production that focuses on a single species, for example, a corn or a Douglas-fir monoculture. Critics argue that monocultures are environmentally unsustainable because they deplete the soil and are vulnerable to pests and diseases.

monophyletic. An evolutionary lineage derived from one shared ancestor.

morphology. The study of external form, for example, the morph of a plant.

mutant. Genetic alteration of an organism that results in a change from typical morphology and/or other characteristics that may be transmitted to successive generations.

mycorrhizae. Fungi in a mutualistic relationship with various plants found in association with the roots. The fungal partner increases water and mineral uptake by the plant in exchange for some of the carbohydrates the plant produces through photosynthesis.

narrow-gauge railroad. A railway with tracks that are narrower than standard tracks. They are cheaper to install and so are more cost-effective in mountainous and/or sparsely populated regions.

Neogene. A prehistoric block of time occurring during the Cenozoic Era, made up of the Miocene and Pliocene epochs, lasting from about 23 million to 2.6 million years ago.

nomenclature. A system of naming applied to organisms and the related groups they occur in. For example, the binomial *Notholithocarpus densiflorus* includes a genus name and a specific epithet. The name of the family it occurs in is Fagaceae.

old growth. A mature forest or tree that has never been logged.

Oligocene. A prehistoric block of time during the Cenozoic Era, between the Eocene and Miocene epochs, lasting from 33.9 million to 23 million years ago.

oospore. A one-celled reproductive structure produced by some water molds, fungi, and algae that is also a thick-walled zygote formed through sexual reproduction.

orographic effect. When a mountain or mountain range forces moisture-laden air to rise, and the air's capacity to hold the water decreases as it rises, which can result in rain or snow. As the air from prevailing storms then descends on the lee side, the air is drier, typically resulting in a rain shadow.

overstory trees. The tallest trees that dominate in a forest and make up the upper canopy.

paleobotany. The study of extinct plant forms, often through the use of macrofossils and/or phytoliths.

paleoendemic. An organism whose geographic distribution has been much restricted due to changes in environmental conditions, such as redwoods.

paleontology. The study of life forms by means of fossils.

paleospecies. Species from the geologic past.

paleotaxa. Taxa from the geologic past.

phloem. Specialized tissue in vascular plants that conducts carbohydrates made through photosynthesis.

phylum. A taxonomic group that ranks above class and below kingdom in a nested and hierarchical taxonomic system of classification used for plants and other living things.

phytolith. Microscopic silica particles produced by many plants between and in cells. These highly decay-resistant silica deposits are used to study vegetation change over time. Through features such as shape, texture, size, and symmetry, phytolith microfossils can indicate the presence of particular plants in the past.

pistil. Female reproductive organ of flowering plants.

plantation. An area, normally of many acres, planted with a commercially valuable crop such as coffee, sugar, tobacco, rubber, or Douglas-fir. Production often exploits labor and typically serves distant markets rather than local needs.

plant pathology. The study of plant diseases.

plant pathologist. A scientist who studies plant diseases.

Pleistocene. A prehistoric block of time during the Quaternary period, between the Pliocene and Holocene epochs, lasting from 2.6 million to about 11,700 years ago.

Pliocene. A prehistoric block of time between the Miocene and Pleistocene epochs, lasting from 5.3 million to 2.6 million years ago. Nested within the Neogene period, formerly placed in the Tertiary period, which is no longer recognized by the International Commission on Stratigraphy.

pollen. A microscopic structure produced by a male organ in a flower or by a male cone; it travels via the wind, insects, birds or other means of transport to female structures in the same species, which it pollinates and fertilizes so that it will produce seeds.

pollen ornamentation. Patterns on the outside of a pollen grain that vary by species. Ragweed pollen, a common irritant for hayfever sufferers, is ornamented with spikes.

pollination. The process by which pollen is transferred to the stigma of a flower.

polyphyletic. An evolutionary lineage derived from multiple ancestors.

pulp. A slurry of cotton, linen, wood, or other plant-based material used in papermaking.

Quaternary. The most recent period in the Cenozoic era, comprising the Pleistocene and

Holocene epochs, that spans from about 2.6 million years ago to the present.

refugia. A safe place where an organism can retreat when under attack or when conditions are not conducive to its survival or capacity to thrive.

rain shadow. An area of reduced rainfall on the side of a mountain or mountains opposite the side that faces the prevailing storms, so that most of the precipitation has already fallen by the time an air mass reaches it, resulting in drier conditions. See "orographic effect."

revolute. Curved backward, as in the edge of a leaf.

root crown. The top of the root system where one or more stems of a plant originate.

rotation. A production regime in which one type of crop plant alternates with another in order to avoid depleting the soil, for example, rotating nitrogen-fixing alders with Douglas-fir.

sapling. A young tree.

sapwood. Younger wood in a tree or shrub that is between the heartwood and the bark.

sawlog. A cut tree trunk of a suitable species that is large enough to be cut into timber.

sawtimber. Trees or logs suitable for making lumber.

scanning electron microscope. A means of high magnification that creates an image of the surface of a specimen using electrons as a source of illumination instead of visible light.

schooner. A ship with fore-and-aft sails on two or more masts, usually with the shorter foremast toward the front and the larger mainmast in the center.

secondary vein. An aggregation of vascular tissue in a leaf that branches off a main midrib or other primary vein.

secondary xylem. Also known as wood, specialized tissue in vascular plants that conducts water and moves minerals. The cells are more lignified than the conducting cells in primary xylem. Unlike primary xylem, wood originates from a lateral meristem called the "vascular cambium."

seed. A reproductive structure found in many plants that contains an embryonic plant along with nutritious tissue to support it and a hardened exterior coat to protect the contents.

seedling. The young plant that establishes after a seed has germinated and the embryo inside has started to grow.

seed set. A measure of reproductive output in a seed plant.

serrate. Regular teeth along a margin or edge, typically of a leaf.

silviculture. The study of how to most efficiently produce lumber and other forest products from trees.

simple leaf. A leaf whose blade or broad section is not divided into leaflets like lupine leaves.

social Darwinism. A system of organizing human society based on essentialist notions about race, class, and gender. Note that Darwin claimed he was not a social Darwinist.

softwood. A conifer tree and the wood generated from a coniferous tree. Contrast with hardwood trees, which are flowering, not cone-bearing, trees.

species. A group of organisms capable of exchanging genes, for example, through breeding, and producing reproductively viable offspring. In a scientific name, the species name follows the genus name.

spike. A kind of aggregation of flowers, also known as an inflorescence, in which each individual flower lacks a stalk.

sporangium. A sack in which spores are made and held until they are dispersed.

spore. A one-celled reproductive structure typically found in plants, fungi, algae, water molds, protozoa, and the like.

sporulate. The act of releasing spores.

sprout. A shoot of a plant, for example, from a seed or a sucker from a tree stump.

stamen. Male reproductive organ of most flowering plants, made up of sacks of pollen inside the anther, which is held up by a stalk called a "filament."

staves. The wooden boards that make up a barrel.

steam donkey. A steam-powered winch formerly used in logging, bark extraction, mining, and other industries that required pulling something or letting it out with a cable, rope, or other line.

stigma. The receptive portion of the female structure in a flower where pollen grains from the same species land or are transported and have the potential to germinate.

style. The middle section of the pistil, or female structure, found in flowers. It connects the stigma with the ovary, which contains one or more seeds when mature.

subfamily. A subcategory in nested classification under the rank of family sometimes used by taxonomists to cluster closely related plants, animals, and other living organisms.

subtend. Attached below, as in the red bracts of a poinsettia that subtend the tiny, inconspicuous flowers.

sucker. A vegetative shoot that grows from a cut trunk or branch or from the roots of a tree or shrub. It typically is straight and as a result is useful when green for making baskets, wattle fences, and other woven items.

tannery. A production facility dedicated to converting animal hides into leather.

tannic acid. A complex mixture of polyphenolic compounds useful for processing animal hides into leather. The mixture varies depending on the source but typically includes compounds derived from tannins that occur naturally in many plants.

taxon, taxa (plural). Any ranked taxonomic group, such as species, genus, family, order, or class.

taxonomist. A scientist who classifies and/or names biological organisms.

tectonic or tectonism. Of or relating to the structure of the earth's crust and its large-scale processes.

Tertiary. A prehistoric block of time, the first period of the Cenozoic era, between the Cretaceous and Quaternary periods, lasting from about 65 million to 1.6 million years ago. An old term found in the scientific literature that the International Commission on Stratigraphy no longer recognizes as a formal unit. Roughly replaced by the Neogene and the Paleogene, which collectively span from 65.5 to 2.6 million years ago.

timber famine. A shortage of wood of suitable qualities for construction and carpentry.

topographic relief. The three-dimensionality of the earth's surface and its graphic representation.

transcendentalism. A philosophical, political, and literary movement that originated in New England in the early nineteenth century and emphasized the divinity in nature and humanity. Key leaders include Ralph Waldo Emerson and Henry David Thoreau.

tree coring. A way of determining the age of a tree using a metal auger that bores into the main trunk and extracts a core without killing the tree. Assuming there is no heart rot and that the auger reached the center of the tree, counting the number of growth rings can provide a relatively accurate measure of age. This method is not accurate for trees in the tropics, which do not form clear annual growth rings.

trunk. The singular woody stem of a tree.

understory. Vegetation growing under the canopy of dominant or mature trees.

unisexual flowers. Flowers with either female or male organs.

vascular system. Specialized conducting tissues in vascular plants. Phloem conducts carbohydrates made by photosynthesis, and xylem moves water and minerals.

vegetation. An aggregation of plants that has a distinctive architecture. For example, a freshwater marsh, forest, scrub, or desert vegetation.

venation. The pattern of veins, typically in a leaf.

water mold. Fungi-like organisms that are more closely related to brown algae and diatoms. They live in water or soil or parasitize other organisms and include some of the most notorious plant pathogens, such as the one that contributed to the Irish Potato Famine.

wooly. Having thick, entangled, dense hairs on a leaf or other plant structure that function to reduce water loss and/or discourage herbivory.

xerophytic species. Plants adapted to dry or droughty environments such as deserts and Mediterranean climates.

xylem. Specialized tissue in vascular plants that moves water and minerals needed for growth.

BIBLIOGRAPHY

Acton, Kelly J., Nilka Ríos Burrows, Kelly Moore, Linda Querec, Linda Geiss, and Michael M. Engelgau. 2002. "Trends in Diabetes Prevalence among American Indian and Alaska Native Children, Adolescents, and Young Adults." *American Journal of Public Health* 92(9):1485–1490. http://www.ncbi.nlm.nih.gov/pmc/articles/PMC1447266/#!po=2.77778 (accessed September 17, 2014).

Agee, James K. 1993. *Fire Ecology of Pacific Northwest Forests*. Washington, D.C.: Island Press.

American Philosophical Society. 2012. "Yuki." Native American audio collections. Philadelphia: American Philosophical Society. www.amphilsoc.org/exhibit/natamaudio/yuki (accessed October 30, 2012).

"Ancient Industry Thrives on Tanbark Oak in California's Humboldt County." 1952. *Timberman* 53(6):82–92.

Anderson, Kat. 1993. "Native Californians as Ancient and Contemporary Cultivators." In *Before the Wilderness: Environmental Management by Native Californians*, ed. Thomas C. Blackburn and Kat Anderson, 151–174. Menlo Park, Calif.: Ballena Press.

Anderson, M. Kat. 2005. *Tending the Wild: Native American Knowledge and the Management of California's Natural Resources*. Berkeley: University of California Press.

Anderson, M. Kat, and Frank K. Lake. 2013. "California Indian Ethnomycology and Associated Forest Management." *Journal of Ethnobiology* 33:33–85.

Anderson, Pamela K., Andrew A. Cunningham, Nikkita G. Patel, Francisco J. Morales, Paul R. Epstein, and Peter Daszak. 2004. "Emerging Infectious Diseases of Plants: Pathogen Pollution, Climate Change and Agrotechnology Drivers." *Trends in Ecology and Evolution* 19:535–544.

Anderson, R. Scott, and Scott L. Carpenter. 1991. "Vegetation Change in Yosemite Valley, Yosemite National Park, California, during the Protohistoric Period." *Madroño* 38(1):1–13.

Animal and Plant Health Inspection Service (APHIS). 2010. United States Department of Agriculture. Confirmed Nursery Protocol. Revised March 31. http://www.aphis.usda.gov/plant_health/plant_pest_info/pram/protocols.shtml#response (accessed February 12, 2013).

———. 2013. "APHIS List of Regulated Hosts and Plants Proven or Associated with *Phytophthora ramorum*." Updated August. http://www.aphis.usda.gov/plant_health/plant_pest_info/pram/downloads/pdf_files/usdaprlist.pdf (accessed September 17, 2014).

Arguello, Leonel. 2006. "Case Study: Managing Cultural and Natural Elements of the Bald Hills of Redwood National and State Parks." In *Restoring the Pacific Northwest*, ed. Dean Apostol and Marcia Sinclair, 86–87. Washington, D.C.: Island Press.

Armstrong, J. B. 1891. "New Uses for Tan-bark Oak." *Pacific Coast Wood and Iron* 15(5):213.

Backhouse, Janet. 1997. *The Illuminated Page: Ten Centuries of Manuscript Painting in the British Library*. Toronto, Canada: University of Toronto Press.

Bacon, Francis. 2002. "New Atlantis." In *Francis Bacon: The Major Works*, ed. Brian Vickers, 457–489. Oxford: Oxford University Press.

Bailey, L. H. 1917. *The Standard Cyclopedia of Horticulture*. Vol. 6. New York: The Macmillan Company.

Baker, Marc Andre. 1981. *The Ethnobotany of the Yurok, Tolowa, and Karok Indians of Northwest California*. Master's thesis, Humboldt State University.

Ball, Betty. 1994. "'Hack and Squirt': The Epitome of Cynicism in Forest Management." *MEC Newsletter*, no. 17 (Fall): no page number. Ukiah, Calif.: Mendocino Environmental Center.

Bandekow, Richard J. 1947. "Present and Potential Sources of Tannin in the United States." *Journal of Forestry* 45(10):729–734.

Barrett, S. A. 1964. *The Beautiful Tree, Chishkale*. Berkeley: University of California Extension Media Center. 16mm film.

Barrett, S. A., and E. W. Gifford. 1970. "Miwok Houses." In *The California Indians: A Source Book*, ed. R. F. Heizer and M. A. Whipple, 276–284. Berkeley: University of California Press.

Barth, Nancy. 1994. "A New Look at Coast Hardwoods." *Real Estate Magazine* 8, no. 7, issue 189 (October 7–20):1–4, 18, 25.

Basgall, Mark E. 1987. "Resource Intensification among Hunter-Gatherers: Acorn Economies in Prehistoric California." *Research in Economic Anthropology* 9:21–52.

Bates, Craig. 1983. "Acorn Storehouses of the Yosemite Miwok." *The Masterkey* 57:19–27.

Bauer, Patricia M. 1954. "The Beginnings of Tanning in California." *California Historical Society Quarterly* 33(1):59–72.

Baumhoff, Martin A. 1963. "Ecological Determinants of Aboriginal California Populations." *University of California Publications in American Archaeology and Ethnology* 49(2):155–236.

———. 1978. "Environmental Background." In *Handbook of North American Indians*, ed. Robert F. Heizer, 16–24. Washington, D.C.: Smithsonian Institution.

Beard, Yolande S. 1979. *The Wappo: A Report*. Morongo Indian Reservation–Banning, Calif.: Malki Museum Press.

Bergemann, S. E., and M. Garbelotto. 2006. "High Diversity of Fungi Recovered from the Roots of Mature Tanoak (*Lithocarpus densiflorus*) in Northern California." *Canadian Journal of Botany* 84:1380–1394.

Bergemann, Sarah E., Nicholas C. Kordesch, William VanSant-Glass, Matteo Garbelotto, and Timothy A. Metz. 2013. "Implications of Tanoak Decline in Forests Impacted by *Phytophthora ramorum*: Girdling Decreases the Soil Hyphal Abundance of Ectomycorrhizal Fungi Associated with *Notholithocarpus densiflorus*." *Madroño* 60(2):95–106.

Berkes, Fikret. 1999. *Sacred Ecology: Traditional Ecological Knowledge and Resource Management*. Philadelphia: Taylor & Francis.

Berlik, Mary, David B. Kittredge, and David R. Foster. 2002. *The Illusion of Preservation: A Global Environmental Argument for the Local Production of Natural Resources*. Harvard Forest Paper no. 26. Petersham, Mass.: Harvard University.

Betts, H. S. 1911. "Utilization of the Wood of Tanbark Oak." In *California Tanbark Oak*, pt. 2, 24–34. USDA Forest Service Bulletin 75. Washington, D.C.: Government Printing Office.

Bicknell, S. H., D. J. Bigg, R. P. Godar, and A. T. Austin. 1993. "Sinkyone Wilderness State Park Prehistoric Vegetation: Final Report." Arcata, Calif.: Humboldt State University, College of Natural Resources. Unpublished report prepared for the California Department of Parks and Recreation, Interagency Agreement no. 4–100–0252. In the Natural Heritage Section files of California Department of Parks and Recreation, Sacramento.

Bledsoe, A. J. 1885. *Indian Wars of the Northwest, a California Sketch*. San Francisco: Bacon & Company, Book and Job Printers.

Block, William M., and Michael L. Morrison. 1987. "Conceptual Framework and Ecological Considerations for the Study of Birds in Oak Woodlands." In *Proceedings of the Symposium on Multiple-Use Management of California's Hardwood Resources, November 12–14, 1986, San Luis Obispo, California*. USDA Forest Service, General Technical Report PSW-100, technical coordinators Timothy R. Plumb and Norman H. Pillsbury, 163–173. Berkeley, Calif.: Pacific Southwest Forest and Range Experiment Station.

Bocek, Barbara R. 1984. "Ethnobotany of Costanoan Indians, California, Based on Collections by John P. Harrington." *Economic Botany* 38(2):240–255.

Bolander, Henry N. 1866. "Remarks on California Trees." *Proceedings of the California Academy of Sciences* 3:225–233.

Bolsinger, Charles L. 1988. "The Hardwoods of California's Timberlands, Woodlands, and Savannas." USDA Forest Service, Resource Bulletin PNW-RB-148. Portland, Ore.: Pacific Northwest Research Station.

Boone, R. Sidney, Michael R. Milota, Jeanne D. Danielson, and Dean W. Huber. 1992. "Quality Drying of Hardwood Lumber: Guidebook—Checklist." USDA Forest Service, General Technical Report FPL-IMP-GTR 2. Madison, Wis.: Forest Products Laboratory.

Bowcutt, Frederica. 1994–1996. "A Floristic Study of Sinkyone Wilderness State Park, Mendocino County, California." *The Wasmann Journal of Biology* 51(1–2):64–143.

———. 1998. "Resistance to Logging." In *Green versus Gold: Sources in California's Environmental History*, ed. Carolyn Merchant, 166–175. Covelo, Calif.: Island Press.

———. 2011. "Tanoak Target: The Rise and Fall of Herbicide Use on a Common Native Tree." *Environmental History* 16(2):197–225.

———. 2013. "Tanoak Landscapes: Tending a Native American Nut Tree." *Madroño* 60(2):64–86.

———. 2014. "Tanoak Conservation: A Role for the California Department of Fish and Wildlife." *California Fish and Game* 100(1):94–113.

Boyd, Robert, ed. 1999. *Indians, Fire and the Land in the Pacific Northwest*. Corvallis: Oregon State University Press.

Brasier, C. M. 2008. "The Biosecurity Threat to the UK and Global Environment from International Trade in Plants." *Plant Pathology* 57:792–808.

Brasier, Clive M., and S. A. Kirk. 2004. "Production of Gametangia by *Phytophthora ramorum* in Vitro." *Mycological Research* 108:823–827.

Briles, Christy E., Cathy Whitlock, and Patrick J. Bartlein. 2005. "Postglacial Vegetation, Fire, and Climate History of the Siskiyou Mountains, Oregon, USA." *Quaternary Research* 64:44–56.

Brockway, Lucile H. 1979. *Science and Colonial Expansion: The Role of the British Royal Botanic Gardens*. New York: Academic Press.

Brown, Beverly A. 1995. *In Timber Country: Working People's Stories of Environmental Conflict and Urban Flight*. Philadelphia: Temple University Press.

Browne, J. Ross. 1959. *The Coast Rangers (A Chronicle of Adventures in California)*. Reprint. Balboa Island, Calif.: Paisano Press. Originally published in 1862.

Brush, Warren. 1947. "Knowing Your Trees: Tanoak *Lithocarpus densiflorus* (Hooker and Arnold) Rehder." *American Forests* (March):126–127.

Buckley, James Michael. 1997. "A Factory without a Roof: The Company Town in the Redwood Lumber Industry." *Perspectives in Vernacular Architecture* 7:75–92.

Bueno, Monica, Janelle Deshais, and Leonel Arguello. 2010. "Waiting for SOD: Sudden Oak Death and Redwood National and State Parks." In *Proceedings of the Sudden Oak Death Fourth Science Symposium*, technical coordinators S. J. Frankel, J. T. Kliejunas, and K. M. Palmieri, 297–301. USDA Forest Service, General Technical Report PSW-GTR-229. Albany, Calif.: Pacific Southwest Research Station.

Bunting, Robert. 1997. *The Pacific Raincoast: Environment and Culture in an American Eden, 1778–1900*. Lawrence: University Press of Kansas.

Bureau of Land Management. 2009. "Applying Glyphosate on Tanoak to Aid in Sudden Oak Death Eradication." Scoping Document, November 9. Environmental Assessment No. DOI-BLM-OR-C040–2010–0002-EA. Coos Bay District, North Bend, Ore. http://www.blm.gov/or/districts/coosbay/plans/files/SODGlyphosateScoping.pdf (accessed September 13, 2014).

———. 2010. "Applying Glyphosate on Tanoak to Aid in Sudden Oak Death Eradication." Environmental Assessment DOI-BLM-OR-C040–2010–0002-EA. Coos Bay District, North Bend, Ore. http://www.blm.gov/or/districts/coosbay/plans/files/SODEA.pdf (accessed May 1, 2014).

Burns, Russell M., technical comp. 1983. *Silvicultural Systems for the Major Forest Types of the United States*. USDA Forest Service, Agricultural Handbook 445. Washington, D.C.

"California As It Is." 1882. *San Francisco Call*, 11.

California Department of Parks and Recreation. 1986. "Sinkyone Wilderness State Park Unit History: Permanent Settlement." Unpublished report. Accessed in the Natural Heritage Section, Natural Resources Division, California Department of Parks and Recreation, Sacramento, California.

California Department of Pesticide Regulation. n.d. "Search for Products by Chemical." California Environmental Protection Agency. http://www.cdpr.ca.gov/docs/label/chemcode.htm (accessed May 16, 2013).

———. 1990. "DPR Registers 17 New Pesticides in 1998." Sacramento: California Environmental Protection Agency. http://www.cdpr.ca.gov/docs/pressrls/archive/1999/990202–1.htm (accessed April 20, 2013).

———. 2010. "Annual Statewide Pesticide Use Report Indexed by Commodity, Mendocino County." Sacramento: California Environmental Protection Agency. http://www.cdpr.ca.gov/docs/pur/pur09rep/comcnty/mendoc09_site.pdf and http://www.cdpr.ca.gov/docs/pur/pur10rep/comcnty/mendoc10_site.pdf (accessed May 10, 2014).

"California Made Leather." 1866. *Napa Register*, December 1, p. 2, col. 3.

California Oak Mortality Task Force. n.d. "Ecology of Tree Diseases." http://www.suddenoakdeath.org/about-sudden-oak-death/ecology-of-tree-diseases/ (accessed May 29, 2011).

"California Oak Tan Bark." 1919. *Timberman* 20(6):50.

"Californians Pioneer Tanoak." 1963. *Forest Industries* 90(11):66–67.

California Senate. 1860. "Majority and Minority Reports of the Special Joint Committee on the Mendocino War." In *Appendix to the Journal of the California Senate*, 11th session.

California State Board of Forestry. 1886. *First Biennial Report of the State Board of Forestry for the Years 1885–1886*. Sacramento: Superintendent of State Printing.

———. 1890. *Third Biennial Report of the State Board of Forestry for the Years 1889–1890*. Sacramento: Superintendent of State Printing.

———. 1890. "Wattles, and Wattle Planting in California." In *Third Biennial Report of the State Board of Forestry for the Years 1889–1890*, pt. 4. Sacramento: Superintendent of State Printing.

Carpenter, Aurelius O., and Percy H. Millberry. 1914. *History of Mendocino and Lake Counties*,

California with Biographical Sketches of the Leading, Men and Women of the Counties Who Have Been Identified with Their Growth and Development from the Early Days to the Present. Los Angeles: Historic Record Company.

Carpenter, Helen M. n.d. "Tan Bark." Collection of the Grace Hudson Museum and Sun House in Ukiah, California.

Carpenter, Roswell D., David L. Sonderman, and Everette D. Rast. Edited by Martin J. Jones. 1989. *Defects in Hardwood Timber.* USDA Forest Service, Agricultural Handbook no. 678. Delaware, Ohio: Northeastern Forest Experiment Station.

Carr, Myra. 1956. "Shoe Trees." *Pacific Discovery* 9(2):6–12.

Carranco, Lynwood, and Estle Beard. 1981. *Genocide and Vendetta: The Round Valley Wars of Northern California.* Norman: University of Oklahoma Press.

Carranco, Lynwood, and John T. Labbe. 1975. *Logging the Redwoods.* Caldwell, Idaho: The Caxton Printers, Ltd.

Carranco, Ruth, and Links Carranco. 1977. "Briceland Once Center of Thriving Tanbark Industry." *Humboldt Historian* 25(6):1, 4.

Carson, Rachel. 1994. *Silent Spring.* New York: Houghton Mifflin Co.

Centers for Disease Control and Prevention. 2013. "Traditional Foods Project, Diabetes Public Health Resource." Updated December. http://www.cdc.gov/diabetes/projects/ndwp/traditional-foods.htm (accessed September 17, 2014).

Chartkoff, Joseph L., and Kerry Kona Chartkoff. 1984. *The Archaeology of California.* Stanford, Calif.: Stanford University Press.

Chestnut, V. K. 1974. "Plants Used by the Indians of Mendocino County, California." In *Contributions from the U.S. National Herbarium*, vol. 7, 295–422. Reprint. Ukiah, Calif.: Mendocino County Historical Society. Originally published in 1902.

Christensen, Glenn A., Sally J. Campbell, and Jeremy S. Fried, technical eds. 2008. "California's Forest Resources, 2001–2005: Five-Year Forest Inventory and Analysis Report." USDA Forest Service, General Technical Report PNW-GTR-763. Portland, Ore.: Pacific Northwest Research Station.

Christopher, A. J. 1984. *Colonial Africa.* Totowa, N.J.: Barnes & Noble Books.

Clark, F. H. 1892. "Forestry; Redwoods." In *Transactions of the Fourteenth State Fruit Growers' Convention in Annual Report of the State Board of Horticulture of the State of California, for 1891.* Sacramento: State Board of Horticulture of the State of California.

Clayton, Carl. 2002. "Tools of the Future: Future Trends in Small Milling, Dehumidification Drying and Mulching." *Timberwest* (November–December), 26–28.

Cobb, Richard C., João A. N. Filipe, Ross K. Meentemeyer, Christopher A. Gilligan, and David M. Rizzo. 2012. "Ecosystem Transformation by Emerging Infectious Disease: Loss of Large Tanoak from California Forests." *Journal of Ecology* 100:712–722.

Cobb, Richard C., David M. Rizzo, Katherine J. Hayden, Matteo Garbelotto, João A. N. Filipe, Christopher A. Gilligan, Whalen W. Dillon, Ross K. Meentemeyer, Yana S. Valachovic, Ellen Goheen, Tedmund J. Swiecki, Everett M. Hansen, and Susan J. Frankel. 2013. "Biodiversity Conservation in the Face of Dramatic Forest Disease: An Integrated Conservation Strategy for Tanoak (*Notholithocarpus densiflorus*) Threatened by Sudden Oak Death." *Madroño* 60(2):151–164.

Colegrove, Nolan. 2005–2006. "The Forest Is in Your Hands." *Evergreen Magazine* (Winter). http://www.evergreenmagazine.com/magazine/issue/Winter_2005_2006.html (accessed October 8, 2014).

Cook, Sherburne F. 1976. *The Conflict between the California Indian and White Civilization.* Berkeley: University of California Press.

Cornford, Daniel A. 1987. *Workers and Dissent in the Redwood Empire*. Philadelphia: Temple University Press.

Coy, Owen C. 1929. *The Humboldt Bay Region 1850–1875: A Study in the American Colonization of California*. Los Angeles: The California State Historical Association.

Crepet, William L. 1989. "History and Implications of the Early North American Fossil Record of Fagaceae." In *Evolution, Systematics, and Fossil History of Hamamelidae*, ed. P. R. Crane and S. Blackmore, 45–66. Oxford: Clarendon Press.

Cronise, Titus Fey. 1868. *The Natural Wealth of California*. San Francisco: H. H. Bancroft Company.

Curtin, Leonora Scott Muse. With historical review and photos by Margaret C. Irwin. 1957. "Some Plants Used by the Yuki Indians of Round Valley, Northern California." *Southwest Museum Leaflets*, no. 27. Los Angeles: Southwest Museum.

Dahms, W. G. 1958. "Chemical Control of Brush and Undesirable Hardwoods on Forest Land of the Pacific Northwest." *Weed Abstracts* 7(12): no page numbers.

Davis, Edward M. 1947. "Machining Madrone, California Laurel, Tanbark Oak, and Chinquapin." Report no. R1727, 1–6. Madison, Wis.: USDA Forest Service, Forest Products Laboratory.

Davis, Frank W., Mark Borchert, Ross K. Meentemeyer, Alan Flint, and David M. Rizzo. 2010. "Pre-impact Forest Composition and Ongoing Tree Mortality Associated with Sudden Oak Death in the Big Sur Region, California." *Forest Ecology and Management* 259(12):2342–2354.

DeCelles, P. G. 2004. "Late Jurassic to Eocene Evolution of the Cordilleran Thrust Belt and Foreland Basin System, Western U.S.A." *American Journal of Science* 304:105–168.

Denk, Thomas, and Guido W. Grimm. 2009. "Significance of Pollen Characteristics for Infrageneric Classification and Phylogeny in *Quercus* (Fagaceae)." *International Journal of Plant Science* 170(7):926–940.

Desprez-Loustau, Marie-Laure, Cécile Robin, Marc Buée, Régis Courtecuisse, Jean Garbaye, Frédéric Suffert, Ivan Sache, and David M. Rizzo. 2007. "The Fungal Dimension of Biological Invasions." *Trends in Ecology and Evolution* 22(9):472–480.

Devine, Warren D., and Constance A. Harrington. 2013. "Restoration Release of Overtopped Oregon White Oak Increases 10-Year Growth and Acorn Production." *Forest Ecology and Management* 291:87–95.

Diekmann, Lucy, Lee Panich, and Chuck Striplen, 2007. "Native American Management and the Legacy of Working Landscapes in California." *Rangelands* 29, no. 3:46–50.

Dillon, Whalen W., Ross K. Meentemeyer, John B. Vogler, Richard C. Cobb, Margaret R. Metz, and David M. Rizzo. 2013. "Range-Wide Threats to a Foundation Tree Species from Disturbance Interactions." *Madroño* 60(2):139–150.

Dizard, Jan E. 1999. *Going Wild: Hunting, Animal Rights, and the Contested Meaning of Nature*. Amherst: University of Massachusetts Press.

Dodd, Richard S., Alejandro Nettel, Jessica W. Wright, and Zara Afzal-Rafii. 2013. "Genetic Structure of *Notholithocarpus densiflorus* (Fagaceae) from the Species to the Local Scale: A Review of Our Knowledge for Conservation and Replanting." *Madroño* 60(2):130–138.

Donoghue, John D., and William C. Denison. 1996. "Commercial Production of Shiitake (*Lentinula edodes*) Using Whole-Log Chip of *Quercus*, *Lithocarpus*, and *Acer*." In *Mushroom Biology and Mushroom Products: Proceedings of the 2nd International Conference*, ed. D. J. Royse, 265–275. University Park: Pennsylvania State University.

Driver, Harold E. 1939. "Culture Element Distributions: X, Northwest California." *University of California Anthropological Records* 1(6):297–433.

———. 1952. "The Acorn in North American Indian Diet." *Proceedings of the Indiana Academy of Science* 62:56–62.

Durkin, Patrick R. 2011. "Imazapyr Human Health and Ecological Risk Assessment: Final Report." Unpublished report produced for the U.S. Forest Service, Southern Region, Atlanta, Georgia (Contract: AG-3187-C-06–0010, USDA Forest Order Number: AG-43ZP-D-11–0012). New York: Syracuse Environmental Research Associates, Inc.

Economic Development Administration. 1968. "The Hoopa Valley Reservation Hardwood Study Report." Economic Development Administration Technical Assistance Project, 1–154. Washington, D.C.: U.S. Department of Commerce.

Ehrlich, Paul R., David S. Dobkin, and Darryl Wheye. 1988. *The Birder's Handbook: A Field Guide to the Natural History of North American Birds.* New York: Simon & Schuster Inc.

Ellwood, Eric L. 1958. "Problems and Prospects in Drying California Hardwoods for High-Quality Use." *California Forest and Forest Products*, no. 8 (December): no page numbers.

Emerson, Ralph Waldo. 1909. "The Fortune of the Republic." In *The Works of Ralph Waldo Emerson*, vol. 11, *Miscellanies*, 393–425. Reprint. Boston: Fireside Edition. Originally published in 1878. Facsimile at http://lf-oll.s3.amazonaws.com/titles/1961/1236.11_Bk.pdf (accessed September 18, 2014).

Engelmann, George. 1876. "About the Oaks of the United States." *The Transactions of the Academy of Science of St. Louis* 3:372–400, 539–543.

Espenas, Leif D. 1953. "The Seasoning of One-Inch Tanoak Lumber." Bulletin 3, 1–46. Corvallis: Oregon Forest Products Laboratory.

Essene, Frank. 1942. "Cultural Element Distributions: XXI Round Valley." *University of California Anthropological Records* 8(1):1–97.

Estes, Kenneth M., and David A. Blakeman. 1970. "Foliar Spraying of Sprouting Tanoak Plants Best in Late Summer." USDA Forest Service Research Note PSW-207. Berkeley, Calif.: Pacific Southwest Forest and Range Experiment Station.

Evans, Edward A. 2004. "Potential Problems Facing the U. S. Nursery Industry." Department of Food and Resource Economics, University of Florida IFAS Extension, EDIS document FE491, no page numbers.

Eyre, C. A., M. Kozanitas, and M. Garbelotto. 2013. "Population Dynamics of Aerial and Terrestrial Populations of *Phytophthora ramorum* in a California Forest under Different Climatic Conditions." *Phytopathology* 103(11):1141–1152. doi: 10.1094/PHYTO-11–12–0290-R.

"Famous Saddle Leather." 1955. *California Magazine of the Pacific* 45(12):6.

Farmer, Jared. 2013. *Trees in Paradise: A California History.* New York: W. W. Norton & Company.

Fattore, Elena, and Roberto Fanelli. 2013. "Palm Oil and Palmitic Acid: A Review on Cardiovascular Effects and Carcinogenicity." *International Journal of Food Sciences and Nutrition* 64(5):648–659.

Fearing, Watson Burbank. 1961. "An Engineering Study of the Solvent Seasoning of Tanoak." Master's thesis, University of California, Berkeley.

Fichtner, E. J., S. C. Lynch, and D. M. Rizzo. 2007. "Detection, Distribution, Sporulation, and Survival of *Phytophthora ramorum* in a California Redwood-Tanoak Forest Soil." *Phytopathology* 97(10):1366–1375.

Filipe, João A. N., Richard C. Cobb, Ross K. Meentemeyer, Christopher A. Lee, Yana S. Valachovic, Alex R. Cook, David M. Rizzo, and Christopher A. Gilligan. 2012. "Landscape

Epidemiology and Control of Pathogens with Cryptic and Long-Distance Dispersal: Sudden Oak Death in Northern Californian Forests." *PLoS Computation Biology* 8(1):e1002328.

Filipe, João A. N., Richard C. Cobb, David M. Rizzo, Ross K. Meentemeyer, and Christopher A. Gilligan. 2010. "Strategies for Control of Sudden Oak Death in Humboldt County—Informed Guidance Based on a Parameterized Epidemiological Model." In *Proceedings of the Sudden Oak Death Fourth Science Symposium, 122–125*. USDA Forest Service, General Technical Report PSW-GTR-229. Albany, Calif.: Pacific Southwest Research Station.

Findlen, Paula. 1994. *Possessing Nature: Museums, Collecting, and Scientific Culture in Early Modern Italy*. Berkeley: University of California Press.

Finlay, Mark R. 2009. *Growing American Rubber: Strategic Plants and the Politics of National Security*. New Brunswick, N.J.: Rutgers University Press.

FIR Report, Winter 1990. Vol. 11, no. 2, 1–12. Southwest Oregon Forestry Intensified Research Program newsletter, Oregon State University Extension Service, Medford. http:// ir.library.oregonstate.edu/xmlui/bitstream/handle/1957/47762/FirReportvol11no2. pdf?sequence=1 (accessed May 3, 2014).

Fisher, W. F. ca. 1950. "Humboldt County Hardwoods." Unpublished internal report on file at Six Rivers National Forest, Eureka, California.

Frankel, Susan J. 2008. "Sudden Oak Death and *Phytophthora ramorum* in the USA: A Management Challenge." *Australasian Plant Pathology* 37:19–25.

Frankel, Susan J., and Everett M. Hansen. 2011. "Forest *Phytophthora* Diseases in the Americas: 2007–2010." *New Zealand Journal of Forestry Science* 41S:S159–167.

Freinkel, Susan. 2007. *American Chestnut: The Life, Death, and Rebirth of a Perfect Tree*. Berkeley: University of California Press.

Fryer, Janet L. 2008. "*Lithocarpus densiflorus* in Fire Effects Information System." USDA Forest Service, Rocky Mountain Research Station, Fire Sciences Laboratory. http://www. fs.fed.us/database/feis/plants/tree/litden/all.html (accessed January 4, 2014).

Gale, Daniel B., and Dee B. Randolph. 2000. "Lower Klamath River Sub-basin Watershed Restoration Plan." Unpublished report produced by the Yurok Tribal Fisheries Program in Klamath, Calif., and the Yurok Tribal Watershed Restoration Program in Orick, Calif. (April), 1. http://www.yuroktribe.org/departments/fisheries/documents/LowerKlamathRestorationPlanFINAL2000_000.pdf (accessed April 20, 2013).

Garbelotto, Matteo, Kelly Ivors, Daniel Hüberli, Peter Bonants, and Art Wagner. 2006. "Potential for Sexual Reproduction of *Phytophthora ramorum* in Washington State Nurseries." In *Proceedings of the Sudden Oak Death Second Science Symposium: The State of Our Knowledge, January 18–21, 2005, Monterey, California*. USDA Forest Service General Technical Report PSW-GTR-196, technical coordinators S. J. Frankel, P. J. Shea, and M. I. Haverty. Albany, Calif.: Pacific Southwest Research Station.

Garibaldi, Ann, and Nancy Turner. 2004. "Cultural Keystone Species: Implications for Ecological Conservation and Restoration." *Ecology and Society* 9(3): article 1. http://www. ecologyandsociety.org/vol9/iss3/art1 (accessed July 1, 2014).

Geospatial Innovation Facility. 2012. "Distribution of Sudden Oak Death as of February 20, 2012." OakMapper: Monitoring Sudden Oak Death. Geospatial Innovation Facility and Kelly Research & Outreach Lab. University of California, Berkeley. www.oakmapper.org/ pdf/California (accessed October 30, 2012).

Gifford, E. W. 1967. "Ethnographic Notes on the Southwestern Pomo." *University of California Anthropological Records* 25:1–48.

———. 1968. "Californian Balanophagy." In *Essays in Anthropology: Presented to A. L. Kroeber in Celebration of His Sixtieth Birthday, June 11, 1936*, 87–98. Reprint. Freeport, N.Y.: Books for Libraries Press, by arrangement with the University of California Press.

Gilliland, Linda Ellen. 1985. "Proximate Analysis and Mineral Composition of Traditional California Native American Foods." Master's thesis, University of California, Davis.

Goodrich, Jennie, Claudia Lawson, and Vana P. Lawson. 1980. *Kashaya Pomo Plants*. American Indian Monograph Series no. 2. Los Angeles: American Indian Studies Center, University of California.

Goss, Erica M., Meg Larsen, Annelies Vercauteren, Sabine Werres, Kurt Heungens, and Niklaus J. Grünwald. 2011. "*Phytophthora ramorum* in Canada: Evidence for Migration within North America and from Europe." *Phytopathology* 101(1):166–171.

Gould, R. A. 1976. "Ecology and Adaptive Response among the Tolowa Indians of Northwestern California." In *Native Californians: A Theoretical Retrospective*, ed. Lowell J. Bean and Thomas C. Blackburn, 49–78. Socorro, N.Mex.: Ballena Press.

Graham, Alan. 1999. *Late Cretaceous and Cenozoic History of North American Vegetation North of Mexico*. New York: Oxford University Press.

Greene, Edward L. 1889. *Illustrations of West American Oaks: From Drawings of the Late Albert Kellogg, M.D.* San Francisco: Published with funds from James M. McDonald, Esq.

Griffin, James R., and William B. Critchfield. 1976. "The Distribution of Forest Trees in California." USDA Forest Service, Research Paper PSW-82. Berkeley, Calif.: Pacific Southwest Forest and Range Experiment Station. Originally published in 1972.

Guerrant, Edward O., Jr. 2012. "Characterizing Two Decades of Rare Plant Reintroductions." In *Plant Reintroduction in a Changing Climate: Promises and Perils*, ed. Joyce Maschinski and Kristin E. Haskins, 9–29. Washington, D.C.: Island Press.

Gysel, Leslie W. 1956. "Measurement of Acorn Crops." *Forest Science* 2(1):305–313.

Hale, H. M. 1906. "Consumption of Tanbark in 1905." USDA Forest Service Circular 42, 1–4. Washington, D.C.: Government Printing Office.

Hall, Guy H. 1998. *The Management, Manufacture, Marketing of California Black Oak, Pacific Madrone, and Tanoak: A Practical Handbook on Successful Hardwood Utilization in California and Southern Oregon*. Camas, Wash.: Western Hardwood Association.

Ham, Sam H. 1992. *Environmental Interpretation: A Practical Guide for People with Big Ideas and Small Budgets*. Golden, Colo.: North American Press.

Hardin, Garrett. 1985. *Filters against Folly: How to Survive Despite Economists, Ecologists, and the Merely Eloquent*. New York: Penguin Book.

Harlow, William M., and Ellwood S. Harrar. 1968. *Textbook of Dendrology: Covering the Important Forest Trees of the United States and Canada*. 5th ed. New York: McGraw-Hill Book Company.

Harper, Paul, Tim Metz, and Robert J. Hrubes. 1995. "An Analysis of the Possible Regional Economic Benefits of Small Scale Sustainable Forestry: Phase 1: Determining the Potential Regional Supply of Certified Timber." Unpublished technical report. Redway, Calif.: Institute for Sustainable Forestry.

Harrington, Timothy B. 1989. "Stand Development and Individual Tree Morphology and Physiology of Young Douglas-fir *(Pseudotsuga menziesii)* in Association with Tanoak *(Lithocarpus densiflorus)*." PhD diss., Oregon State University.

Harrington, Timothy B., and John C. Tappeiner II. 1997. "Growth Responses of Young Douglas-Fir and Tanoak 11 Years after Various Levels of Hardwood Removal and Understory Suppression in Southwestern Oregon, USA." *Forest Ecology and Management* 96:1–11.

———. 2009. "Long-Term Effects of Tanoak Competition on Douglas-Fir Stand Development." *Canadian Journal of Forest Research* 39:765–776.

Harrington, Timothy B., John C. Tappeiner II, and Thomas F. Hughes. 1991. "Predicting Average Growth and Size Distributions of Douglas-Fir Saplings Competing with Sprout Clumps of Tanoak or Pacific Madrone." *New Forests* 5(2):109–130.

Harris, Esmond, Jeanette Harris, and N. D. G. James. 2003. *Oak: A British History*. Macclesfield, U.K.: Windgather Press Ltd.

Harvey, Athelstan George. 1947. *Douglas of the Fir: A Biography of David Douglas, Botanist*. Cambridge, Mass.: Harvard University Press.

Hawk, Steve. 2014. "Branching Out: How a Little-Known U.S. Trade Law Has Clipped the Global Market for Illegal Lumber." *Sierra* 99(6):46–47.

Hayden, Katherine J., Alejandro Nettel, Richard S. Dodd, and Matteo Garbelotto. 2011. "Will All the Trees Fall? Variable Resistance to an Introduced Forest Disease in a Highly Susceptible Host." *Forest Ecology and Management* 261(11):1781–1791.

Heizer, Robert F., and Albert B. Elsasser. 1980. *The Natural World of the California Indians*. Berkeley: University of California Press.

Helgerson, Ole T. 1990. "Response of Underplanted Douglas-Fir to Herbicide Injection of Sclerophyll Hardwoods in Southwest Oregon." *Western Journal of Applied Forestry* 5(3):86–89.

Hendryx, Michael, with Barbara J. Davis. 1991. *Plants and the People: The Ethnobotany of the Karuk Tribe*. Yreka, Calif.: Siskiyou County Museum.

Henry, Christopher D. 2009. "Uplift of the Sierra Nevada, California." *Geology* 37(6):575–576.

Hight, Jim. 1997. "Value Added: Local Woodworkers Turn Hardwoods into Gold." *North Coast Journal of Politics, People & Art* 8, no. 6 (June): no page numbers.

Hilgard, E. W. 1894. "The Canaigre, or Tanners Dock." University of California Agricultural Experiment Station, Berkeley, California, Bulletin no. 105, 1–9.

Hirsch, Jerry. 2004. "Nursery Group Wins Dispute." *Los Angeles Times*, August 3.

History of Humboldt County, California, with Illustrations: Descriptive of Its Scenery, Farms, Residences, Public Buildings, Factories, Hotels, Business Houses, Schools, Churches, Etc. 1881. San Francisco: Wallace W. Elliott & Co., Publishers.

Hittell, John S. 1882. *The Commerce and Industries of the Pacific Coast of North America Comprising the Rise, Progress, Products, Present Condition, and Prospects of the Useful Arts on the Western Side of Our Continent, and Some Account of Its Resources*. San Francisco: A. L. Bancroft & Co., Publishers.

———. 1901. "Autobiography and Reminiscence of John Shertzer Hittell (Deceased)." The Society of California Pioneers Collection of autobiographies and reminiscences of early pioneers. Unpublished manuscript written by the author on October 5, 1894, and compiled by the society after his death. California Digital Library. http://content.cdlib.org/ark:/13030/kt4k4020qr/?order=3&brand=calisphere (accessed November 9, 2012).

Hobbs, S. 1987. "Reforestation without Herbicides." Forestry Intensified Research Report, Oregon State University Extension Service 8(4):13–14.

Holling, C. S., and Gary K. Meffe. 1996. "Command and Control and the Pathology of Natural Resource Management." *Conservation Biology* 10(2):328–337.

Holschuh, Arno. 2000. "The New Face of Forestry." *North Coast Journal of Politics, People & Art* 11, no. 7 (July): no page numbers.

Hooker, William Jackson, and G. A. Walker Arnott. 1840. *The Botany of Captain Beechey's Voyage*. Part 9. London: Henry G. Bohn. Originally published in February–March and reprinted in 1841. http://www.biodiversitylibrary.org/item/6486#page/1/mode/1up (accessed February 21, 2014).

Hooker, William Jackson, 1841. *Icones Plantarum; or Figures, with Brief Descriptive Characters and Remarks of New or Rare Plants, Selected from the Author's Herbarium.* Vol. 4. London: Longman, Orme, Brown, Green, and Longmans. Facsimile, Biodiversity Heritage Library, http://ia600605.us.archive.org/21/items/mobot31753002356464/mobot31753002356464.pdf (accessed October 10, 2014).

Hosten, Paul E., O. Eugene Hickman, Frank K. Lake, Frank A. Lang, and David Vesely. 2006. "Oak Woodlands and Savannas." In *Restoring the Pacific Northwest: The Art and Science of Ecological Restoration in Cascadia,* ed. Dean Apostol and Marcia Sinclair, 63–96. Washington, D.C.: Island Press.

Hough, Franklin B. 1882. *Report on Forestry, Submitted to Congress by the Commissioner of Agriculture.* Washington, D.C.: Government Printing Office.

Howes, F. N. 1953. *Vegetable Tanning Materials.* London: Butterworths Scientific Publications.

Huber, Dean W., and Philip M. McDonald. 1992. "California's Hardwood Resource: History and Reasons for Lack of a Sustained Hardwood Industry." USDA Forest Service, General Technical Report PSW-GTR-135. Berkeley, Calif.: Pacific Southwest Research Station.

Hurtado, Albert L. 1988. *Indian Survival on the California Frontier.* New Haven, Conn.: Yale University Press.

Integrated Taxonomic Information System (ITIS). n.d. http://www.itis.gov (accessed February 28, 2014).

Ivors, K., M. Garbelotto, I. D. E. Vries, C. Ruyter-Spira, B. TE. Hekkert, N. Rosenzweig, and P. Bonants. 2006. "Microsatellite Markers Identify Three Lineages of *Phytophthora ramorum* in US Nurseries, yet Single Lineages in US Forest and European Nursery Populations." *Molecular Ecology* 15(6):1493–1505.

Jacknis, Ira, ed. 2004. *Food in California Indian Culture.* Berkeley: Phoebe A. Hearst Museum of Anthropology, University of California.

Jackson, Kenneth T. 1985. *Crabgrass Frontier: The Suburbanization of the United States.* New York: Oxford University Press.

Jacob, James R. 1998. *The Scientific Revolution: Aspirations and Achievements, 1500–1700.* The Control of Nature Series. Amherst, N.Y.: Humanity Books.

Jaramillo, Annabelle E. 1988. "Growth of Douglas-fir in Southwestern Oregon after Removal of Competing Vegetation." USDA Forest Service Research Note PNW-RN-470. Portland, Ore.: Pacific Northwest Research Station.

Jepson, Willis Linn. 1909. *The Trees of California.* San Francisco: Cunningham, Curtis & Welch.

———. 1910. *The Silva of California: Memoirs of the University of California.* Vol. 2. Berkeley, Calif.: The University Press.

———. 1911. "Tanbark Oak and the Tanning Industry." In *California Tanbark Oak,* part 1, 5–23. USDA Forest Service Bulletin 75. Washington, D.C.: Government Printing Office.

———. 1951. *A Manual of the Flowering Plants of California.* Berkeley: University of California Press.

Kay, Burgess L., Oliver A. Leonard, and James E. Street. 1961. "Control of Madrone and Tanoak Stump Sprouting." *Weeds* 9(3):369–373.

Kelly, Morgan. 2011. "Erratic, Extreme Day-to-Day Weather Puts Climate Change in New Light." *News at Princeton.* http://www.princeton.edu/main/news/archive/S32/13/25I02/index.xml?section=topstories (accessed February 10, 2013).

Kliejunas, John T. 2010. "Sudden Oak Death and *Phytophthora ramorum*: A Summary of the Literature." USDA Forest Service, General Technical Report PSW-GTR-234. Albany, Calif.: Pacific Southwest Research Station.

Kluza, D. A., D. A. Vieglais, J. K. Andreasen, and A. T. Peterson. 2007. "Sudden Oak Death: Geographic Risk Estimates and Predictions of Origins." *Plant Pathology* 56(4):580–587.

Knapp, Friedrich. 1921. "Nature and Essential Character of the Tanning Process and of Leather." *Journal of the American Leather Chemists Association* 16:658–681.

Kniffen, Fred B. 1939. "Pomo Geography." *University of California Publications in American Archaeology and Ethnology* 36(6):353–400.

Knighten, Claude, and Jerry Redding. 2004. "USDA Takes Action in Three States to Halt Spread of Plant Fungus." News release, United States Department of Agriculture Animal and Plant Health Inspection Service. http://www.plantmanagementnetwork.org/pub/php/news/2005/sod/ (accessed October 11, 2014).

Kodizumi, G. 1916. "Classification of Castaneaceae." *Botanical Magazine* 30:199.

Kramer, Andrea T., and Valerie Pence. 2012. "The Challenges of *Ex-situ* Conservation for Threatened Oaks." *International Oak Journal*, no. 23:91–108.

Kroeber, A. L. 1919. "Sinkyone Tales." *Journal of American Folk-Lore* 32(124):346–351.

Kroeber, A. L., and E. W. Gifford. 1949. "World Renewal, a Cult System of Native Northwest California." *University of California Anthropological Records* 13(1):1–156.

Lake, Frank. 2007. *Traditional Ecological Knowledge to Develop and Maintain Fire Regimes in Northwestern California, Klamath-Siskiyou Bioregion: Management and Restoration of Culturally Significant Habitats.* PhD diss., Oregon State University.

Langston, Nancy. 1995. *Forest Dreams, Forest Nightmares: The Paradox of Old Growth in the Inland West.* Seattle: University of Washington Press.

Lavy, T. L., L. A. Norris, J. D. Mattice, and D. B. Marx. 1987. "Exposure of Forestry Ground Workers to 2,4-D, Picloram and Dichlorprop." *Environmental Toxicology and Chemistry* 6:209–224.

Lee, Chris. 2009. "Sudden Oak Death and Fire—2009 Update." California Oak Mortality Task Force. http://www.suddenoakdeath.org/pdf/summary%20of%20fire%20and%20p%20ramorum%20issues%20v5.3.pdf (accessed January 15, 2012).

Legrève, Anne, and Etienne Duveiller. 2010. "Preventing Potential Disease and Pest Epidemics under a Changing Climate." In *Climate Change and Crop Production*, ed. Matthew P. Reynolds, 50–70. Oxfordshire, U.K.: CAB International.

Lehmann, Susan. 2000. "Industrial Development: Tanneries." In "Economic Development of the City of Santa Cruz, 1850–1950," ch. 3, context I, of *Fully Developed Context Statement for the City of Santa Cruz.* Unpublished report prepared for the City of Santa Cruz Planning and Development Department. Santa Cruz Public Library, http://scplweb.santacruzpl.org/history/work/edindtan.shtml (accessed September 11, 2014).

Leopold, Aldo. 1991. "'Piute Forestry' vs. Forest Fire Prevention." In *The River of the Mother of God and Other Essays by Aldo Leopold*, ed. Susan L. Flader and J. Baird Callicott, 68–70. Madison: The University of Wisconsin Press. Originally published in 1920.

Levene, Bruce, and Sally Miklose. 1989. *Fort Bragg Remembered: A Centennial Oral History.* Fort Bragg, Calif.: Fort Bragg Centennial.

Lewis, Henry T. 1993. "Patterns of Indian Burning in California: Ecology and Ethnohistory." In *Before the Wilderness: Environmental Management by Native Californians*, ed. Thomas C. Blackburn and Kat Anderson, 55–116. Menlo Park, Calif.: Ballena Press.

Libby, W. J. 1996. "Ecology and Management of Coast Redwood: Keynote Address." In *Proceedings of the Conference on Coast Redwood Forest Ecology and Management*, Humboldt State University, Arcata, California, June 18–20. Internet Archive Wayback Machine, http://web.archive.org/web/20050210232412/http://cnr.berkeley.edu/~jleblanc/WWW/Redwood/rdwd-Ecology.html (accessed July 7, 2014).

Lightfoot, Kent G. 2005. *Indians, Missionaries, and Merchants: The Legacy of Colonial Encounters on the California Frontiers.* Berkeley: University of California Press.

Logan, William Bryant. 2005. *Oak: The Frame of Civilization.* New York: W. W. Norton & Company.

Loo, Judy A. 2009. "Ecological Impacts of Non-indigenous Invasive Fungi as Forest Pathogens." *Biological Invasions* 11(1):81–96.

Loud, Llewellyn L. 1918. "Ethnography and Archaeology of the Wiyot Territory." *University of California Publications in American Archaeology and Ethnology* 14(3):221–436.

Lowry, Judith Larner. 1999. *Gardening with a Wild Heart.* Berkeley: University of California Press.

Luppold, William G., and R. Edward Thomas. 1991. "New Estimates of Hardwood Lumber Exports to Europe and Asia." USDA Forest Service, Research Paper NE-652. Radnor, Pa.: Northeastern Forest Experiment Station.

MacLeod, Alan, Marco Pautasso, Mike J. Jeger, and Roy Haines-Young. 2010. "Evolution of the International Regulation of Plant Pests and Challenges for Future Plant Health." *Food Security* 2:49–70.

Manos, Paul S., Charles H. Cannon, and Sang-Hun Oh. 2008. "Phylogenetic Relationships and Taxonomic Status of the Paleoendemic Fagaceae of Western North America: Recognition of a New Genus, *Notholithocarpus.*" *Madroño* 55(3):181–190.

Manos, Paul S., and Alice M. Stanford. 2001. "The Historical Biogeography of Fagaceae: Tracking the Tertiary History of Temperate and Subtropical Forests of the Northern Hemisphere." *International Journal of Plant Science* 162, no. 6, supplement: S77–S93.

"The Mark of the Range." 1954. *Fortnight,* October 20, p. 29.

Marsh, George P. 1864. *Nature and Man or, Physical Geography as Modified by Human Action.* New York: Charles Scribner. Republished in *Man and Nature by George Perkins Marsh,* ed. David Lowenthal. Cambridge, Mass.: The Belknap Press of Harvard University Press, 1965.

Marston, D. S. 1955. "Leather with Personality [A. K. Salz Company]." *Rohm & Haas Reporter* 13(1). http://www.santacruzpl.org/history/articles/83/ (accessed October 23, 2012).

Mascheretti, S., P., J. P. Croucher, A. Vettraino, S. Prospero, and Matteo Garbelotto. 2008. "Reconstruction of the Sudden Oak Death Epidemic in California through Microsatellite Analysis of the Pathogen *Phytophthora ramorum.*" *Molecular Ecology* 17(11):2755–2768.

Mast, Fred R. 1968. "Tanoak Utilization Story: New Applications Pay Off." *Forest Industries* 95(9):31–33.

McCarthy, Helen. 1993. "Managing Oaks and the Acorn Crop." In *Before the Wilderness: Environmental Management by Native Californians,* ed. Thomas C. Blackburn and Kat Anderson, 213–228. Menlo Park, Calif.: Ballena Press.

McDonald, Philip M. 1977. "Tanoak . . . A Bibliography for a Promising Species." USDA Forest Service, General Technical Report PSW-22. Berkeley, Calif.: Pacific Southwest Forest and Range Experiment Station.

McDonald, Philip M., and Gary O. Fiddler. 1993. "Feasibility of Alternatives to Herbicides in Young Conifer Plantations in California." *Canadian Journal of Forest Research* 23:2015–2022.

———. 1996. "Development of a Mixed Shrub-Tanoak-Douglas-Fir Community in a Treated and Untreated Condition." USDA Forest Service, Research Paper PSW-RP-225. Albany, Calif.: Pacific Southwest Research Station.

McDonald, Philip M., Gary O. Fiddler, and Henry R. Harrison. 1994. "Repeated Manual Release in a Young Plantation: Effect on Douglas-fir Seedlings, Hardwoods, Shrubs, Forbs, and Grasses." USDA Forest Service, Research Paper PSW-RP-221. Albany, Calif.: Pacific Southwest Research Station.

McDonald, Philip M., and Dean W. Huber. 1994. "California's Hardwood Resource: Status of the Industry and an Ecosystem Management Perspective." USDA Forest Service, General Technical Report PSW-GTR-153. Albany, Calif.: Pacific Southwest Research Station.

———. 1995. "California's Hardwood Resource: Managing for Wildlife, Water, Pleasing Scenery, and Wood Products." USDA Forest Service, General Technical Report PSW-GTR-154. Albany, Calif.: Pacific Southwest Research Station.

McDonald, Philip M., and John C. Tappeiner II. 1987. "Silviculture, Ecology, and Management of Tanoak in Northern California." In *Proceedings of the Symposium on Multiple-Use Management of California's Hardwood Resources, November 12–14, 1986, San Luis Obispo, California*, technical coordinators Timothy R. Plumb and Norman H. Pillsbury, 64–70. USDA Forest Service, General Technical Report GTR-PSW-100. Berkeley, Calif.: Pacific Southwest Forest and Range Experiment Station.

McDonald, Philip M., Detlev R. Vogler, and Dennis Mayhew. 1988. "Unusual Decline of Tanoak Sprouts." USDA Forest Service, Research Note PSW-398. Berkeley, Calif.: Pacific Southwest Forest and Range Experiment Station.

McPherson, Brice A., Sylvia R. Mori, David L. Wood, Andrew J. Storer, Pavel Svihra, N. Maggi Kelly, and Richard B. Standiford. 2005. "Sudden Oak Death in California: Disease Progression in Oaks and Tanoaks." *Forest Ecology and Management* 213:71–89.

Medvigy, David, and Claudie Beaulieu. 2012. "Trends in Daily Solar Radiation and Precipitation Coefficients of Variation since 1984." *Journal of Climate* 25:1330–1339.

Meentemeyer, Ross K., Brian L. Anacker, Walter Mark, and David M. Rizzo. 2008. "Early Detection of Emerging Forest Disease Using Dispersal Estimation and Ecological Niche Modeling." *Ecological Applications* 18:377–390.

Meentemeyer, Ross K., Nik J. Cunniffe, Alex R. Cook, João A. N. Filipe, Richard D. Hunter, David M. Rizzo, and Christopher A. Gilligan. 2011. "Epidemiological Modeling of Invasion in Heterogeneous Landscapes: Spread of Sudden Oak Death in California (1990–2030)." *Ecosphere* 2, no. 2, article 17:1–24.

Meentemeyer, Ross K., Nathan E. Rank, Brian L. Anacker, David M. Rizzo, and J. Hall Cushman. 2008. "Influence of Land-Cover Change on the Spread of an Invasive Forest Pathogen." *Ecological Applications* 18:159–171.

Meentemeyer, Ross, David Rizzo, Walter Mark, and Elizabeth Lotz. 2004. "Mapping the Risk of Establishment and Spread of Sudden Oak Death in California." *Forest Ecology and Management* 200:195–214.

Mendell, Brooks C., and Amanda H. Lang. 2012. *Wood for Bioenergy: Forests as a Resource for Biomass and Biofuels*. Durham, N.C.: Forest History Society.

Mendocino Redwood Company and Humboldt Redwood Company. 2002. "Tanoak." Mendocino Redwood Company and Humboldt Redwood Company Archive. http://www.mrc.com/archives/tanoak/ (last updated October 18, 2002, accessed September 4, 2012).

Merchant, Carolyn. 1996. *Earthcare: Women and the Environment*. New York: Routledge, Inc.

Merriam, C. Hart. 1918. "The Acorn, a Possibly Neglected Source of Food." *National Geographic Magazine*, no. 34:129–137.

Merriman, John M. 1975. "The Demoiselles of the Ariège, 1829–1831." In *1830 in France*, 87–110. New York: New Viewpoints.

Metz, Margaret R., Kerri M. Frangioso, Ross K. Meentemeyer and David M. Rizzo. 2011. "Interacting Disturbances: Wildfire Severity Affected by Stage of Forest Disease Invasion." *Ecological Applications* 21(2):313–320.

Meyers, Katherine J., Tedmund J. Swiecki, and Alyson E. Mitchell. 2006. "Understanding the Native Californian Diet: Identification of Condensed and Hydrolyzable Tannins in Tanoak Acorns (*Lithocarpus densiflorus*)." *Journal of Agricultural and Food Chemistry* 54(20):7686–7691.

————. 2007. "An Exploratory Study of the Nutritional Composition of Tanoak (*Lithocarpus densiflorus*) Acorns after Potassium Phosphonate Treatment." *Journal of Agricultural and Food Chemistry* 55:6186–6190.

Michaux, François André. 1865. *The North American Sylva, or, a Description of the Forest Trees of the United States, Canada, and Nova Scotia Considered Particularly with Respect to Their Use in the Arts and Their Introduction into Commerce, to Which Is Added a Description of the Most Useful of the European Forest Trees.* Translated and with notes by J. Jay Smith. Philadelphia: W. M. Rutter.

Middleton, Beth Rose. 2011. *Trust in the Land: New Directions in Tribal Conservation.* Tucson: The University of Arizona Press.

Miller, Char. 2000. "130 Years Ago—the Pivotal Decade: American Forestry in the 1870s." *Journal of Forestry* 98(11):6–10.

Mitchell, Ann Lindsay, and Syd House. 1999. *David Douglas: Explorer and Botanist.* London: Aurum Press Ltd.

Moritz, Max A., and Dennis C. Odion. 2005. "Examining the Strength and Possible Causes of the Relationship between Fire History and Sudden Oak Death." *Oecologia* 144(1):106–114.

Muir, John. 1961. *The Mountains of California.* Reprint. New York: Doubleday & Company. Originally published in 1894.

Munz, Philip A., in collaboration with David D. Keck. 1973. *A California Flora with Supplement.* Berkeley: University of California Press.

National Park Service. n.d. "Sudden Oak Death." Redwood National and State Parks. http://www.nps.gov/redw/naturescience/sod.htm (accessed February 10, 2013).

National Parks Conservation Association. 2008. "Redwood National and State Parks: A Resource Assessment." Unpublished report. http://www.npca.org/about-us/center-for-park-research/stateoftheparks/redwood/REDW_Report.pdf (accessed May 10, 2014).

Nelson, Donald. 1993. Transcript of Doweloc panel discussion, December 11, 1993, College of the Redwoods. Hosted by the Mendocino Forest Conservation Trust and facilitated by Don Nelson. Excerpts from tape number 1, side 1 (Disk-Hardwood/File-1dl1293). Copies of the transcript were deposited at the Mendocino County Museum in Willets, California, and the Guest House Museum in Fort Bragg, California.

"New Ways to Cure Leather." 1957. *P G & E Progress* 34(7):3.

Nixon, Kevin C. 1989. "Origins of Fagaceae." In *Evolution, Systematics, and Fossil History of Hamamelidae,* ed. Peter R. Crane and Stephen Blackmore, vol. 2, *"Higher" Hamamelidae,* 23–43. Systematics Association Special Volume, no. 40B. New York: Oxford University Press; Oxford: Clarendon Press.

———— 1997. "Fagaceae." In *Flora of North America: North of Mexico,* ed. Flora of North America Editorial Committee. Vol. 3, *Magnoliophyta: Magnoliidae and Hamamelidae,* 436–506. Oxford: Oxford University Press.

Nomland, Gladys A. 1935. "Sinkyone Notes." *University of California Publications in American Archaeology and Ethnology* 36(2):149–178.

Norgaard, Kari Marie. 2004. "The Effects of Altered Diet on the Health of the Karuk People: A Preliminary Report." Karuk Tribe of California, http://www.trunity.net/files/71201_71300/71222/health-effects-of-altered-diet.pdf (accessed July 1, 2014).

North, Malcolm P., Jerry F. Franklin, Andrew B. Carey, Eric D. Forsman, and Tom Hamer.

1999. "Forest Stand Structure of the Northern Spotted Owl's Foraging Habitat." *Forest Science* 45(4):520–527.

Nuttall, Thomas. 1865. *The North American Sylva; or, a Description of the Forest Trees of the United States, Canada, and Nova Scotia Not Described in the Work of F. Andrew Michaux, and Containing All the Forest Trees Discovered in the Rocky Mountains, the Territory of Oregon, Down to the Shores of the Pacific, and into the Confines of California, as Well as in Various Parts of the United States.* Vol. 1. Philadelphia: Rice, Rutter & Co.

Olson, W. Z. 1955. "Gluing Characteristics of Chinquapin, Tanoak, California Laurel, Madrone." Report 2030, 1–7. Madison, Wis.: USDA Forest Service, Forest Products Laboratory.

Oppmann, Andrew W., Jr. 1991. "Spray Areas Detailed." *Triplicate*, March 15, 3A.

Oregon Department of Agriculture. n.d. "Search Pesticide Products Information." http://oda.state.or.us/dbs/pest_productsL2K/search.lasso (accessed September 27, 2014).

Oregon Flora Project. 2012. "Oregon Plant Atlas." Oregon Flora Project. Oregon State University, Corvallis. www.oregonflora.org/atlas.php (accessed November 26, 2012).

Oregon Washington Railroad & Navigation Company v. Washington, 270 U.S. 87, 103 (1926). (McReynolds & Sutherland, JJ., dissenting).

Ørsted, A. S. 1866. "Bidrag til Egeslægtens Systematik." In *Videnskabelige Meddelelser fra den Naturhistoriske Forening i Kjöbenhavn*, no. 1–6, published by Selskabets Bestyrelse, 11–88. Copenhagen: Bianco Lunos Bogtrykkeri ved F.S. Muhle. Facsimile, Biodiversity Heritage Library, http://www.biodiversitylibrary.org/item/110790#page/274/mode/1up (accessed October 9, 2014).

Ortiz, Beverly R. 2008. "Contemporary California Indian Uses for Food of Species Affected by *Phytophthora ramorum*." In *Proceedings of the Sudden Oak Death Third Science Symposium*. USDA Forest Service, General Technical Report GTR-PSW-214, technical coordinators, S. J. Frankel, J. T. Kliejunas, and K. M. Palmieri, 419–425. Albany, Calif.: Pacific Southwest Research Station.

Oswald, Daniel D. 1972. "Timber Resources of Mendocino and Sonoma Counties, California." USDA Forest Service, Resource Bulletin PNW-40. Portland, Ore.: Pacific Northwest Forest and Range Experiment Station.

Palmer, Lyman L. 1880. *History of Mendocino County, California: Comprising Its Geography, Geology, Topography, Climatography, Springs, and Timber.* San Francisco: Alley, Bowen & Co.

Parke, J. L., E. Oh, S. Voelker, E. M. Hansen, G. Buckles, and B. Lachenbruch. 2007. "*Phytophthora ramorum* Colonizes Tanoak Xylem and Is Associated with Reduced Stem Water Transport." *Phytopathology* 97(12):1558–1567.

Peattie, Donald Culross. 1991. *A Natural History of Western Trees.* Reprint. Boston: Houghton Mifflin Company. Originally published in 1953.

Peluso, Nancy Lee. 1992. *Rich Forests, Poor People: Resource Control and Resistance in Java.* Berkeley: University of California Press.

Perry, David A. 1998. "The Scientific Basis of Forestry." *Annual Review of Ecology and Systematics* 29:435–466.

Peterson, Wesley. 2001. "One Man's Trash . . .: California's Hardwood Utilization Project." *Forest Products Equipment* (May): 11–16.

Pfeiffer, Jack R. 1956. "The Case for Northwest Hardwoods: A Look into the Future." *Pacific Coast Hardwoods* (March): 10–11.

Philp, Tom. 1994. "Poison Programs Raise North Coast Fire Fears." *The Sacramento Bee*, August 21, B5.

Piirto, Douglas D., Brenda Smith, Eric K. Huff, and Scott T. Robinson. 1997. "Efficacy of Herbicide Application Methods Used to Control Tanoak (*Lithocarpus densiflorus*) in an Uneven-Aged Coast Redwood Management Context." In *Proceedings of a Symposium on Oak Woodlands: Ecology, Management, and Urban Interface Issues, March 19–22, 1996, San Luis Obispo, California,* technical coordinators Norman H. Pillsbury, Jared Verner, and William D. Tietje, 199–208. USDA Forest Service, General Technical Report PSW-GTR-160. Albany, Calif.: Pacific Southwest Research Station.

Plumb, Timothy R., and Philip M. McDonald. 1981. "Oak Management in California." USDA Forest Service, General Technical Report PSW-GTR-54. Berkeley, Calif.: Pacific Southwest Research Station.

Ponder, Felix, Jr., and Calvin F. Bey. 1981. "Effects of Calcium Cyanamide on the Growth of Planted Hardwoods." USDA Forest Service, Research Note NC-266. Saint Paul, Minn.: North Central Forest Experiment Station.

Porter, Read D., and Nina C. Robertson. 2011. "Tracking Implementation of the Special Need Request Process under the Plant Protection Act." *Environmental Law Reporter* 41(11):11000–11019.

Powell, J. W. 1879. *Report on the Lands of the Arid Region of the United States.* 2nd ed. Washington, D.C.: Government Printing Office.

Prain, D., ed. 1917. *Curtis's Botanical Magazine, Illustrating and Describing Plants of the Royal Botanic Gardens of Kew and of Other Botanical Establishments.* Vol. 13 of the 4th series. London: L. Reeve & Co., Ltd.

Preston, William. 1998. "Serpent in the Garden: Environmental Change in Colonial California." In *Contested Eden: California before the Gold Rush,* ed. Ramón A. Gutiérrez and Richard J. Orsi, 260–298. Berkeley: University of California Press.

Pyne, Stephen J. 1982. *Fire in America: A Cultural History of Wildland and Rural Fire.* Princeton, N.J.: Princeton University Press.

———. 2010. *America's Fires: A Historical Context for Policy and Practice.* Durham, N.C.: Forest History Society.

Radosevich, S. R., P. C. Passof, and O. A. Leonard. 1976. "Douglas Fir Release from Tanoak and Pacific Madrone Competition." *Weed Science* 24(1):144–145.

Radtke, Leonard B. 1937. "The Tan Oak, Friend of the Hoopa Valley Indians: Shall We Destroy It?" In *Indians at Work.* Washington, D.C.: Office of Indian Affairs.

———. 1939. "Notes on the Mast Trees of the Hoopa." Hoopa, Calif.: U.S. Indian Service. Unpublished report.

Rajala, Richard A. 1998. *Clearcutting the Pacific Rain Forest: Production, Science, and Regulation.* Vancouver: University of British Columbia Press.

Raphael, Martin G. 1987. "Wildlife-Tanoak Associations in Douglas-Fir Forests of Northwestern California." In *Proceedings of the Symposium on Multiple-Use Management of California's Hardwood Resources, November 12–14, 1986, San Luis Obispo, California.* USDA Forest Service, General Technical Report PSW-100, technical coordinators Timothy R. Plumb and Norman H. Pillsbury, 183–189. Berkeley, Calif.: Pacific Southwest Forest and Range Experiment Station.

Raphael, Ray. 1974. *An Everyday History of Somewhere, Being the True Story of Indians, Deer, Homesteaders, Potatoes, Loggers, Trees, Fishermen, Salmon, & Other Living Things in the Backwoods of Northern California, as Written Down by Ray Raphael, and Pictured from Original Sources by Mark Livingston.* New York: Alfred Knopf.

Reed, Lois J., and Neil G. Sugihara. 1987. "Northern Oak Woodlands—Ecosystems in Jeopardy or Is It Already Too Late?" In *Proceedings of the Symposium on Multiple-Use Management of California's Hardwood Resources, November 12–14, 1986, San Luis Obispo, California,* USDA

Forest Service, General Technical Report PSW-100, technical coordinators Timothy R. Plumb and Norman H. Pillsbury, 59–63. Berkeley, Calif.: Pacific Southwest Forest and Range Experiment Station.

Rehder, Alfred. 1960. *Manual of Cultivated Trees and Shrubs: Hardy in North America Exclusive of the Subtropical and Warmer Temperate Regions*. 2nd ed. New York: The Macmillan Company. Originally published in 1940.

Rizzo, D. M., M. Garbelotto, J. M. Davidson, G. W. Slaughter, and S. T. Koike. 2002. "*Phytophthora ramorum* and Sudden Oak Death in California: I. Host Relationships." In *Proceedings of the Fifth Symposium on Oak Woodlands: Oaks in California's Changing Landscapes, October 22–25, 2001, San Diego, California*, 733–740. USDA Forest Service, General Technical Report PSW-GTR-184, technical coordinators R. B. Standiford, D. McCreary, and K. L. Purcell. Albany, Calif.: Pacific Southwest Research Station.

———. 2002. "*Phytophthora ramorum* as the Cause of Extensive Mortality of *Quercus* spp. and *Lithocarpus densiflorus* in California." *Plant Disease* 86(3):205–214.

Rizzo, Dave M., and G. W. Slaughter. 2001. "Root Disease and Canopy Gaps in Developed Areas of Yosemite Valley, California." *Forest Ecology and Management* 146:159–167.

Rizzo, David M., and Matteo Garbelotto. 2003. "Sudden Oak Death: Endangering California and Oregon Forest Ecosystems." *Frontiers in Ecology and the Environment* 1(5):197–204.

Rizzo, David M., Matteo Garbelotto, and Everett M. Hansen. 2005. "*Phytophthora ramorum*: Integrative Research and Management of an Emerging Pathogen in California and Oregon Forests." *Annual Review of Phytopathology* 43:309–335.

Romero, A-Dae. 2013. "Tribal Consultation: Time for FDA to Recognize Sovereignty Principles." *Food Safety News*, November 21. http://www.foodsafetynews.com/2013/11/tribal-consultation-a-tribal-sovereignty-principle-non-existent-for-fda/#.U1NJNcYXdSU (accessed April 19, 2014).

Rowland, Jeannette. 1960. "Early Santa Cruz Industry." *News and Notes from the Santa Cruz Historical Society*, no. 17 (October): 1.

Roy, D. F. 1956. "Killing Tanoak in Northwestern California." USDA Forest Service, Forest Research Notes no. 106, 1–9. Berkeley: California Forest and Range Experiment Station.

———. 1957. "A Record of Tanoak Acorn and Seedling Production in Northwestern California." USDA Forest Service, Forest Research Notes no. 124, 1–6. Berkeley: California Forest and Range Experiment Station.

———. 1957. "Silvical Characteristics of Tanoak." USDA Forest Service, Technical Paper no. 22. Berkeley: California Forest and Range Experiment Station.

Roy, Douglass F. 1962. "California Hardwoods: Management Practices and Problems." *Journal of Forestry* 60(3):184–186.

Sahlins, Peter. 1998. *Forest Rites: The War of the Demoiselles in Nineteenth-Century France*. Cambridge, Mass.: Harvard University Press.

Sander, G. H. 1958. "Oregon Hardwoods: Management, Marketing, Manufacture." Extension Bulletin 775. Corvallis: Oregon State University Extension.

Sander, Ivan L., and Howard N. Rosen. 1985. "Oak: An American Wood." USDA Forest Service, FS-247. Washington, D.C.

Sargent, Charles Sprague. 1895. *The Silva of North America: A description of the trees which grow naturally in North America exclusive of Mexico*. Vol. 8. New York: Houghton, Mifflin and Company.

———. 1965. *Manual of the Trees of North America exclusive of Mexico, Second Corrected Edition in Two Volumes*. Vol. 1. Reprint. New York: Dover Publication Inc. Originally published in 1922.

Schaeffer, Claude E. 1959. "Indian Tribes and Languages of the Old Oregon Country: A New Map." *Oregon Historical Quarterly* 60:129–133.

Schenck, Sara M., and E. W. Gifford. 1952. "Karok Ethnobotany." *University of California Anthropological Records* 13(6): 377–392.

Schiebinger, Londa. 2004. *Plants and Empire: Colonial Bioprospecting in the Atlantic World.* Cambridge, Mass.: Harvard University Press.

Schniewind, Arno P. 1958. "The Strength and Related Properties of Tanoak: I. General Description and Strength Properties in the Green Condition." *California Forestry and Forest Products* (7): no page numbers. Berkeley: Forest Products Laboratory, California Agricultural Experiment Station, University of California, Berkeley.

Schofield, W. R. 1950. *Forest Laws of California: History of Forest and Fire Laws, Summary of Forest Practice Act.* Portland, Ore.: Western Forestry and Conservation Association.

Schorn, Howard E., Jeffrey A. Myers, and Diane M. Erwin. 2007. "Navigating the Neogene: An Updated Chronology of Neogene Paleofloras from the Western United States." *Courier Forschungsinstitut Senckenberg*, no. 258:139–146.

Schowalter, Timothy, Everett Hansen, Randy Molina, and Yanli Zhang. 1997. "Integrating the Ecological Roles of Phytophagous Insects, Plant Pathogens, and Mycorrhizae in Managed Forests." In *Creating a Forestry for the 21st Century: The Science of Ecosystem Management*, ed. Kathryn A. Kohm and Jerry F. Franklin, 171–189. Washington, D.C.: Island Press.

Schubert, G. H. 1950. "Control of Sprouting of Tanoak and Madrone Stumps." USDA Forest Service, Forest Research Notes no. 74, 1–2. Berkeley: California Forest and Range Experiment Station.

Schwantes, Carlos Arnaldo. 1996. *The Pacific Northwest: An Interpretive History.* 2nd ed. Lincoln: University of Nebraska Press.

Senos, René, Frank K. Lake, Nancy Turner, and Dennis Martinez. 2006. "Traditional Ecological Knowledge and Restoration Practice." In *Restoring the Pacific Northwest*, ed. Dean Apostol and Marcia Sinclair, 393–426. Washington, D.C.: Island Press.

Séquin, Margareta. 2012. *The Chemistry of Plants: Perfumes, Pigments, and Poisons.* Cambridge, U.K.: RSC Publshing.

Shanks, Ralph, and Lisa Woo Shanks, ed. 2006. *Indian Baskets of Central California: Art, Culture, and History.* Novato, Calif.: Costaño Books in association with Miwok Archeological Preserve of Marin. Distributed by University of Washington Press.

Shelly, John R. 1997. "An Examination of the Oak Woodland as a Potential Resource for Higher-Value Wood Products." In *Proceedings of a Symposium on Oak Woodlands: Ecology, Management, and Urban Interface Issues, March 19–22, 1996, San Luis Obispo, California*, technical coordinators Norman H. Pillsbury, Jared Verner, and William D. Tietje, 445–455. USDA Forest Service, General Technical Report PSW-GTR-160. Albany, Calif.: Pacific Southwest Research Station.

———. 2001. "Does It Make 'Cents' to Process Tanoak to Lumber?" Unpublished report prepared and edited by Adina Merenlender and Emily Heaton, University of California, Oak Woodland Conservation Workgroup. http://ucanr.edu/sites/oak_range/Oak_Articles_On_Line/Oak_Woodland_Products_Range_Management_Livestock/Does_It_Make_Cents_to_Process_Tanoak_to_Lumber/ (accessed March 2, 2014).

Shelly, John R., and Stephen L. Quarles. 2013. "The Past, Present, and Future of *Notholithocarpus densiflorus* (Tanoak) as a Forest Products Resource." *Madroño* 60(2):118–125.

Sherry, S. P. 1971. *The Black Wattle (Acacia mearnsii* De Wild.). Pietermaritzburg, South Africa: University of Natal Press.

Sims, Hank. 2009. "Pulp Mill Closes for Good." *North Coast Journal of Politics, People & Art.* Posted October 20. http://www.northcoastjournal.com/blogthing/archives/2009/10/20/pulp-mill-closes-for-good/ (accessed April 7, 2013).

Snyder, George. 1992. "Yuroks Fear Cancer from Spraying." *San Francisco Chronicle*, July 7, A1, A6.

Stewart, Omer C. Edited and with an introduction by Henry T. Lewis and M. Kat Anderson. 2002. *Forgotten Fires: Native Americans and the Transient Wilderness.* Norman: University of Oklahoma Press.

Stine, Raymond. 1980. "Economics of Utilizing Oak for Energy." In *Proceedings of the Symposium on Ecology, Management, and Utilization of California Oaks, June 26–28, 1979, Claremont, California.* USDA Forest Service, General Technical Report PSW-44, technical coordinator Timothy R. Plumb. Berkeley, Calif.: Pacific Southwest Forest and Range Experiment Station.

"Stockton." 1920. *Timberman* 21(11):48.

Storer, Tracy I., and Robert L. Usinger. 1963. *Sierra Nevada Natural History.* Berkeley: University of California Press.

Sudworth, George B. 1967. *Forest Trees of the Pacific Slope.* Reprint. New York: Dover Publications. Originally published in 1908.

Sullivan, William J. ca. 1986. "Economic Potential of the Tanoak Timber of the North Coast Region of California: A Sabbatical Report." Arcata, Calif.: Humboldt State University, Library Special Collections Archives.

Swiecki, Ted, Elizabeth Bernhardt, Matteo Garbelotto, and Yana Valachovic. 2014. "Management of *Phytophthora ramorum* (Sudden Oak Death) in Tanoak and Oak Stands." *Phytosphere Research*, no page numbers. Updated June. http://phytosphere.com/publications/sodmanagementstudy.htm (accessed September 30, 2014).

Swiecki, Tedmund J., and Elizabeth A. Bernhardt. 2013. "A Reference Manual for Managing Sudden Oak Death in California." USDA Forest Service, PSW-GTR-242. Albany, Calif.: Pacific Southwest Research Station.

"Tanbark Industry on the Coast." 1973. *Mendocino County Historical Society Newsletter* 12(1):2–3.

"Tanbark Oak of California Yields Riches." June 1918. *Timberman* 19(8): 36.

Tappeiner, John C., II, Timothy B. Harrington, and John D. Walstad. 1984. "Predicting Recovery of Tanoak (*Lithocarpus densiflorus*) and Pacific Madrone (*Arbutus menziesii*) after Cutting or Burning." *Weed Science* 32(3):413–417.

Tappeiner, John C., II, and Philip M. McDonald. 1984. "Development of Tanoak Understories in Conifer Stands." *Canadian Journal of Forest Research* 14:271–277.

Tappeiner, John C., II, Philip M. McDonald, and Douglass F. Roy. 1990. "*Lithocarpus densiflorus* (Hook. & Arn.) Rehd. Tanoak." In *Silvics of North America*, vol. 2, *Hardwoods*, technical coordinators Russell M. Burns and Barbara H. Honkala, 417–425. USDA Forest Service, Agricultural Handbook 654. Washington, D.C.

Teague, Vera Snider. 1975. *From Buckskin to Teambells as Told by John Snider.* Ukiah, Calif.: The Letter Shop.

"This Sort of Thing Even the Senate Bill Should Stop." 1947. *American Metal Market* 54 (May 24):6.

Tucker, John M. 2012. "Fagaceae." In *The Jepson Manual: Vascular Plants of California*, ed.

Bruce G. Baldwin, Douglas H. Goldman, David J. Keil, Robert Patterson, Thomas J. Rosatti, and Dieter H. Wilken, 802–808. 2nd ed. Berkeley: University of California Press.

Tucker, John M., William E. Sundahl, and Dale O. Hall. 1969. "A Mutant of *Lithocarpus densiflorus*." *Madroño* 20(4):221–225.

Tyrrell, Ian. 1999. *True Gardens of the Gods: Californian-Australian Environmental Reform, 1860–1930*. Berkeley: University of California Press.

UC Berkeley Forest Pathology and Mycology Laboratory. 2012. SODMAP project. University of California, Berkeley. www.sodmap.org (accessed December 6, 2012).

United States Department of Agriculture, Research, Education, and Economics Information System. n.d. "Enhancing Tribal Health and Food Security in the Klamath Basin of Oregon and California by Building a Sustainable Regional System." http://www.reeis. usda.gov/web/crisprojectpages/0230374-enhancing-tribal-health-and-food-security-in-the-klamath-basin-of-oregon-and-california-by-building-a-sustainable-regional-food-system.html (accessed May 3, 2014).

United States Forest Service. 1907. "Consumption of Tanbark and Tanning Extract in 1906." USDA Forest Service circular 119, 1–9. Washington, D.C.: Government Printing Office.

Van Strum, Carol. 1983. *A Bitter Fog: Herbicides and Human Rights*. San Francisco: Sierra Club Books.

Vander Wall, Steven B. 2001. "The Evolutionary Ecology of Nut Dispersal." *Botanical Review* 67:74–117.

Vitousek, Peter M., Carla M. D'Antonio, Lloyd L. Loope, and Randy Westbrooks. 1996. "Biological Invasions as Global Environmental Change." *American Scientist* 84(5):468–478.

Wade, Walter. 1809. *Quercus; or Oaks: From the French of Michaux, Histoire des Chênes de l'Amérique Septentrionale, with Notes and an Appendix*. Dublin: Graisberry and Campbell.

Wallace, William. 1978. "Hupa, Chilula, and Whilkut." In *Handbook of North American Indians*, ed. Robert F. Heizer, 164–179. Washington, D.C.: Smithsonian Institution.

Walstad, John D. 1992. "History of the Development, Use, and Management of Forest Resources." In *Reforestation Practices in Southwestern Oregon and Northern California*, ed. Stephen D. Hobbs, Steven D. Tesch, Peyton W. Owston, Ronald E. Stewart, John C. Tappeiner II, and Gail E. Wells, 26–46. Corvallis: Forest Research Laboratory, Oregon State University.

Walstad, John D. and Frank N. Dost. 1986. "All the King's Horses and All the King's Men: The Lessons of 2,4,5-T." *Journal of Forestry* 84:28–33.

Warburton, Austen D., and Joseph F. Endert. 1966. *Indian Lore of the North California Coast*. Santa Clara, Calif.: Pacific Pueblo Press.

Weiser, Andrea, and Dana Lepofsky. 2009. "Ancient Land Use and Management of Ebey's Prairie, Whidbey Island, Washington." *Journal of Ethnobiology* 29:184–212.

Wheeler, James. 1747. *The Modern Druid, Containing Instructions Founded on Physical Reasons, Confirmed by Long Practice, and Evidenced by Precedents, for the Much Better Culture of Young Oaks More Particularly, . . .* London: printed for the author and sold by C. Davis; and J. Clarke.

White Residents of Mendocino to Robert. 1855. Letters Received by the Office of Indian Affairs, 1824–1881. National Archives Mf., record group 75, series microcopy no. 234, roll 34.

Whiteside, Thomas. 1979. *The Pendulum and the Toxic Cloud: The Course of Dioxin Contamination*. New Haven, Conn.: Yale University Press.

Wieck, Roger S., William M. Voelkle, and K. Michelle Hearne. 2000. *The Hours of Henry*

VIII: A Renaissance Masterpiece by Jean Poyet. New York: George Braziller Publisher in association with The Pierpont Morgan Library.

Wiemann, Michael C. 2010. "Characteristics and Availability of Commercially Important Woods." In *Wood Handbook: Wood as an Engineering Material*, ed. Robert J. Ross, 2-1 to 2-45 USDA Forest Service, General Technical Report FPL-GTR-190. Madison, Wis.: Forest Products Laboratory.

Wilkinson, William H., Philip M. McDonald, and Penelope Morgan. 1997. "Tanoak Sprout Development after Cutting and Burning in a Shade Environment." *Western Journal of Applied Forestry* 12(1):21–26.

Williams, Gerald W. 2007. *The Forest Service: Fighting for Public Lands.* Westport, Conn.: Greenwood Press.

Williams, Michael. 1989. *Americans and Their Forests: A Historical Geography.* Cambridge: Cambridge University Press.

———. 2003. *Deforesting the Earth: From Prehistory to Global Crisis.* Chicago: The University of Chicago Press.

Williams, Robert D., and Sidney H. Hanks. 1994. *Hardwood Nurseryman's Guide.* Rev. ed. USDA Forest Service, Agriculture Handbook no. 473. Originally issued March 1976.

Wolf, Carl B. 1945. *California Wild Tree Crops: Their Crop Production and Possible Utilization.* Anaheim, Calif.: Rancho Santa Ana Botanic Garden.

Wood, Mary Christina, and Zachary Welcker. 2008. "Tribes as Trustees Again (Part I): The Emerging Tribal Role in the Conservation Trust Movement." *Harvard Environmental Law Review* 32(2):373–432.

Wright, Jessica W., and Richard S. Dodd. 2013. "Could Tanoak Mortality Affect Insect Biodiversity? Evidence for Insect Pollination in Tanoaks." *Madroño* 60(2):87–94.

Yahnke, Amy E., Christian E. Grue, Marc P. Hayes, and Alexandra T. Troiano. 2013. "Effects of the Herbicide Imazapyr on Juvenile Oregon Spotted Frogs." *Environmental Toxicology and Chemistry* 32:228–235. doi: 10.1002/etc.2048. http://www.ncbi.nlm.nih.gov/pubmed/23147474.

Yoon, Carol Kaesuk. 2000. "Puzzling Disease Devastating California Oaks." *New York Times*, August 13. http://www.nytimes.com/library/national/science/081300sci-trees.html (accessed April 29, 2014).

INDEX

Page numbers in *italic* refer to illustrations or tables.